My Husband's Women

BY

ADRIANE WILLIAMS

Preface

This book, originally written in 2001 as a labor of love, is being re-published with the same captivating storyline. However, it has undergone more thorough editing this time around. To all my fellow writers—keep writing. You never know when or where your breakthrough might come.

Thank you for your support, and may God bless you.

My Husband's Women

by Adriane Williams

Originally copyrighted on January 7, 2002 (TX0001036717)

chardanbooks@gmail.com

Paperback: ISBN 978-8-218-50777-0

eBook: ISBN 979-8-330-399-338

Prologue

Marriage to the man of your dreams isn't always as simple as it seems. There are unforeseen challenges along the way, like navigating relationships with your husband's female family members or friends. While some women are wonderfully supportive and embrace sharing their loved one with the person he loves, others may view a wedding or marriage as a competition. This dynamic can place both the husband and the new spouse in an uncomfortable position.

In the story of Racquel Middleton and Marcus Collin, you'll witness their journey to becoming and staying Mr. and Mrs. Collin, despite the challenges they face.

Amen.

Table of contents

Chapter 1 1

Chapter 2 7

Chapter 3 39

Chapter 4 63

Chapter 5 73

Chapter 6 101

Chapter 7 110

Chapter 8 131

Chapter 9 146

Chapter 10 151

Chapter 11 156

Chapter 12 174

Chapter 13 176

Chapter 14 188

Chapter 15 198

Chapter 16 208

Chapter 17 217

Chapter 18 238

Chapter 19 247

Chapter 20 257

Chapter 21 263

Chapter 22 275

Chapter 23 285

Chapter 24 296

Chapter 25 312

Chapter 26 316

Chapter 27 326

Chapter 28 329

Chapter 29 335

Chapter 30 341

Chapter 31 348

Epilogue 359

Chapter 1

As tears rolled down my face, my heart was bitter. Along with the animosity, there was an inexplicable emotion. Yes, I felt sadness, but there was also a sense of euphoria. She was finally dead! "Diva Evil" was my pet name for her. I had many other names, but as a God-fearing woman, I'll try not to expose her for the interesting person she truly was. Throughout the days when my marriage teetered on the brink of destruction, she reveled in my misery.

She even told me, "I was here before you, and I will be here after you." Nothing would have pleased her more than seeing Marcus Collin leave me. If I had died, she probably would have danced at my funeral and served champagne. She wanted him for herself, wanted him to come home so she could take care of him— I was convinced of it. Oh God! If my husband knew I even thought that, he'd divorce me. He, of course, was uncontrollable with grief. As his wife, I did my best to stand by him and offer moral support, no matter what I was feeling. I consoled my husband by holding him; saying anything would have been pointless, and offering any words of sympathy would have been a lie.

As tears rolled down his face, and as he put his tough façade away for a moment, I wondered if this could really be happening. Was my arch-rival truly gone? She was gone, alright. The casket that lay before us would soon be closed. "Yeah," I whispered to myself, "Gone, just not defeated." Her memory would linger. I might have to accept that she had graduated to sainthood in my husband's eyes, in whom he could see no wrong.

I gently tapped him and said, "Honey, soon you must go up and say a few words." In a raspy baritone, he replied, "I can't go up there." I tried a little more firmly, "Listen, all these people expect you…"

Marcus stopped me. "Babe, I can't."

"What about Mildred?" I asked. "Where is she?"

"She fainted. Steve carried her off."

My mind was racing—what should I do next? The reverend then asked to speak with me.

"Sister Racquel, if Brother Marcus is unable to stand, is it possible…."

I thought, *Oh no. This is a bad dream. Is he really going to ask what I think he is? Lord, no. Please do not ask me to stand and speak about how wonderful that woman was. Please. I'm begging to be delivered from this situation.*

"I greatly appreciate your help. Thank you, Sister."

I simply nodded and smiled. "Of course, Reverend Steele."

Returning to my husband's slumped figure, I placed my hand under his chin, lifted his head, and looked into his sorrow-filled face. His eyes were red and worn. I secretly wondered if he would react the same way if I died. Ashamed of that selfish thought, I excused myself. In the safety of the ladies' room, I refreshed myself and prayed for strength, asking God to guide my heart, mind, and words. Walking back out with a wet paper towel in hand, I gently cleaned my husband's face and then guided him to the podium. Hand in hand, we joined the reverend and the choir.

I softly asked them to sing "Amazing Grace." The standing-room-only crowd at Chadmeyer's Funeral Parlor murmured softly, with only a few choosing to sing along. When I turned to Marcus, I asked for his prepared words. His blank stare told me all I needed to know—he didn't have a damn thing ready. I straightened my back, placed both hands on the podium, closed my eyes, and then looked down at Sister Gloria Collin.

Even in death, she looked formidable. I took a deep breath and began to summarize all of her less offensive characteristics.

"Mrs. Collin, or Sister Gloria, as many of you here know her, her stay on this earth was much too short. But God's knowledge is infinite. It was God's choice to call His devoted child home. Though we may not understand His ways, our sweet and merciful

Creator, who is immeasurable in wisdom, guides us through life from birth to death."

"Amen," someone added.

I continued, determined not to lose my focus.

"Sister Gloria was one of the most generous members of our congregation. There wasn't a charity or event she didn't contribute to, and not a single person in need was ever turned away by Sister Gloria."

I then turned to my husband, hoping he was composed enough to continue. Marcus seemed surprised by the kind things I'd said about his mother. *What did Marcus expect?* I thought to myself. *She was angelic to everyone but me.*

He hesitated briefly before signaling that he was ready to take over. Relieved to see his calm, I turned from the pleased but baffled Marcus and addressed the audience:

"As you all know, this is her son, my husband, Marcus Collin. He can share one of the many lovely personal memories his family had with Sister Gloria."

Marcus stepped in front of me.

"Before I start, I just want to thank my wife for speaking so I could get it together."

He began, "A night at the Collin house was never a dull moment…." Marcus then proceeded to tell the audience a comical story, practically reliving it as he spoke. As I sat down, I remembered the first time I met Marcus and his mother. I was just a little girl then. Thinking back, I realized it really didn't look too promising for Marcus and me.

Two different people, two different backgrounds. I recalled meeting his mother after my own mother had passed. As a good Christian, Sister Gloria offered her condolences, although they had never met. I remember her assessment of me must not have been much, judging by the way she looked me over.

She exclaimed in her thick West Indian accent, "You poor child, who will take you in now?"

Embarrassed, I replied, "I live with my Aunt Lynn."

"How very lucky for you," she said, sounding condescending.

Her son Marcus added, "You're almost homeless."

The dislike was almost instant. Unbeknownst to me, I met my future husband that day at Holy Trinity Baptist. Marcus T. Collin. He was dressed neatly, with a mischievousness lurking in his inquisitive obsidian gaze. An impish dimple on the side of his youthful face hinted at his charm. I remember the day clearly—January 5, 1980. The Collin family hailed from St. Thomas and had left five years earlier. Trevor Collin was a physician, and

Gloria Collin had the luxury of staying home. While Dr. Collin was humble, his wife was rumored to be arrogant.

Some church members felt she behaved as though she herself had earned that medical degree. It was safe to say they lived comfortably. Mrs. Collin insisted on being called;

"Mrs. Dr. Collin," and just about everyone agreed, except Reverend Steele, he called her Sister Gloria.

Chapter 2

Racquel

I did everything I could to avoid going to Aunt Sarah Lynn's church without my mom. Going to church had always been something my mother and I did together, before she went upstairs to see her main man, Jesus. Near the end of her illness, she became fond of saying, "I'm going upstairs to meet my main man."

That was her personal joke about death. It made me cry, but she would always say, "It's alright, I'll be fine." My mother, Susan Ann Middleton, passed away in early 1979 from cancer. I was ten years old at the time; she was thirty-two. It had already been decided that I would either live with my Aunt Sarah Lynn or go into foster care. Aunt Lynn was certainly the lesser of the two evils.

So, I began living with my Auntie Lynn, her husband Herbert Baker, and their daughter, Grace. Aunt Sarah Lynn's daughter was my age. My cousin Grace had sun-kissed brown skin just like mine. My hair was longer, but Grace had beautiful glittery green eyes, so our cuteness evened out, eliminating any jealousy. And since we had stuck safety pins in our index fingers and put them together, she was also my blood sister.

Aunt Lynn lived in a split-level, two-story home in Jackson Heights, New York. The transition from my mom's neat but confined Brooklyn one-bedroom apartment was the least of my worries. It was adjusting, not just to new surroundings but new people. Through a sheen of tears, I said goodbye to my once happy, paint-chipped palace. The arrival at the Baker household was quiet and unceremonious. Instead of raining, as I had wished it would, the evening was clear and beautiful.

The fading twilight gave way to a purple, twinkling sky. It felt as if my mother was saying, "Okay, honey, this is where I want you to live, and everything will be alright." My uncle Herbert helped me upstairs to the second floor, carrying my suitcase. Holding my duffel bag tightly, I finally let it drop to the floor. He patted my head and kindly closed the door, giving me some privacy.

The guest bedroom, hardly ever used, was now mine. The room wasn't very large, and my meager possessions did little to make it feel like home. It felt as empty as the space in my heart—just one suitcase, one duffel bag, and two pictures of my mother. One was a faded photo of a young Susan holding a smiling baby—me. The other was a picture of her alone.

In that photo, she's sitting at an outdoor restaurant, waving with a wry smile, her lips painted red, I assumed, though the black-and-white photo made it hard to tell. I briefly traced her image with my finger, then set about putting my clothes away.

When I finished unpacking, I looked around, turning in a complete circle, surveying the place I would call home for the next few years. I stuffed my empty duffel bag in the closet and slid my suitcase under the bed. Sitting down, I thought about how unfair my mother's death was. Why couldn't it have happened to someone else? Lying in what felt like a borrowed bed, watching every corner of the room, I felt my usual nighttime jitters. I missed my night light but was too afraid to ask for one. The shadows seemed to unsettle me, I would have ask, for a light, It was not a big deal.

My cousin Grace came into the room to say good night and gave me one of her favorite dolls to keep me company as I slept. It took some time, but with each passing day, my heart slowly began to heal.

Church had been something my mother and I enjoyed together. At first, it seemed impossible to go without her. But Aunt Lynn was determined that something as small as 'death' wouldn't stop me from attending service. Needless to say, it was customary to go to church every Sunday. And on religious holidays, it was sometimes standing room only.

One particular week, I was forced out of my church strike. I had only missed three Sundays, but it was duly noted, and the grieving period was over. My Aunt Lynn decided it was time for me to attend church again, saying it was "time to make my peace with God." Although I felt it was God who should apologize for taking my mother away, I guess I was just spoiled. I had been used to just me and my mom for so long. Susan Ann Middleton was all I knew; she was the only parent I had.

If I didn't mention my father, it wasn't by accident—I didn't know him, had never met him, and therefore didn't miss him. My mom never discussed him; as previously, she never had a positive or negative thing to say about him. I had stopped asking about him, but sometimes, I wondered about who he was. He must have been a bad man if she didn't want to discuss him. I wished I could forget him entirely.

I remembered the last gift my mother gave me: an outfit for Aunt Lynn's second wedding. It was the cutest dress she could find at Dresses for Less, where designer dresses were sold at half price. The dress was white with small pink flowers on the sleeves, and I had a matching pink and white hat to go with it. It was so cute. Nonetheless, my mother was an excellent seamstress. Most times she made my dress for events. Mama always said that only rich people and fools spent a fortune on clothes. I thought she said that to make herself feel better about not affording the things she liked.

We weren't rich, nor did we pretend to be, but we occasionally shopped for bargains at higher-priced stores like Macy's. Although

Momma didn't shop at Saks Fifth Avenue or Neiman Marcus, she felt there was no reason not to look like she did. Since it was Easter Sunday and the last dress my mom had given me, I saw no reason not to wear it again. It was my favorite—and practically my only dress—except for the ugly blue one Aunt Lynn bought. Momma always said Aunt Lynn wasn't blessed with the same fashion sense she had.

Needless to say, I wore the white dress one to three times a week. Aunt Lynn didn't consider that very ladylike. I was still full of anger and looked for ways to rebel. Aunt Lynn often threatened to spank me if I didn't take off the dress. Yet, knowing its sentimental value, she just complained instead of following through with a spanking.

Despite not having much money, my mother was well-known and had many friends. A few were too snooty to talk to us, but Momma would say they just needed a little Jesus in their lives. At my young age, I didn't quite understand this, as we were almost always in church when she said it.

My mother, Susan, believed in honesty, kindness, and self-control—a true lady in every sense of the word. I admired her and vowed to be like her one day. This might sound corny, but I felt her spirit around me. When I felt sad, I'd think of her and become calm, collected, and strong.

Over time, Aunt Lynn became my legal guardian, which I didn't mind. She reminded me of my mother in many ways: she looked like her and had a daughter just like Momma. The main difference between them was how they acted. Aunt Lynn was as enthusiastic about playing the lottery at the local grocery store as she was about church. Unlike my mother, who was calm and quiet, Aunt Lynn spoke her mind and didn't care who liked it. I heard her say so on many occasions. If it weren't for her college degree in communications, one might think Aunt Lynn's degree was in telling people where to go.

Cousin Grace was my age and my best friend. Since we looked alike, everyone thought we were sisters. We would lie and say that we were. I was the younger sister, and she was the oldest. We both enjoyed Sunday school; it was a place where we did almost everything a regular school would do, except class work and homework.

On Easter Sunday, during class, I ended my strike and we talked about Jesus dying and coming back from the dead. I thought, if He could do it, then maybe we all should be able to. I still harbored old resentments against God. After all, Mama wasn't there, so I felt justified.

During the Sunday service, I felt a bit melancholy and needed to be alone. I wanted to say a prayer for my mom. Asking the teacher to be excused under the pretense of going to the bathroom, I wandered my way to the choir room.

How peaceful it was when no one was around. As I tried to say a silent prayer, I was disturbed by three boys who had also escaped their Sunday school teacher: Marcus, Steven, and Timothy.

"Hey, what are you doing here? This is the choir room; ain't nobody supposed to be in here," Marcus, the leader of the group, said. His tone was more of a command than a question.

I replied, "Well, what are you doing here? I left my bag in here and was just getting it." With my bag in hand, there was no way he could call me a liar. Marcus looked at his friends and said, "Ah, come on," then looked at me as if I had ruined some grand plan.

Moments later, Grace walked in and asked if everything was alright. I told her "yeah," not wanting to worry her. Together, we walked back to our class. I quickly said a prayer for my mother before I could forget. On the way out of Sunday school, Marcus, the troublemaker, spotted me again. Every time he saw me, he had something mean to say.

He clearly thought he was hot stuff. I was determined to ignore him. Thankfully, Aunt Lynn's service had finished, and I saw her up ahead. I had no time to deal with Marcus. Sure enough, Marcus raced past me, and Grace asked, "Oh, what is that boy doing now?"

No sooner had Grace asked than Marcus approached with a pleased expression, eager to tell on me. "Mrs. Baker, Racquel was playing in the choir room," he announced, his beady eyes twinkling with satisfaction.

I should have known. "The weasel." Aunt Lynn did not tolerate any disrespect towards the Lord. She fixed me with her sternest stare, curled her lip, and in her most hushed voice said, "The Lord's house isn't for playing. If I catch you... I'ma tan you, I know my sister taught you bettah."

This brought on a fit of stifled giggles from Marcus, the so-called clown. My response at that moment was simply, "Yes, ma'am," since trying to explain myself always had the opposite effect and only made Aunt Lynn more displeased. As I watched Marcus practically skip away, I came up with a new nickname for him: Little Asshole. I feared Aunt Lynn's wrath too much to utter it aloud in front of the whole congregation.

I was humiliated and hurt that Aunt Lynn used my deceased mother as a way to chastise me. With my arms folded and eyes shooting daggers at Marcus' back, one solitary thought played in my clever little mind: 'This means war.'

The procession from church was always slow, with some members discussing the sermon and others talking about their cooking. Everyone was watching everyone else. Church members, some loudly remarking on who wore what or who should not have worn this or that, and who looked like they'd been dragged in by a cat. The ones who felt they were appointed by God to judge the rest had bold identification cards: colorful totes and scarves with "I Love Jesus" written in gold, and voluminous hats perched on their heads. It was as if to say, "World, look at me, I am one of His people."

When we reached home, changing from my dress into sweats and then sitting in front of the TV with milk and cookies was by far my favorite part of the Sunday ritual. I really didn't like milk, but I drank it for its growing properties. Grace would sit and read or watch a Sunday classic with me.

Aunt Lynn would finish cooking Sunday dinner while listening to an afternoon service playing on the radio. The service was often loud and spirited. I always prayed that Aunt Lynn would finish cooking before she caught the Holy Ghost. I'd sit and look heavenward, checking for the spirits she seemed to catch so often. The smell of the one-generation-removed Southern food would make my mouth water: lightly seasoned baked chicken, yams, yellow rice, string beans, and sweet buttery cornbread. But no ham.

Ever since Aunt Lynn took that health class years ago to monitor her cholesterol, she'd sworn off pork. And since her husband mentioned that lately his angel was "sprouting wings," she decided not to make Sunday dessert. At the dinner table, Uncle Herbert would lead us in the blessing of the food, a ritual that usually took about ten minutes, and if he had something special to say, it could take nearly fifteen. Grace and I would watch with one eye open, waiting for the blessing to be over so we could dig in. But sometimes we could not wait and we'd dip our hands into the hot plate and stuff food in our mouths.

Before Uncle Herbert lifted his head and opened his eyes, Aunt Lynn sometimes spied on us and punished us by making us repeat the "grace" out loud before eating. Although the Bakers seemed like a regular family, we were not. The sole disciplinarian was Uncle Herbert. According to him, he was up-to-date with the times, and the tricks we might pull on Aunt Lynn had no effect on him. In my mind, he was anything but regular. He claimed that God had given him special powers to see through liars. He was like Superman, but lying was not his kryptonite. He convinced us that stealing and lying both earned us an express ticket to hell, describing in vivid detail what awaited us there.

As Grace's stepfather, he was not allowed to spank her—that was Aunt Lynn's job—but he could lecture us to death. At that point, it seemed better to just accept physical punishment. Before Grace and I were out of our teens, we both audaciously prayed for scholarships to college, hoping to move out of the house, even if only temporarily.

As Grace grew older and became more daring with her replies to everything Aunt Lynn said, and with my own growing tendency to find excuses to stay out of the house, the adults blamed our behavior on our changing hormones. It was decided that when Grace and I reached our teens, we should join the young Christians group. Its sole purpose seemed to be keeping track of us; to me, it felt like babysitting.

With every graduation there was a new teacher. Now, we were sitting in Sister Brenda Wood's class, she was the middle school church teacher on Saturdays and Sister Sandra Du Bois's on Sundays. Aunt Lynn was afraid that if we mixed with the wrong crowd, we might get "into trouble or in the family way," as she put it. I complained, "Man, that means we'll be in church twice a week," unable to hold my tongue.

"Mommy, that leaves us no time for ourselves," Grace argued.

We thought of every reason and excuse not to go. "Why do we have to go? You can trust us," Grace tried once again to change her mind. But Aunt Lynn's response was firm: "You both are going. And I don't want to hear anything else."

"Grace, unfold your arms. I am the only one who pays the bills around here. Anyone who gets an attitude will have to deal with me."

Aunt Lynn wasted no time making it clear that, as long as we lived with her, if she wanted us to attend church five times a week, we had no say in the matter. We learned quickly not to push the limits; Aunt Lynn was from the old school and had no qualms about reminding us that she was the captain and we were the sailors.

As church members aged, it was common for them to actively join the various committees at church.

Aunt Lynn and Uncle Herbert were no exception. They joined the fundraising board at church, which left Grace and me with more free time than just attending Sunday services. We used that time to hit the mall, where we could indulge in some unsupervised fun. Despite being only a few months apart in age, Grace usually had to convince me to loosen up and break the rules a bit.

Once she had persuaded me to join one of her excursions, I always ended up having a great time.

On one of our mall trips, I asked her, "Grace, you've been so quiet lately. What's going on?"

"What's going on? Are you still a virgin? I hope you didn't go and sleep with Steve," I asked. Grace glanced at me and rolled her eyes.

"I'll take that as a no," I continued, pressing on. "Let me guess—you're pregnant? Girl, I hope you didn't let that fool get you pregnant."

Grace looked up again, clearly unimpressed by my rambling, while I remained oblivious to the blank look she was giving me.

"Because if you're pregnant, you'll have to get rid of it. Aunt Lynn won't let you bring a baby into the house. Both of you are unemployed, still in high school, and I thought we were heading to college."

She quickly cut me off.

"Racquel, if I'm technically still a virgin, how the hell could I be pregnant?"

"Oh… What's up then? Tell me." First, she swore me to secrecy, which seemed odd. I felt silly crossing my heart; we were almost sixteen, for goodness' sake. It was my turn to roll my eyes and show her how unnecessary and mysterious she was being. Why was she acting so cryptic?

"My stepfather has been seeing Sister Frances from the fundraising committee at church for years."

"That's it? That's the big secret?"

Talk about dramatics. I was expecting something more scandalous, like her stepfather making a pass at her or something. I guess there was a little drama in me, too.

"Well, it's a relief it's not those other things I mentioned. So, you should tell your mother."

"Racquel, she already knows."

I was a bit shocked. Aunt Lynn, despite her role as a good Christian soldier, wasn't enough to keep Uncle Herbert faithful. It certainly changed my perspective on things, like marriage.

"Grace, your mom's grown; she can handle it. She must have her reasons for not blowing up yet."

"I know, it's just that she waited so long to remarry. Even though she gets on our nerves, I still want her to be happy too. Trust me, the happier she is, the less grief she gives us," Grace added.

"I know that's right," I replied. "But you're not off the hook yet. What's this 'technical virgin' stuff?" I asked, feeling out of the loop and a bit embarrassed. When Grace started to smile, my eyes widened in alarm.

Well, I'll be damned—little Gracie isn't so innocent after all. I looked at her and said, "Give me the goods, girl."

"Well, there's not much to tell. I am still a virgin. Nothing's happening, just a little touching and this and that. I like Steven and all, but I've got a future. I'm not trying to have any kids or anything, and I definitely don't want him bragging to his friends about us."

"Forget it, I see you're not going to tell me."

How different we were—if I had something juicy to share, I wouldn't be able to keep it to myself. Except I had nothing to share.

In the mall, Grace and I put on our mature charade, pretending to be much older. We wanted the guys to think we came from some off-Broadway play, not from Sunday school. It wasn't a complete falsehood; I did come from church, so it wasn't much of a stretch. We browsed through every store, not letting on that we didn't have a dime to our names. I learned that trick from my mama.

"Well, well, well," a voice exclaimed. "What do we have here? You girls just coming from Sunday school?" Of course, he emphasized the Sunday school part.

It was Marcus and his two sidekicks, Steven and Tim—or T-ski, as his so-called new name went. I personally thought it was dumb. I guessed they hung out at the mall too. The leader of the pack had traded his Sunday clothes for jeans and a white top with bold, colorful letters spelling "Benetton."

Instead of feeling embarrassed about having our cover blown, my best defense was to ignore him. It had worked all these years, so why stop now? I looked at him as if he were beneath my notice and said, "We were just leaving."

Marcus asked, "Do you need a ride? My car is right outside." He clearly wanted to show off his birthday present. I replied, "No, thank you." Grace's answer, however, was "Yes"—she was positively car-crazy. Grace nagged until I gave in and let Marcus drive us home.

He tried to keep up a conversation, but it all became background noise to me, so I completely tuned him out. Steven Bowers, Grace's steady boyfriend, was in the backseat with her, kissing and whispering. Even though Steven didn't have a car, he had an after-school job, which Grace considered essential for dating her. She had already decided that once she found a boyfriend with a vehicle, she would dump Steven.

Grace might have been a bit shallow, but she was cool otherwise. In my eyes, she wasn't fast—just an opportunist. I envied her ability to take advantage of situations, but I lacked the courage to do the same. As a fatherless and motherless child, I felt the weight of needing to succeed, and growing up too fast was simply not an option for me.

My dreams were focused on getting a scholarship and going to college, not on guys and cars. Now, don't get me wrong—I went out occasionally and even let some overly eager boy shove his tongue down my throat, leaving slobber all over my mouth. I couldn't understand the appeal; it just made me want to gag. I figured maybe I needed an older guy—someone who actually knew how to kiss without making it feel like a dental procedure. But that seemed like a far-off possibility. "We're going to see *The Last Dragon* next Sunday; our entire Sunday school class is going!"

"Let me guess, Steven's going, right?"

"Shh! Keep it down before my mother hears you, girl." I didn't blame her; Aunt Lynn had a radar for adolescent conversations. More than once, she'd recounted in full detail things we'd said in the privacy of our rooms.

The following Sunday, our hair was pressed (since Aunt Lynn wasn't ready to agree to perms), and we were all set to go. One wrong move at church, though, and she would've revoked our get-out-of-jail-free passes.

At the movies, Steve and Marcus made fun of us, claiming that Taimak, the lead star, was a fruit. But Vanity's in it," Grace countered.

"We're not impressed," Marcus retorted.

Steve added, "I'm not paying my money to watch a fruitcake."

"I've seen it a million times, and trust me, he's fruity," Steven insisted.

"No, he isn't," Grace shot back.

"Yes, he is," Steve reiterated.

"Then why did you watch it millions of times?" Grace challenged, hands on her hips.

"I've got two older brothers and three younger sisters, remember?"

"Come on, little lady," he said, throwing his arm over her shoulder. "We're hanging out together today, right?"

With that weak line, he convinced Grace to see a scary movie with him. I stuck to my plan, bought a ticket for *The Last Dragon*, and stood in line at the concession stand.

Marcus joined me. "If you want, you could change your ticket and sit with us."

"Nope. I came here to see *The Last Dragon*, and that's what I'm gonna do."

"Do you have enough money?"

"This is not a date, Negroid. I've got my own," I said, pulling out eight crisp dollars and waving them in his face.

"Why you gotta call me names? I'm just asking."

Despite my objections, from that day on, the five of us occasionally hung out outside of church. Although Marcus was still a pest, I started to see another side of him. He was intelligent, funny as hell, and, honestly, kind of handsome.

The next time all five of us made plans to hang out was at a party four years later. It was the first time Grace and I ever snuck out. Timothy's friend Bernard was hosting it at his house. We said good night to Aunt Lynn and Uncle Herbert at our usual eleven o'clock, then went to bed fully dressed. Holding my robe tightly over my party outfit, I pretended to use the bathroom so I could listen for their snores. Mission accomplished: their bedroom television was off, and they were catching some serious zzz's. By midnight, we were out the door. I was grateful Aunt Lynn hated dogs, especially with how we climbed out the window and onto the tree. My only fear was falling.

"We're going to get caught," I whispered as Grace eased the car out of the garage. She was the only one between us who'd taken the driver's ed.

"No, we ain't. Now shut up; you're making me nervous," she snapped, putting the parked Celica in reverse while I pushed on the hood. "Watch how a pro does it," Grace said, just before backing into our garbage cans. "Oops," she muttered.

"I thought you knew how to drive."

"I do. You made me nervous," she shot back, turning on the engine and putting her mom's car in drive. My heart was pounding. I thought we were caught for sure.

But the lights at the Bakers' house remained off.

"They must sleep like the dead," I muttered to myself. If this is what excitement feels like, I'm staying home next time, I thought, convinced a beatdown was waiting for us when we returned.

"Racquel, live a little," Grace said, cutting through my wariness.

Bernard's parents both worked the night shift, leaving him in charge of himself and his younger brother, Kwame. With Presidents' Day that Monday and no school, his parents were working double shifts. Bernard had their schedule down to a science and threw parties three times a month around it. The tiny two-bedroom apartment was transformed into a makeshift nightclub. It smelled dank and was dimly lit, except for two red bulbs—one in the living room and the other in the hallway.

His parents' room was closed off. His own room was a mess, with sneakers and clothes strewn everywhere, and his brother, Kwame, was laid out on the lower bunk, watching late-night specials while we danced to KRS-One's new tape. Grace spotted Steve in the corner of the living room, talking to a girl who looked familiar as we walked closer. I led the way, with Grace right behind me. The new girl was licking the edges of what looked like a cigarette, then dipped it into her mouth, finally lighting it. She inhaled and promptly choked.

"Doesn't she go to our church?" Grace asked as we watched from a distance. I looked her up and down.

"They just let anyone in nowadays," I muttered.

After staring for a moment, the girl finally addressed us: "Whatcha you goodie goodies doing here?"

"Chill, Danielle, chill," Steve said. "This is my girl, Grace, and her cousin Racquel." Instead of greeting us, Danielle rolled her eyes and turned away, pretending to stretch. Timothy walked over and shouted over the blaring rap music that Marcus couldn't make it. Marcus must have had better things to do—who could blame him?

I sat on the leather sofa next to Timothy while Grace and Steve danced together. Their intricate dance moves left little room for anyone else. They danced or sat together for most of the time we were there. At ten to four, I tapped Grace on the shoulder. It was time to leave. Grace gave Steve one last lingering kiss before we headed out the door. There was no need to drive him home since he had his father's car. The cool blast in the building's hallway was a welcome relief after the humid and cramped apartment.

During the drive back, we joked about the weed head, Danielle, and laughed at the buckshots that peeked out from underneath her lopsided weave. When we got out of the car two houses down, we pushed Aunt Lynn's car back to the side of the house. Then, we climbed the tree to my bedroom window. I went first, reaching the escape route. I grabbed the sill, but it was jammed. I pushed and pulled. "What the hell are you doing up there?" Grace hissed at me.

"It's stuck!!!" I whispered back.

"Oh shit," Grace said, wiggling her hands as if she needed to pee. "Hurry up." At last, as if by magic, the window was up. I quietly climbed into my room and looked around. Grace followed me through the window seconds later. She opened the door, peeked out, and then went into her own room. After I undressed, I lay in bed, thinking about how easy it all was, and fell asleep shortly after.

At six in the morning, I felt a tap on my shoulder. It was Aunt Lynn, standing over me, while Grace leaned in my doorway, looking more asleep than awake, her head wrapped in her usual scarf.

"You girls sure think you're slick, Well you ain't." Aunt Lynn said. I flinched, bracing myself for the Auntie Lynn special.

"Get…your…ass…up. I want this house cleaned from top to bottom—every closet, every corner, doorframe, and windowsill—before you head off to school. When you get home, don't even think about leaving this house to go to the store. Y'all are making me gray before my time. Well, guess what? You both are grounded until I say otherwise. If you even look outside, I'll jump on both your backs and beat you like you stole something—like my damn car."

We were punished for four months, and unlike Grace, I didn't mumble a word. By all accounts, we could have been beaten about our heads as soon as we stepped out of the car.

It was our final year of high school, and both Gracie and I were accepted to Morgan State in Maryland. I had received a full scholarship, while Grace had secured grants and taken out a loan. Aunt Lynn couldn't understand why we wanted to go so far away, or why we chose a historically Black college. "Why?" she would ask. "The whole world isn't Black."

Grace and I chose to ignore her questions and made plans to go anyway. Everyone knew that the best sorority and fraternity parties were at Black campuses. Steve applied to Morgan as well, which irritated Grace, who had hoped to meet an "older college man." Meanwhile, Marcus was graduating from a Catholic high school he attended, despite not being Catholic himself. His mother believed he was receiving the best education her husband could afford, but she was deeply disappointed when Marcus decided to live with relatives in St. Thomas for a year before starting college. He had received a partial scholarship to Columbia University in New York and planned to study medicine, after his time in St. Thomas or wherever he was going.

Marcus' friend Timothy decided to stay in New Jersey and go to trade school. He wanted to become a mechanic and open his own shop. We all thought he was crazy, especially after learning from mutual friends that it was financially impossible for him to attend college. Marcus' mother, Mrs. Collin, tried to find ways to raise money to help him out since he was also a member of Holy

Trinity. By the following year, he would have the option to attend college if his trade school plan didn't work out.

It seemed like everyone had their plans sorted out. Weeks before prom night, it felt like everyone was paired up except for me. Studies occupied most of my time, and when Gracie urged me to "jump on this Financial Aid," I should have listened. But if I had, I wouldn't have pushed myself as hard, and I wouldn't have had a choice. I was attractive enough to get a date, but after neglecting my social life for my books, I had alienated any hopeful prospects. I was dateless.

Marcus did cross my mind. His school had already had their prom. On second thought, it might have made me seem desperate. I decided against it and got ready as though I had a date anyway.

Gracie and I had shopped for our dresses last week. I bought a burgundy off-the-shoulder gown, while Grace opted for a black sleeveless dress. I was determined to look good and dance like everyone else. My hair was upswept with cascading curls, and Grace sported a short haircut, claiming it was her "I'm going to college" look. On prom night, we looked fabulous.

My cousin let me travel in the limo that Steve had rented. She also hinted that I should bring cab fare for later. Steve was a gentleman and didn't mind me hitching a ride. Instead, he insisted we all take pictures together before we left Aunt Lynn's house. When we arrived, I saw a familiar car.

"Who invited him?"

The limo pulled into the driveway. "Steven, give me a few minutes, okay?"

Gracie turned to me and said, "Look, I invited Marcus so you wouldn't be alone."

"What? Girl, are you crazy? I see nothing wrong with dancing by myself."

"Come on, you know that's no fun. Just get out and have a good time."

As I stepped out of the car, Marcus extended his hand to assist me. It was the first thoughtful gesture he had ever made towards me. He was dressed in a black tuxedo, and his cocoa-brown skin contrasted sharply with the formal attire. His haircut was neat and clean, and the peach fuzz on his upper lip was meticulously shaped. "All this for me?" I thought, feeling a mix of nervousness and excitement.

I managed a shaky "Hi" and added, "How are you?" Marcus grinned, seemingly amused by his own private joke, while his eyes scanned me from head to toe. "I'm okay," he replied, though his gaze lingered a bit too long on my chest before he finally met my eyes again. With a courteous nod, he escorted me into the hall.

"You look like you hit the lottery tonight," he said with a smile.

The attempt at flattery was weak but passable. I replied with a simple "thank you," trying not to laugh. Marcus had gone through all this effort for me, so I vowed to be on my best behavior, even if he did step on my toes.

"Tell me," I asked, "does your girlfriend Tracy know you're on a charity date?"

"The answer to your question is no, and this isn't a charity date—I wanted to be here."

He tried to smile, but it wasn't my intention to annoy him. As we walked through the doors, I felt the magic of the moment hit me. I squeezed Marcus's arm, trying to calm my giddiness and not act like I'd never been anywhere. I asked for a drink, taking in the fairytale theme of the place. I was glad I'd brought my camera.

The venue was adorned with soft, colorful track lighting, light mist, man-made willow trees, silver and dark blue balloons, mirrors, faux candles, and other small lighting fixtures. I wanted to take pictures but decided to wait, not wanting to disrupt the mood. Marcus returned with our drinks.

"Man, this place is amazing; my school never did anything like this. My mom chaperoned the prom and complained to anyone who would listen about how cheap it was." He gave the impression he was embarrassed by the episode. I laughed at his comment, a freeing and unguarded laugh. "This place looks really nice," I finally said. Marcus just watched me.

"Your eyes sparkle when you smile."

This time, I was genuinely flattered. "Thank you," I said for the second time that night.

"Let's dance," he suggested.

"Alright," I agreed, hoping to avoid any more compliments. I wasn't easily swayed. After all, this person, my date, had been a nemesis for so long, and it was strange to see him acting so normal. Marcus led me to the dance floor just as the Beastie Boys' "Brass Monkey" started playing. The fast-paced song gave Marcus a chance to show off his moves. He was an average yet confident dancer. We danced to a few more songs and then took a seat. I pulled out a Kleenex for him, since he was sweating. Excusing myself, I found Grace and went to the bathroom, which was actually the information exchange office—a place to have uninterrupted talks, usually about guys.

I pulled out a Kleenex for him, since he was sweating. Excusing myself, I found Grace and went to the bathroom, which was actually the information exchange office—a place to have uninterrupted talks, usually about guys.

Marcus was growing me, just a little. The attempt at flattery was weak but passable. I replied with a simple "thank you," trying not to laugh. Marcus had gone through all this effort for me, so I vowed to be on my best behavior, even if he did step on my toes.

"Tell me," I asked, "does your girlfriend Tracy know you're on a charity date?"

"The answer to your question is no, and this isn't a charity date—I wanted to be here."

He tried to smile, but it wasn't my intention to annoy him. As we walked through the doors, I felt the magic of the moment hit me. I squeezed Marcus's arm, trying to calm my giddiness and not act like I'd never been anywhere. I asked for a drink, taking in the fairytale theme of the place. I was glad I'd brought my camera.

The venue was adorned with soft, colorful track lighting, light mist, man-made willow trees, silver and dark blue balloons, mirrors, faux candles, and other small lighting fixtures. I wanted to take pictures but decided to wait, not wanting to disrupt the mood. Marcus returned with our drinks.

"Man, this place is amazing; my school never did anything like this. My mom chaperoned the prom and complained to anyone who would listen about how cheap it was." He gave the impression he was embarrassed by the episode. I laughed at his comment, a freeing and unguarded laugh.

"This place looks really nice," I finally said. Marcus just watched me.

"Your eyes sparkle when you smile."

This time, I was genuinely flattered. "Thank you," I said for the second time that night.

"Let's dance," he suggested.

"Alright," I agreed, hoping to avoid any more compliments. I wasn't easily swayed. After all, this person, my date, had been a nemesis for so long, and it was strange to see him acting so normal. Marcus led me to the dance floor just as the Beastie Boys' "Brass Monkey" started playing. The fast-paced song gave Marcus a chance to show off his moves. He was an average yet confident dancer. We danced to a few more songs and then took a seat.

"Having a good time?" Grace finally asked.

"Yes," I answered. So it turns out Marcus isn't the jerk I long thought him to be. "Stop playing, girl," she interjected. "Don't front—he looks fine as hell tonight. If Steven and Marcus weren't friends, I'd be all over him. Believe that."

The night continued with Marcus still acting normal. When the prom ended at two a.m., Marcus drove me around for a while. Steven had rented a room, so I guess this was Grace's big night. We had to spend an hour or two meeting up with Grace and Steven back at the hotel.

"Did you have a good time?" To my surprise, I answered "yes."

"Marcus, can I ask you something personal?"

"That depends on what it is." He looked at me. "I already know—you want to know if Tracy and I..."

"Hey, listen," I said, "I'm not nosy. Just curious."

"Right," he said, unconvinced. "The answer is yeah, a while ago. I was her first, so to speak."

"Oh, so you loved her?"

"Hell no. I liked her a lot, yeah, but she wasn't a forever kind of thing. She started bugging out—where am I going, who am I with. It was like I was married or something. She had our whole future planned after high school. That kind of thing can suffocate a guy. Shit, I just started to live."

I was listening and definitely learning at the same time.

"Are you still with her?" I asked.

"Please," he said. "I already have a mother; I don't need two. I'm leaving her here in the States. She's trying to convince me to stay and go to UCLA with her. I told her my grandmother needs me. Some people can't take a hint. Plus, I started seeing Benita a month ago." He added, sounding perturbed, "Tracy was stressing me out."

'A liar and a cheat, I was right—he's still a weasel,' I thought, assessing the situation.

"Well, what about you? Are you letting a brother in or what?"

"Huh?" I answered, coming out of my reverie to focus on his question. "If you mean am I having sex, the answer is no. I'm not having sex, and I don't plan on it."

"What, and who are you waiting for? I know you're not one of those girls who make a brother beg and wait damn near a lifetime."

"Marcus, I have goals right now, and I won't let anyone or anything get in my way. Besides, I want my first time to be special."

"I don't want to waste something like that on just any knucklehead." It was on the tip of my tongue to add, "like you," but I held back. I wanted to talk about something else, but since Marcus had already started telling me about other methods he used to avoid Tracy, I decided to shift the topic. "So, what about your parents?" I asked.

"I remember you mentioned that your family is from St. Thomas. If I recall correctly, you had a bit of a funny accent when we were kids. What year did you come here?"

"I remember my first year here like it was yesterday," Marcus admitted. He described the day as cold and rainy. Then, eager to shift the focus back to me, he changed the subject and began asking more personal and probing questions.

Chapter 3

Marcus

My family moved from St. Thomas to America in the early 1970s. I was only five or six at the time, and despite my protests, my mother was adamant that we had to leave. I didn't want to come to America—I couldn't understand why we should leave behind everything we had back home. I was convinced this new place would be cold and damp, and I had heard that gray, hard brick was everywhere. Saint Thomas was sunny and beautiful, and I wanted to stay with my grandmother. However, I was told I was my mother's child and needed to help pack our clothes.

My grandmother packed enough food for the trip, saying something about not trusting airplane food. Saying goodbye to my grandmother and cousins was heart-wrenching. I promised I would run away and catch a plane back as soon as possible. My mother rolled her eyes at this, trying not to laugh, while dragging me along. After kissing her relatives goodbye, we took a taxi to the airport. My parents chatted excitedly as we boarded the plane, but I was sullen and refused to talk to anyone. My father wanted to cheer me up, but my mother didn't allow it—she was firmly against spanking and preferred talking things through.

Looking back, I realize that her approach was a way of guilt-tripping me into behaving. I took full advantage of this, and my mother spoiled me rotten, which sometimes frustrated my father. On occasion, she had to physically intervene to prevent him from disciplining me, crying out, "No! Don't you hit my baby." He would then warn her that I needed discipline. I wasn't a problem child—just intelligent and willful, like many boys my age. When we finally arrived, it was cold and raining. The sky matched how I felt. It was August 28, 1975, and I hoped the dreary weather might persuade my parents to reconsider.

"See, look, the place isn't ready for us. Let's come back another day," I suggested.

"Shut up, Marcus," my mother snapped, clearly irritated and unwilling to let me spoil her excitement. I was beginning to wear on her nerves. I didn't understand what the fuss was about—Taratola was far nicer than this place. My father's cousin Milford was supposed to pick us up from JFK Airport. "He might be running late," my father informed us.

"Let's just get our bags and wait where he said," my mother decided.

We waited near the baggage claim area. After twenty minutes of waiting and hearing my mother click her tongue in annoyance, a tall, dark-skinned man approached us, catching my father off guard. With a bear hug and a hearty laugh, he said, "So, you're finally here."

"Man, it's been too long," my father replied.

"Let me see that beautiful wife you married," he said, planting a juicy kiss on Mom's cheek. "Gloria, looking lovelier all the time." I made a face. My father didn't seem angry at all, so I smiled.

"Take your bloody hands off my wife," Dad jokes.

"Where's de boy cousin?" Milford asked, looking over the space above my head.

"Here I am," I said, stretching my neck to get noticed. Milford said, "I don't see him." I started jumping up and down.

"There you are," he said. "You've grown so tall."

"Gimme five, my man."

"What's that?" I asked, crinkling my nose.

"That's slang around here. I'm hip. I'm cool," he said, educating us.

"My son won't start talking like that!" Mom said with disdain.

"Uh-oh. We better head out," Milford said, looking sheepish but still smiling. The car he drove was a 1968 Buick.

It was quite a hot car back then, and pride was written all over his face as he told us about the special details of his Buick.

"This is my blue baby. My Lucille," he said. During the ride to Milford's house, he turned on the radio, which I think was to put Mom in a calm, relaxed mood.

It was clear that the hustle and bustle of the city excited and frightened her. "Everybody and everything moves so fast here," she said. Unable to believe this place was such a big deal, she looked nervous. Dad reached over and touched her hand. Looking back, I feel it was an invisible strength he lent her.

The radio was playing "Everybody Plays A Fool," a song my cousin turned up, claiming it was 'righteous tunes.' His voice and accent blended with the song. My mother rolled her eyes with a grin. Although it was apparent that Cousin Milford had adopted an American culture considered substandard, he was a serious pharmacist both back home and now in America. He was a partner at Queens Pine Valley Pharmaceuticals where he lived.

It was his dream to open his own pharmaceutical company. My father, knowledgeable in biology and medicine and a businessman at heart, hoped for an alliance with our cousin in the future. By the time we reached the house, exhaustion had begun to set in, and we were all too tired to admire the house before us. I lumbered out of the car, tired yet anxious to meet cousins my own age. I was rewarded as the children ran out of the house. "They're here! They're here!" they said simultaneously. My mother and father greeted them, hugging the children they had never met. I guess the boldest of the three asked, "Are we related?"

"Yes," was my dad's reply. "Your father is my first cousin, which also makes you my little cousins." The bold one looked up at my dad and felt what I usually feel; he was great, especially when he wasn't trying to "discipline" me.

There were two boys, Glen and Michael, and their sister, LaShawn. Glen was closest to my age; we were a year apart. The trio were stair-step children, each a year apart. "Come in and meet my wife," said Cousin Milford. "Then I'll take you up to a room where you can nap. Marcus can go into one of the children's rooms."

"Denise, come out here," Milford called in a loud, boisterous voice. Now you're waking up the neighbors, I thought, as his wife came out laughing with her American accent. Denise was a social worker at a local high school, Milford said with pride. Mrs. Denise Jacob was beautiful. I believe she was my first real crush. She had enormous, expressive eyes and a full smile. Her afro was brown and curly. I looked up at her with childhood wonder. She was like a new character in my life. The difference between Denise and my mother was so vivid—from the hair right down to the shoes they wore. The first day they met, my mother was dressed in a knee-length skirt with a floral blouse. Denise wore an African print shirt with bell-bottom jeans slung low on her hips. My mother wore flat sandals; Cousin Denise wore platforms.

Her Angela Davis afro was picked out to perfection, and large hoops swung from her earlobes, unlike my mother's small pearl earrings. Whenever Denise was asked about her Afro, she would raise a fist and respond with, "Power to the people," or my favorite, "Right on." Her completion was the color of honey. My mother, with her dark brown skin and long black hair kept in a tight coil at the back of her head, saw Denise as a rival. I noticed my mother's posture became a bit more rigid upon their introduction, though she made an effort not to show her disappointment or jealousy.

"Hello," my mother said, her voice melodious.

"Nice to meet you, Gloria."

"I've heard so much about you and your husband. Milford was so excited when you decided to move here. I guess he feels homesick sometimes."

"Yes, dear," he said, "I feel homesick until I look at my bank statement and you."

"Can you dig it?"

"Oh, I can," Gloria replied.

They kissed. We felt uncomfortable, like we didn't belong there. They were so absorbed in each other, engaging in the kind of love talk my parents would have. Michael, Glen, and I exchanged glances, while Lashawn decided to voice his distaste with a "yucky." If Mrs. Jacob noticed my mother acting standoffish, she didn't let on. "Please come on up, Gloria," Denise led the way, and my mother followed. My parents' room was in the attic. The attic was spacious, with a large bed, a dresser, and a small bathroom. It was modestly decorated.

Denise maintained a one-sided conversation, informing my mother that she could make changes if she liked. My mother finally said, "Thank you." I felt embarrassed; it was the first time I remembered Mom being so curt. Once we were out of earshot, I asked her if she liked it.

"She probably had help getting the job done," my mother said.

"Huh?" I asked, confused.

"Oh, nothing," she replied. "We're staying here only a little while until we can afford our own house."

"Will we have a house like this?" I asked.

"Bigger," she said. "Much bigger."

I smiled, pleased to see her happy again. Denise, the new love of my life, and my cousin went downstairs to prepare dinner. My father took a tour of the house, the garage, and the backyard, talking guy stuff with Milford. I sought out my new-found friends while Mom stayed upstairs to unpack. Our first evening ended quietly.

Tomorrow was a full day ahead, with talk of church in the air since it would be Sunday. After a restful night, everyone was in high spirits. Denise offered to cook a big Sunday breakfast, and to my surprise, my mother offered to help. The aromas of American cooking blended with back-home flavors. It was a blessing that cousin Milford had enough ingredients to make my mom feel a bit more at home.At the table, Denise insisted on drawing my mom out. "Gloria, I know this city might seem a little overwhelming, but just ask about anything you're unfamiliar with, okay? We're family, and I'm here to help until you guys find a place."

Switching tactics, she asked, "How are the churches in Saint Thomas?"

"I suppose they're not too different from the churches here," my mother responded, slipping into that odd, familiar demeanor.

"Ha! Got you, Gloria!" Denise exclaimed, her tone bubbly. "It's not the same," she continued. "The churches here are more or less a pageant show and gossip station." A genuine smile broke across my mother's pretty face.

The men at the table chimed in with their own witty remarks. My father, usually so reserved in both behavior and speech, seized the opportunity to address the female company. "I believe," he stated, "it's the men who take the idea of church and God seriously." His laughter during the little speech didn't go unnoticed.

"Yeah, right," Denise replied, accompanied by my mom's "Oh! Please." Milford then added, "Let's get ready; service starts at twelve sharp." "This morning, I refuse to let you make me late," Milford said to his wife. They exchanged looks and eyebrow movements. I couldn't help but think about how much fun it was going to be living there.

My parents loved each other, but they lacked the magic I saw between my cousin and his wife. Even at that young age, I knew I wanted a Denise of my own someday.

Milford and his wife attended a church called Holy Trinity somewhere in Brooklyn. At eleven sharp, the Buick was packed and ready to go. The last call for the bathroom was made, and everyone, well-dressed and neat, declined. We were off to Holy Trinity.

The church wasn't as nice as our church back home, but it was okay. At that tender age, I was completely prejudiced about things from home. I remember the shiny, polished wood floors at Holy Trinity that gleamed under the colorful patterns of stained glass windows. Everyone was dressed elegantly, with hats that grew bigger and brighter. Just like our church back home.

"Come on," said Michael, and Glen informed me that Sunday school was downstairs. "Afterwards, we get treats." Lashawn called, "Wait up," as we left her behind. As I rushed ahead, my mother reminded me to walk. Ms. Billington, my Sunday school teacher, didn't sound very American. "Are there any visitors here today?" she asked. My cousins made pointing gestures toward me. I felt embarrassed and annoyed at being singled out.

"Let's not be shy," she gently urged.

"I'm Marcus Collin," I said.

"Where are you from, Marcus?" she asked, excited to have a fellow islander in her class.

"My family is from St. Thomas."

"That's lovely. Do you like it here so far?" she inquired.

"So far, yes, but this is just my second day."

"Where are your parents?" she asked next.

"Upstairs," I answered.

"You must introduce me to them. I'm from Trinidad," she said.

"Let's sing the welcome song for Marcus, class!" she announced. The class began singing, "Welcome, welcome, we are so glad you're here…." The next three hours were spent talking about Jesus' commandments and coloring. At the end, just as Michael promised, we were all given three cookies each and milk.

Michael went to the next class to get his sister. Glen and I stayed where the cookies were. As I came downstairs, I noticed my mother's disapproving look, which made me stop at my fourth cookie. I looked down at the crumbs on my clothes. She gave me a stern look.

"Hello," she said, "I'm Mrs. Collin, Marcus's mother," shaking hands with Ms. Billington.

"Great, I don't have to look for you. I'm Ms. Billington, the Sunday school teacher." They shook hands. "I hear you've only just arrived."

"Yes, we came in the day before yesterday from Saint Thomas. How long have you lived here?" my mother asked Ms. Billington. "I see you're also visiting from somewhere else."

"Yes," Ms. Billington explained, "I was telling Marcus that I'm from Trinidad. This is only my first year here. Who are you here with?"

"My husband's cousin, Milford Jacob."

Suddenly realizing the time, my mother turned to leave. I thought to myself that this woman asked a lot of questions, almost as if she wanted our whole life story. My mother seemed to find it easier to talk to Ms. Billington than to Cousin Denise, whom I liked. "This is my number," Ms. Billington said, scribbling on a piece of paper. "Call me; I can show you around and pass on any needed information. I've picked up a few tips from living here. I stay with my sister Ann. Well, see you next Sunday, young man," she said, shaking my hand.

My mother located Milford and my father; they were "fellowshipping." My cousin had promised the pastor and other members of the church that he would bring our family back. "I really enjoyed today's service," Denise said to no one in particular.

"Yes," my father agreed, "very inspirational." My mother said she enjoyed the music. Milford added that he "needed a short nap."

I said I wanted to watch television since it was too chilly to play outside. "You just have to get used to the weather," Michael said. "Trust me, it gets a lot colder than this." "Don't remind us," my father replied. "We might turn around and go back home."

Finding a school for me to attend should have been straightforward, but leave it to my mother to complicate things. She was determined for me to go to a Catholic school, believing it was the only place where a child could receive a proper education. Despite Denise's attempts to convince her otherwise, my mother was unyielding. It didn't matter to her that our family had just arrived in the country.

These strong opinions of my mother led to frequent disagreements between my parents. Yet, my mother was also supportive and comforting to my father. Her ideals of life often clashed with his. My father initially worked as a biology teacher at a public school, just as he did in St. Thomas. He saved diligently for medical school, knowing that one day he'd leave teaching behind to pursue his dream.

My mother found employment as a cleaning lady in an east side Manhattan apartment, vowing that once my father graduated from medical school, it would be her last day as a toilet washer. We still lived with cousin Milford and his family, which irritated my mother, but she remained focused on the bigger picture. She hoped that the sacrifice would eventually lead to having her own house. "Sometimes you have to stoop to conquer," she would say.

During the time my father was in school and my mother was working as a cleaning lady, money was tight. When I was five years old, it wasn't a big deal, but as I grew older, especially on Sundays and weekends, I felt out of place. My accent made me the target of many jokes at school. Both white and black American children would tease me, telling me to get back on my "banana boat" and return to my own country.

Initially, I didn't like America. My mother told me they were all jealous because our home country was beautiful, while this country was just a concrete jungle. I didn't fully understand what she meant at the time, but I agreed. My mother reassured me that things wouldn't always be this way, as my father was going to be a doctor. One day, we would have everything we wanted, and the opinions of others wouldn't matter.

My father graduated from medical school in 1979 and began his internship at Brooklyn Jewish Hospital. My mother seized every opportunity to mention my father's accomplishments to members of the church. She didn't brag; she just worked his achievements into conversations. Curiously, she stopped referring to him as Trevor or her husband and began calling him Doctor Collin.

The same year my father graduated from medical school, we officially became U.S. citizens. The day passed with little fanfare for my mother, but for us, it was a significant milestone.

But my father was pleased, as it fit perfectly into his carefully crafted plans. In the beginning, my mother still acted like a well-adjusted visitor, ready to flee at a moment's notice. Her adjustment was very gradual; she was caught between two worlds, uncertain about embracing a new, unfamiliar country and calling it home.

Once my father became a doctor, the ladies at church began to treat my mother with more kindness. She started receiving invitations to various social events and church functions. It was also clear that Ms. Hazel Billington, my Sunday school teacher, had her own aspirations. She became my after-school sitter, which was not something I particularly enjoyed.

The occasions when my mother couldn't pick me up from the sitter, my father made time to collect me. We would spend quality time together, going to the park or for ice cream. What my mother did not see, I experienced firsthand. He always made extra dinner for my father when he picked me up, offering things she had prepared or adjusting her hair and makeup if she knew he was on his way over. My mother was oblivious to this; to me, Ms. Hazel was a friend, but to my mother, she had become much more.

My mother and Ms. Hazel became inseparable. Ms. Hazel was constantly dragging my mother to various Caribbean social gatherings. Looking back, I can understand how my mother became so trusting; Ms. Hazel shared a familiar Caribbean background and made my mother feel at ease. My mother leaned on that connection.

The only place my mother and Denise went together was church. My mother was polite to Milford's wife, Denise, but not particularly friendly. Denise, with her grace and forethought, understood that my mother was missing her home and still felt like a stranger in this new country.

At night, it was my custom to kiss my parents goodnight. One evening, I overheard my mother telling my father, "This country is always at war with another. America has drugs and drug addicts aplenty, and the lazy black folks here keep talking about 'the man.'" My father asked if Ms. Hazel allowed my mother to tape record their conversations or if she wrote everything down for remembrance. "Good night, Gloria."

I was surprised and embarrassed by my mother's views, hoping she had not been overheard by anyone else.

While my mother busied herself with becoming Mrs. Dr. Collin, trouble was brewing in her backyard. Looking back, I'm sure that if my mother hadn't been so preoccupied with her new role, she might have seen Ms. Billington for the woman she truly was.

I saw right through her, no matter how nice she was to me. I chose to believe the same about my father. I think the only reason he didn't get upset about her flirting was that he sometimes enjoyed it. Whenever my father got caught up in any "small talk," I had no trouble reminding him that my mother was waiting for us. Yet, I was nothing compared to Ms. Hazel—she had her game down to a science. She wasn't deterred by me at all. Whether my mother saw Ms. Billington's attraction to my father and his 'potential,' or was oblivious to it, I wasn't sure, but I didn't like it. All I could do was sit and watch the events unfold.

With all this going on, my favorite part of the week became Sundays. In junior high school, I made friends outside of my cousins, and as I grew older, my accent became less prominent.

My father, Dr. Collin, provided us with more—like a new car, which drew increased attention from the parishioners at church, new clothes for me, and a new house for my mother. With this new wealth came newfound respect from many parishioners who had initially shunned her for her attitude. After buying the house, it finally sank in for Ms. Hazel: she didn't stand a chance.

I suppose my mother had her game down to a science as well. Her elevated status at church became the highlight of her week as a housewife. On Sundays, she was Mrs. Dr. Collin.

Entering high school, I barely scraped by. I was an average student, though my mother liked to say I was on the honor roll. I still had no clear idea of what I wanted to do after high school. My mother suggested it would be nice to have two doctors in the family, but while my father enjoyed his work, I wasn't excited about the idea of seeing someone's insides. Junior High had revealed my talent for math, and since math to me meant money, it was easy to grasp. If I pursued anything in the future, it would definitely be accounting, not medicine.

At fifteen, I was still forced to go to church with my parents. It was embarrassing and did nothing for the cool image I was trying to cultivate. One Sunday, I told my mother I was an atheist, hoping it would convince her to let me stay home.

"What's that? We are going to church like the God-fearing people we are," she said. In my mind, she was just trying to maintain appearances.

Meanwhile, I was more interested in girls, dedicating all my spare time to studying them. I considered myself a ladies' man and managed to score at least once a week. Once I learned how to use my "hidden talent," I wasted no time applying it wherever I could.

Special girls in my life, or rather, the ones who came and went quickly, often didn't last long around my mother. She had a talent for making them uncomfortable, whether the discussion was about religion, social issues, or finances.

"Mom, I'm dating, not looking for a wife," I had to tell her repeatedly. On this particular Sunday, the topic was my current girlfriend, Tracy.

"What's wrong with her, Mom?"

"I just want the right kind of girl for my son. It's my job to protect you."

"Protect me from what?"

"From young girls who don't have anything."

"My father gave me 'the talk' when I was thirteen. Sorry to shock you," I said, trying to sound confident and unbothered.

"For a smart boy, you're pretty naive," was her only response. This was a conversation I'd rather avoid.

"Mom, Dad told me to run an errand before church. I'll meet you there."

There was one girl who stood out as a bit of a nerd. I used to pick on her every chance I got. I wanted to get to know her, but it was like she saw right through me and couldn't be bothered. Her name was Racquel, and I knew her from church. I was certain she was the only one my mother would find no fault in. She was a church girl and a bookworm, always with her nose in the air.

When we were younger, she wanted nothing to do with me, so every Sunday I made it my mission to harass her. She found every way possible to avoid my attempts, which only made me try harder. This went on for years until I decided to get to know her better and offered to be her date for the prom.

How was I to know she would undergo such a transformation? I had already had my prom and had heard from my friend Steve that she was going solo. Since Steve had plans to go to a hotel with his girl afterward, I decided to help a friend in need. I hoped it might also turn out to be my lucky night.

I was surprised by how attractive she looked and wondered if it was too late to make a move. She obviously knew about Tracy, but who told her? It seemed she didn't appreciate me taking her out, asking stupid questions and getting on my nerves within the first fifteen minutes. Eventually, she quieted down, and we began to have a good time. The hall looked nice—nicer than our own prom.

We danced a little, and I tried to compliment her throughout the night, hoping to improve my chances. She made it clear, without much effort, that she hadn't changed her mind about me. In truth, all I really wanted was to sleep with her. I wasn't interested in her thoughts or opinions and lacked the finesse to pretend otherwise.

Towards the end of the night, I realized it hadn't been a complete waste of time. I decided to shift my approach; rather than trying to win her over, I focused on understanding what made her tick. I wasn't surprised when she mentioned she was a virgin; in fact, I would have been more surprised if she weren't. The night concluded on a positive note overall. She was set to attend Morgan in the fall, while I was planning to take a year-long vacation before starting college.

Racquel

The night went fairly well, though to my annoyance, he didn't try to kiss me goodnight—he just hugged me. I suppose he understood that if I had waited this long, I wasn't about to get caught up in the moment. Gracie, on the other hand, had a lot to share about her night. She recounted everything, revealing that sex was painful and lasted only a few minutes. I thought to myself, what a waste—I'm not missing a thing.

The next morning, Aunt Lynn asked if we had a good time and if we had conducted ourselves like ladies, fixing us with her "I've got my eye on you" stare. We assured her we had, and we put prom night behind us, focusing on college.

Aunt Lynn then asked to speak with me privately, claiming it was important. I assumed she was going to lay down extra rules for our time away. Gracie had gone out with Steve, and after prom, they were inseparable. Alone without my sidekick, Aunt Lynn saw the perfect opportunity to talk to me. Her serious expression was a bad sign. She told me she knew it was hard not having my mother around and that, given the circumstances, she was proud of how hard I'd worked.

It was clear she was about to say something significant, so I tried to mask my impatience. I said thank you, trying not to look too eager to move on. Then she dropped a bombshell: "There was some money left in a trust for you by your father." She didn't even flinch.

How was I supposed to react to that a week before leaving for college? I was already stressed about being smart enough to handle college and fitting in, and now this. "What?" was all I managed to say. After a moment of processing this unexpected news, I felt betrayed and asked her, "How long have you known about this?" I asked, my anger and confusion bubbling over. I wasn't sure who to blame, but I knew Aunt Lynn was just the messenger, not the cause of my pain. That knowledge offered little comfort. It wasn't her fault, but it didn't lessen the hurt I felt. After the initial shock, my questions came pouring out.

"Who is he? Why did I never hear from this man? Why didn't you warn me? Why didn't my mother tell me?"

"She didn't think you were ready to handle it at the age of ten," Aunt Lynn said with a hint of frustration. "Now that you're all grown up, I believe you deserve to know the truth."

"Yeah, but Aunt Lynn, why now, right before I go off to school? Why didn't you tell me last year or the year before?"

"Your mind was on your studies, and this would have only distracted you. If now isn't the right time, then when?" Aunt Lynn said.

"Well, he can't buy my forgiveness. I don't forgive him," I replied, meaning every word.

"Child, don't be foolish. Take the money; you'll need it. Whatever you want to work out with your father can be handled in time."

My father? What a joke—I don't have one. After Aunt Lynn's grandstanding, she left me alone in the kitchen to think.

With my hands folded and determination written all over my face, I felt an agonizing ache and emptiness in my heart. A traitorous tear slid down my cheek, and I cried for the second time in my life. The first time was after my mother died; the second time was learning that my father was alive. I washed my face and went on with my day, discussing the money with Aunt Lynn. I wasn't going to be anyone's fool. I didn't mention Robert Scylas again; it was as if he didn't even exist.

A new chapter was calling, and I had to pack and prepare for it. Aunt Lynn drove us to our new residence in her old jalopy, but we were unconcerned. Independence was right around the corner, and it didn't matter what means got us there.

I was so nervous that my stomach felt like it had just come off a roller coaster. My palms started to sweat, and all I could think was, please God, don't let me do or say anything noticeably stupid. With the extra money I was given, I bought a little "I'm proud of me" wardrobe and saved the rest. Grace was convinced I should have bought a car or jewelry.

How differently we think. I was assured that a part-time job would give me all the "essentials" I needed. Listening to her, the ten thousand I had left would soon turn into ten dollars. When Aunt Lynn left, I was relieved. She inspected everything—our shared dorm room, the shower stalls, and even the cafeteria, despite the rules. It was embarrassing. When we hugged her, she was actually crying, mentioning she needed to check her numbers now that we were in college, and she had to hit her targets. She memorized our housing address to track us. For me, she couldn't leave fast enough.

Settling into our new home, dorm room number five, the gray walls made the place look like a tomb. I looked around, trying to think of ways to make it comfortable. "This is our own private prison cell," Grace commented. "There you go, being dramatic," I said.

"Look, I'm going to find Steve."

"Grace, have you become whipped or something? Give the boy a chance to settle in. There are a lot of people on campus, and I thought you were planning to branch out."

"Don't be jealous that I have a man and you don't. And just like you said, there are plenty of guys on campus, so get busy."

She laughed to soften the sting of her words, but it was too late—the jab had already left me thinking about my own romantic situation.

Chapter 4

Marcus

My moms didn't want me going to St. Thomas. She came up with every excuse, starting with college being a top priority. I told her I was finally taking control of my own life and that college would still be there for me next year. I reassured her that her plans for my future were what I had in mind for myself, though she didn't need to know I was bending the truth.

I planned to take a hiatus for a year and then return to the States with a clear direction for my future. Trying to explain this to my parents felt like trying to teach trigonometry to our dog, Blaze. I was determined to go, and nothing was going to change my mind. My mother packed various items for different family members, and I wondered if they would even remember me.

In a raspy voice, she assured me they would, and handed me a photo of my grandmother and cousins to take with me, just in case I forgot. On the day I was leaving, I considered calling Racquel but decided against it. I hadn't left her with the best impression, and by this time, she should be in school.

As always, my father was absorbed in his work but took the time to talk with me the night before. "Don't worry about your mother. This is the first time you'll be gone for so long."

My moms didn't want me going to St. Thomas. She came up with every excuse, starting with college being a top priority. I told her I was finally taking control of my own life and that college would still be there for me next year. I reassured her that her plans for my future were what I had in mind for myself, though she didn't need to know I was bending the truth.

I planned to take a hiatus for a year and then return to the States with a clear direction for my future. Trying to explain this to my parents felt like trying to teach trigonometry to our dog, Blaze. I was determined to go, and nothing was going to change my mind. My mother packed various items for different family members, and I wondered if they would even remember me. In a raspy voice, she assured me they would, and handed me a photo of my grandmother and cousins to take with me, just in case I forgot. On the day I was leaving, I considered calling Racquel but decided against it. I hadn't left her with the best impression, and by this time, she should be in school. As always, my father was absorbed in his work but took the time to talk with me the night before.

"Don't worry about your mother. This is the first time you'll be gone for so long."

"Okay, Ma, I gotta go," I said, freeing myself from her iron grip. Boarding the plane, I felt a surge of freedom. Since the plane was 'blessed' and my money securely tucked away in my worn Jockeys, I took a nap. When I woke up, I wasn't aware that we had landed.

Transferring the money to my wallet and then placing the wallet in my sock, I exited the plane. Hungry from not eating, I looked around as I walked off the ramp, marveling at how colorful and beautiful the place was. My heart ached at the thought of a missed childhood on this island. I drew a deep breath, savoring the air as much as I could, wondering if I could somehow bring some of this life back with me when I return to the States. The island smelled of fragrant natural adornments—rich soil, beautiful flowers, vegetables, fruit trees, and the salted blue-green water. Yes, the air was sweet.

The stench of New York was a distant memory after leaving Newark airport. It was incomprehensible that anyone would want to leave here.The Newark waste management plant topped any stench that New York could produce. Since it has been around for decades, the residents were probably used to it. But back home I was finally breathing breathable air. This small island provided all the necessities to survive. But as a wise man once told me—my father—why just survive when you can live? I caught sight of the sun reflecting off the white sand against the blue-green water, mesmerizing. It was hot, yet not the dry, humid heat I was used to. The island's surrounding water provided a natural cooling effect to the hot air. A gentle breeze pushed through the tropical plants, making them sway. I was tempted to take off my shoes right then and there to feel the earth beneath my feet.

The accents around me sounded comforting and familiar. People were friendly and helpful, a welcome change from the New York attitude I was accustomed to. Returning gave me a glimpse of what my parents must have felt when they left. I began to understand what my father and mother missed and what they gave up to live in America. My mother was right—New York was a rat race. Everything here was smooth, uncomplicated, and relaxed. Now that I had become a tourist in a place that was once home, naming places and faces was a small challenge. The sooner I met up with my family, the better. There was so much to see, and I didn't want to miss anything.

Then I spotted her—the matriarch of our family, Grandmother Ruby, my father's mother. Her face was creased with age, her eyes still bright with a lifetime of wisdom. How could I have thought we would not recognize each other? Our faces were so similar that if it weren't for the fifty-year gap between us, I could have been called her son. Needless to say, I favored my father, who greatly resembles his mother. Seeing her, I was glad that she was still alive. After all, it had been thirteen years since we left for the

States, and she was seventy-eight. I hugged her gently, afraid to hurt her frail body. "You forgot me already?" my Aunt Mildred inquired.

"Nah, I can never forget you, Aunt Mildred," I said, embracing her and affecting a long-missed accent. Standing next to my aunt was an unfamiliar face.

"Hello. Welcome back, Marcus." I stared at Aunt Mildred, hoping she would say something.

"I'm sorry," I said apologetically. "Are we family?"

"No," she replied. "I'm a friend of the family." Thank God, I thought, because this would be the first time I'd met her and maybe she would see a movie after I gathered the courage to ask.

"Hi," I said, flashing my best mix of confidence and shyness. This was going to be one hell of a summer. It didn't matter that this woman was at least ten years my senior. Outwardly, I shook hands respectfully with Sophie, a family friend, but in my mind, I was already plotting my game plan.

Racquel

Buckling down to study seemed straightforward enough. I set up my study and class schedule, peeking out occasionally to savor the college experience I had earned. Gracie, as always, spent most of her time socializing and studying minimally. She seemed to know everyone, from the football coach to the chemistry majors, thriving in her element. On rare occasions, I tried to join in, but I never felt quite at ease.

I found most of my freshman classmates vain and superficial, wondering how some had even graduated high school. On reflection, I wondered if this was what people meant by being "deep" or at least trying to be. As for the guys, I found nothing worth pursuing. I categorized everyone I met, unaware that I was building a shell around myself.

The exception to my scrutiny was a guy dressed in jeans and a baseball jersey. He always walked alone, lost in thought, with a bag slung over one shoulder. From his demeanor, it was clear he was not a freshman; he took school seriously. He was tall, with a rich chocolate-brown complexion, a square chin, and full, soft-looking lips—no ash, which was a plus. He always kept his hair cut low and rarely smiled, but when he did, it felt like the stars came out just for me. His dimples made my heart do somersaults. I didn't usually venture out as much as Grace, but meeting him inspired me to make slight changes to my daily routine. I had never been so interested in anyone before. It became a mission to meet him, yet I was determined to play it cool and not let him see how eager I was.

Hating to admit Grace was right, I realized I needed a car. She thought a nice 1987 model would be perfect and made plenty of jokes when I settled on a lesser model—a modest car, nothing extravagant, just something to get me around. My first vehicle, and I was so proud of it, was a 1976 brown Pontiac.Never mind, I paid five hundred dollars for it, and every week something needed fixing. It was mine—my first major purchase. As I became more upwardly mobile, I had more things to do and rarely stayed in, as had been my habit. With my new interests, I became more social, overlooking things in people that used to annoy me. I was eager to meet this guy, but he didn't socialize in the same circles as my cousin. How would I ever see him if he only came out for classes? Grace, who was a mastermind at arranging things like this, told me to let her handle it. Skeptical of her abilities, I drove out to the mall in the area, wind in my hair. I had a spending limit for myself, so after purchasing one blouse and two pairs of pants from Eddie Bauer, I left the mall before I could be tempted into any other store, which might have led me to overspend.

On the way back, my little car finally gave out. I cursed up a storm, calling the absent used car dealer every name I could think of. Lifting the hood of the car, I choked on the smoke, my hair was tangled, and my hands were dirty. There was nothing to do but wait for help. After waiting for at least three hours and with my nerves on edge, no help arrived. Finally, someone stopped—I guessed he saw the desperation in my face and took pity. A white Honda

Accord stopped in front of the wreckage, and out stepped my mystery man.

"Can I be of some help?" he asked. I wanted to turn and run, but I knew he would think I was crazy.

"Yeah, my car is acting up," I answered, trying not to sound helpless. "My car sort of broke down. I bought it four months ago, and it's practically brand new."

The look on his face made his thoughts clear. "Let me take a look. It seems your transmission is shot and you've got an oil leak." I had no idea what he meant. I mentally noted that once I landed a good job after college, I'd definitely buy a new car.

"I guess I'll have to get that fixed."

"No," he said with a grin. "Your car is down for the count." He chuckled at his own joke.

"Great," I said, "just the perfect end to a perfect day."

Seeing my frustration, he introduced himself. "Hi, I'm Franklin, and my girlfriend Janice and I were on our way back to school…" The mention of "girlfriend" made me wish for a crack in the pavement to swallow me up.

"Do you go to Morgan?"

"Yes," I mumbled in response to a barely heard question. I climbed into the back seat of his car and muttered a "hello" to

Janice. The car door made soft clicking sounds as it opened, and the vehicle itself looked brand new. Franklin wasn't arrogant or showy; his politeness only made me more frustrated, knowing my dream guy was with someone else. Janice was nice, not at all upset about her man stopping to help me out. I wouldn't be either if I looked like her. With a simple ponytail and makeup applied as if by a professional, she seemed effortlessly put together. I noted that day as one of the worst.

The drive back to campus wasn't as quiet as I'd hoped. Janice was incredibly friendly and insisted on chatting, despite my minimal responses. Maybe if I had bluntly said, "I'm a horny virgin; let me sleep with your fine man," it would have been more effective.

The car slowed as Franklin's Honda pulled up in front of the girls' dormitory. I managed a polite "thank you" before making my way into the dorm and straight to my room. Grace and Steve (the frequent visitor) were there, looking like two peas in a pod. "What happened to you?" Grace asked.

"Don't ask," I replied, laughing to keep from crying over the situation. "By the way, my car is dead."

"What happened?" Steve asked, finally grasping that he'd never be driving it again.

"It's dead, and I can't drive it anymore," I said, my agitation rising. "It broke down on the side of the road. And to top it off, guess who finally shows up after an eternity of waiting—Franklin, the guy I've been wanting to meet. He picks me up, with his girlfriend in the car. And look at me—oil in my hair and my clothes."

"Embarrassing," Grace said, always stating the obvious. Ignoring her, I muttered, "Did I actually say 'road'? Lord, I've been here too long."

It seems the car was a pile of junk, and my lack of knowledge about cars made it easy for the dealer to reel in another sucker.

"The next time I buy a car, I'll make sure to bring someone with me."

"Is the car permanently damaged? Are there any laws against this kind of thing?" Grace asked, her voice filled with indignation.The realization that they were both in a tight spot finally sank in.

Chapter 5

Marcus

The house appeared small yet inviting. Inside, everything had its place, meticulously structured and orderly. I didn't remember the house seeming this small, or perhaps my perception as a child made it seem much larger. It was a single level with three bedrooms, one bath, a large kitchen, and a sitting room. It put my mother's home to shame with its acquired glamor and shine. Hand-sewn curtains and sturdy wooden furniture adorned the place.

Sterling silver plates and serving bowls, relics of old wedding gifts, rested on mantels and were showcased in dining cabinets. On the main mantel, a faded photograph captured a young couple. The woman, clearly my grandmother Ruby, sat gracefully, while a stern-looking young man stood behind her—my grandfather, Elliot Marcus Collin, after whom I was named. His manner and expression spoke volumes about his character.

When my grandmother spoke of him, it was always with a conservative, dignified tone. Despite her reserved demeanor, her love for him was evident in every word she said. He had passed away eight years earlier. Initially, she was alone. My father had offered to bring her to America, but she declined, preferring to spend her final days in St. Thomas, in the house she had shared with him. She believed it would be a sinful shame not to be buried next to him. Now my grandmother lived with her remaining brother, Stewart, whom she cared for, and her daughter, Aunt Mildred. Later that day, I learned that my grandfather had crafted many of the pieces in the house with his own hands and a carving knife, a testament to their generation's self-sufficiency.

They were a generation wary of the fluctuating Caribbean government but not consumed by it. They embraced hard work as a part of life's gifts, often finding satisfaction in it. My grandmother, despite her age, was undeterred. It was not uncommon to see her traveling the countryside to handle various tasks. She was relentless, only stopping when it was time to be laid to rest. For such a small woman, she moved with impressive independence and agility.

She took pride in her farm, which boasted numerous cows and chickens. Grandma showed me her mango and pear trees and also owned a small canned food supply store. Needless to say, my father's money was unnecessary for her survival; she was a woman who never needed saving.

"How's my son?" she asked.

"Oh, Dad is great," I replied.

She inquired about everyone's well-being in detail, even asking about Milford and Denise. "Such a nice girl, Denise."

"Gran, you've met her."

"Of course I did, child. This is where they were married—right here in this house," she said with pride. "There's a realness to the girl that's not often found in many people. In realness, there's honesty," she added, shaking a finger.

"Do you have pictures?"

"I sure do," she replied, struggling to retrieve what all ladies over a certain age treasure: pictures. Milford should bring his family home more often. She worried they might be too Americanized to appreciate it. Opening an album, she flipped through pages, explaining that since her sister Clovine passed away, she had kept the pictures of her son's wedding.

"Hey, there's my dad," I interjected, spotting my father standing next to Milford in a suit. My grandmother and her sister were beside them. Next was a picture of Denise with her hair pressed and curled, wearing a white dress.

"How did they meet?"

"Her father came here to play jazz music for some American naval officers stationed here at the time. I believe he was a bass player."

She took off her glasses and closed the book, looking tired. "Denise was so happy. I hated to see them leave."

"My mother doesn't like Denise much," I told her.

"I'm not surprised," she replied, her tone nonchalant as she noticed my expression and chose not to elaborate. Turning to my mother, she asked, "How's Gloria?" Her eyes conveyed a lack of genuine concern, as if asking out of routine. "My mom's fine," I replied, still trying to understand the unspoken rules among the women in my family. "Yup, Dad's doing great," I added, feeling uncomfortable and sensing a strain in the relationship between my mother and grandmother.

As an afterthought, I remembered the things my parents had sent for her. I rummaged through my belongings and produced a package and a letter. I handed them to my grandmother, who read the letter but set the package aside.

"Why does your father send so much money?" she asked, pulling out three hundred dollars. "He should be saving for a rainy day." Despite the amount seeming modest to me, considering my father had given me his visa card and travelers' checks for the trip and my bank account was at my disposal, I knew he wasn't being stingy. My mother, on the other hand, would have complained and demanded more. My grandmother tucked the money away in her secret compartment, which also served as a makeshift bra drawer, and then asked if I was hungry.

I had learned that for many Black people, food is a way of expressing love. So, when she wanted to feed me, I let her. In her house slippers and colorful apron, she eventually stood up and walked toward the kitchen, still not ready to open my mother's package. Though she appreciated that I cleaned up after myself, she was content handling everything else—washing, cooking, and running errands—without assistance, refusing any offered help.

By my first night, after a few hours, I felt as if I were truly home. Following my grandmother's advice, I refrained from exploring until the next day. When I awoke to the sunrise, it was the most memorable I had ever seen. From my grandmother's property, I could see the shore. The sun's rays glistened off the water, and the trees were bathed in golden light. It looked as though heaven itself had opened up and poured out its rays. The birds were chirping cheerfully. I was sure there was no more beautiful place in the world. After a week in St. Thomas, I learned the island like the back of my hand. If it wasn't for Olivia and her cousin Eugene taking me out, life on that beautiful island would've become as monotonous as over-staying in a fancy hotel. We spent a lot of time exploring the bustling streets of Charlotte Amalie, where vibrant markets and lively local spots kept the days full of discovery and excitement.

I treated Olivia like a science project, content to learn her and wait for the right time to advance. She was different from other girls I knew; she was a woman. Intelligent, independent, she said what she wanted but knew the right time to broach any subject. She had an ease and style that girls my age lacked. Looking back, I realize that women were more complex than I had thought, and each woman has her own set of rules. There is really no grouping together everyone of that sex.

Olivia matured me to some degree. Without my experiences with her during that year alone, I wouldn't have learned the lessons I needed to know to deal with women from that day forth. To occupy my spare time, occasionally I would help my grandmother run her store in the bustling market in St. Thomas, where food and various wares were sold. I learned the barter system she sometimes used.

My favorite of all her customers was Mr. Cicely, a rotund man with visible gold caps in his mouth. He had an agitated leg that caused him to have a pronounced limp and salt-and-pepper hair, which covered only half his head due to its receding nature. He kept his little half-fro neatly combed.

While in the store, it was his habit to rub his pot belly and release a belch, as Mr. Cicely was not one for pleasantries like "excuse me." Grandma always gave him the evil eye and would stare him down while he ordered and left. "Nasty ass," she'd remark as soon as the door chimed to signal his departure. Grandma Ruby thought he was a disgusting old man, although his appearance was spotless. "All that belching he does; what rolly polly needs is a good cleaning out," my grandmother would add with a laugh. "A few hours squatting in the bathroom will help him to stop belching all over. Next time he's here, I'll slip him some of my special herbs in his tea." She looked over at me with a conspiratorial smile. "Shh, don't tell him."

Racquel

It was the fall of my second semester at Morgan. The first year had passed so quickly. By the third week of the semester, I was juggling two papers and an upcoming quiz. I had learned the ropes, so to speak. No longer did I feel intimidated by the place; I had settled in quite easily. I attended school activities regularly. Although my cousin Grace and I ran in different circles, we remained close. I understood that she might not see life as I did, and this year, I was more grounded, finally serious about earning a degree in something beyond popularity.

My romantic life was still nonexistent. I had friends and knew guys, but I found them unworthy. By this point, I was familiar with the ins and outs of the school, the familiar faces, and the key players on campus. Waiting for my dream man was beginning to feel like just that—a dream. I grew tired of waiting. Instead of holding out for Mr. Right, I decided to hold out for Mr. Alright.

Instead of taking pride in my virginity, I wanted to rid myself of this encumbrance. I decided this would be the year of my enlightenment. How to go about it was a mystery. According to Grace, I should just let it happen, so I decided not to be so particular and to follow her lead.

I ventured into the study hall to work on my recent chemistry project, only to find the Alpha Phi Alpha Fraternity members making a commotion in a place meant for studying and solitude. The Big Brothers had their pledges running around the study hall in nothing but their briefs, clearly thinking it was the height of hilarity.

One of the Big Brother's second-in-command called out to me. "Hey, you!" he said. "How you doing? What? You too good to talk to me, sweetheart? Don't you know it's a pleasure just to be seen with me?" His "brothers" joined in, creating a scene. "What's up, 'G'? She won't give you any play?"

"I told her she was crazy," he replied.

In a sweet, gentle voice, I responded, "I'm flattered that someone as important as yourself would give me the time of day. If you don't mind, I'd like to open this book right here and read it."

"Oh, it's like that," he said.

"Yes, it is," I replied. I dismissed him entirely by adjusting my position and turning a page, pretending to read. The art of ignoring someone was a skill I had mastered long ago.

I wanted to find a man but had no intention of getting involved with any guys from fraternities. I'd heard enough sob stories from the girls my cousin knew. She would share their horror stories with me, often calling the girls and their problems "whack." I didn't want to become a victim or a statistic.

One girl had even accused a guy of videotaping her without her permission. As if giving permission would have made it any better. The tape, which I heard was spread around campus, featured stereo sound effects and a soprano-pitched orgasm. I thankfully stayed a virgin this long to avoid being labeled as a garden tool.

The frat brothers' displayed charm was wasted on me. If I had realized that insulting him would make me a challenge in his eyes, I wouldn't have bothered to say anything. The lessons I learned from Gerald taught me that telling a brother "no, I'm not interested" was like declaring war. The game he had planned for me was one I wasn't ready to play.

Gracie and Steve did eventually break up over the summer. She said she needed space. However, the moment Steve started dating someone else, Adriane Williams, Grace decided she no longer needed space and instead wanted to track his every move. I found her insecurity surprising and unlike her usual self. Many nights, I played the role of psychologist, trying to help her with her deflated ego.

Instead of taking my advice to give each other space, Grace wasted no time finding a backup plan in case the breakup was permanent. She said, "I'm not waiting around until he dumps me. I gotta have backup plans." It was interesting how she brought all her ghetto euphemisms with her to this place of higher learning.

I told her about the study hall incident with Gerald. Grace was convinced I should have been flattered. Gerald is an ape—a conceited ape. He would only be wasting his time pursuing me. I don't want to become one of those sorry sisters she always called "whack." That was my first and last encounter with "G" until I began to notice him studying occasionally in study hall. At first, I was surprised, expecting more of his usual cocky behavior. But he ignored me completely—no smiles, no winks, nothing. This continued for weeks until he finally approached me. He asked me a physics question. I smiled and said, "You're taking physics? So am I."

"Excuse my earlier rudeness," he said. "I'm just a serious student."

"No problem," I replied. "So am I, that is, when I'm not clowning around with my friends. Being in a fraternity comes with certain obligations," he explained.

"Of course," I agreed, feeling awkward and needing something to say.

"So, what's your name?"

"Racquel," I answered.

"I'm Gerald Smith," he said, extending his hand.

I shook it, surprised by how his actions didn't match his randy reputation. "My name is pretty common, right?" he said with a sideways smile, looking for confirmation.

"Yes, it sounds common," I replied, waiting for the jerk in him to reveal itself so I could deflate his overinflated ego.

We fell easily into conversation about general topics—nothing too personal. I thought to myself that this couldn't be an act; his manner was so sincere. "You're not at all what I expected," I said.

"It's easy to misjudge me because I'm in a fraternity. We're not all bad."

"Whoa, look at the time," he said, glancing at his watch. "I really have to go, but there's a party at the frat house next Wednesday. Before you say no, think about it. Here's my number." He scribbled it on a piece of paper and handed it to me. "Just in case you tell me you lost it," he added with a grin. Then he made his exit. He wasn't what I expected, so I might think about it. Maybe. The rest of the day went on as though Gerald and I had never spoken. The next day, everything was back to normal—no Gerald in study hall.

I held on to Gerald's number, debating whether or not to call. After returning to my dorm, I received a call from Mr. Scylas asking to see me this coming Wednesday. I couldn't help but think of how avoiding him felt similar to dodging an absentee father— something *he* has been doing for years. "I can't," I said to myself, "I have a date." It was Wednesday night, and it was official—I had a date with Gerald. With no classes on Thursday, it was doable. Gracie was excited, but I wasn't as hyped about the idea as she was. It was just something to do. He wasn't taking me out to dinner or even to the movies; we were just hanging out at the infamous frat house.

I decided on a short black linen dress and a little perfume, hoping it might change his mind about the venue. Before Gerald picked me up, Gracie reminded me to relax, enjoy myself, and make it clear to him about anything I didn't want to do.

"Since when did you age ten years older?"

"Here," she said, handing me a condom.

"It's not that type of party," I replied.

"Hey, you never know."

"Okay, fine," I conceded, taking it with her better-safe-than-sorry look.

The den mother announced that I had a visitor—Gerald was downstairs. He was prompt, arriving at exactly nine-thirty. As I reached the last landing, I felt disappointed to see he was wearing his frat colors. I felt foolishly overdressed.

"Give me a minute, Gerald. I'll change."

"No, don't bother," he said. "I might have to change later anyway."

Gerald drove a 1987 Cressida, a gift for graduating high school. As it turns out, his mother is a nurse in D.C., and his father is a patrol officer, also in D.C. He opened the car door for me and waited while I got in. During the drive, he seemed content to hear his own voice, so I let him ramble on about himself, his fraternity, the frat house, and the football team he played on.

He was on an athletic scholarship, recruited by the Bears' football team from high school. Gerald also held a 3.7 GPA. I was again impressed, wondering how I could have been so wrong about him before. He was a serious student.

"So, why haven't you found a sorority to join?"

"I'm here on a full scholarship," he said. "From what I see, it takes up a lot of time. I didn't want anything to detract from my studies. I didn't want to risk my GPA falling."

"Oh, okay," I replied.

"Besides, my cousin Grace joined, and they had her running around like she was crazy. She dropped out after her second week of pledging."

I spoke only briefly about myself—there wasn't really much to say.

Approaching the place, there was no need to see it; we heard the music from a mile away. The music sounded like an explosion echoing within the walls of the simple two-story frame house. "I guess the party is in full swing," I told Gerald.

"Yup," he answered, wiggling his thick eyebrows. The Black and Gold Alpha colors were proudly displayed in front. One drunk "Alpha" asked Gerald where he had disappeared to before passing out on the stairs. I held Gerald's hand as I crossed the threshold into what he assured me would be a good time. Upon entering the infamous A Phi A house, the smell of smoke, spilled beer, and athlete's foot was overpowering. As a non-smoker, I gagged on the smoke fumes, wanting nothing more than to empty my already empty stomach.

Gerald was beaming with pride after another successful party and took a moment to introduce me to a few of his friends. "Racquel, this is everyone. Everyone, this is Racquel." The sound of a dog barking greeted me, and I forced a smile, saying how charming it was. Gerald took my hand and led me to a quieter part of the house. "I'll be right back," he said before leaving. When he returned, he handed me a couple of beers in plastic cups, the foam spilling over the sides and the cups icy to the touch. Why not? I thought, deciding to let loose a bit.

Had I known more about drinking back then, I would have realized the importance of *not* drinking on an empty stomach, avoiding unfamiliar drinks, and drinking in moderation. Gerald's easy smile made me feel so at ease, I let myself relax. As the night went on, the beers kept flowing and the music grew louder. By 2 a.m., I was laughing uncontrollably, almost losing control of my bladder. I was drunk and starting to feel nauseous. I asked Gerald to take me home, but he always found an excuse, insisting I just needed to lie down. He knew a place. With his brothers cheering him on, he led me to an upstairs room.

As I stumbled into the dimly lit room, I collapsed face down on the bed. I turned to see Gerald closing the door and leaning against it. At this point, the pounding in my head was relentless.

"Gerald, I really need to go," I said weakly.

"Just relax, baby. I'll take care of everything," he replied, as he started to get undressed.

I turned to see what he was doing. "What the hell are you doing?" I demanded, taking in the scene as Gerald's shirt came off and his pants followed quickly.

"Shh…baby," he said soothingly.

"Where did all this baby shit come from," I said, struggling to stand.

"Relax," he said with a forceful push, I landed on the bed. Then he joined me on the twin with a plop. Lips found me quickly, his hands grabbed every possible area. At that moment his hands were palming my vagina, my intentions were to stop him before my panties were lying on the floor.

"Wait, Gerald, I feel ill."

"Don't worry baby," was his reply."

Little did I know the situation was already beyond my control. My drunken arms were no match for him. The more I struggled the more he held me. There we were tussling about like children absorbed in tug of war battle, Fear overriding common sense, I finally reached back to slap Gerald. My palm collided with a crack across his solid cheek, it was an action that caused no effect and did little to stop his octopus-like arms. He hooked his fingers at the sides of my bikinis; I squirmed and shifted my body angle on my side. At this vantage point my pitiful movements were slowed and uneventful. The rip alerted me to the fact my panties were in fact a shredded memory.

"Stop it," I demanded, close to hysterical, and attempted to hit him again, he only laughed at my clumsy movements. Smirking he said: "so you're into the rough stuff. Okay then, that's what I'm talking about." He then gave a hard tweak to one of my nipples. The beer inevitably made its steady path up causing me to vomit first on him then on myself. Although I was horrified, I was relieved. Gerald yelledgoddamnit, then released me cursing as he walked to the bathroom.

"What the fuck is wrong with you? Dumb bitch."

Am I to assume this is my fault, I wondered. Taking advantage of his immovable six two frame was off of me. I stood up on unsteady legs. This was my opportunity to escape taking his shirt and melted ice. I cleaned my face and tied my hair back leaving as quietly as I could out the back of the crowded fraternity house putting an end to my date with Gerald.Walking back to my dorm room, the cool night air relaxed me. Myheadache somewhat eased and the pounding from the music in my ears stopped, I still reeked of vomit. I made a mental note to have a good soak soon as I reached back. Upon reaching the dormitory, Ms. Graves, the den mother, told me a person named Robert Scylas stopped by, and handed me two envelopes. I replied, "Great." Taking the notes, I slowly climbed the stairs to my floor feeling as if I jogged home in my heels then walked. Never mind that I smelled like I rolled myself in garbage.

Marcus

Before Tinder and Netflix and Chill, there was something called dates. And Olivia and I spent a lot of time together during those first few months on St. Thomas, much to my grandmother's dismay. She didn't hide her feelings and often mentioned how she wished her grandson would find someone his own age. "Granny, how do you expect me to enjoy myself and learn to get around without going out? Olivia and I are just friends," I insisted, putting on an innocent face. My grandmother's sharp eyes studied me. After a brief pause, she said, "Alright, just be careful."

The next few days were filled with work at the store—organizing supplies, fixing shelves, taking inventory—you name it, my grandmother had me doing it.

Meanwhile, Olivia took the opportunity to reintroduce me to my mother's side of the family. My father's mother always claimed she couldn't stand them, but she didn't object when Olivia offered to take me.

It seemed absurd that the Hartfords lived only three miles from my father's family, yet despite sharing a grandson, they found it unnecessary to be civil to one another. According to Gran, Ellen—my other grandmother—had tried to cheat her over store supplies more than twenty years ago, and the incident had left a lasting sour taste.

Grandmother Ellen, however, had a different version of events, blaming my other grandmother for the whole ordeal. And so the saga continued, I thought. Gran Ruby often declared she had no time for "those people," passionately expressing her disdain for liars and cheats, calling them evil and "of the devil." I had hoped to escape the religious mumbo jumbo in America, but apparently not.

After a few months on the island, I grew homesick. Despite the island's beauty, my desire to stay began to fade. I missed America, especially the hustle and bustle of New York. The idea of winning over Olivia seemed less likely, and boredom started to creep in. She was kind enough but remained distant, likely due to the difference in our ages.

One day, I decided to take a chance and asked Olivia out to dinner at a resort hotel where my father's cousin, Randal, worked. She agreed. "This is my chance," I thought as I meticulously chose my clothes for the evening. Determined not to appear too young in her eyes, I dressed in a royal blue shirt and khaki pants. When we were finally seated across from each other on what felt like our first official date, I felt a wave of unease. The hotel was near the beach, and we could hear the ocean lapping at the shoreline. The scent of sea salt filled the air, and if we closed our eyes and focused, we could almost feel the spray of the water on our faces. It was something I knew I would miss once I left St. Thomas.

Usually, the hotel dining area was reserved for hotel guests, but with a relative working in the kitchen, it wasn't hard to secure a table. I had hoped to impress Olivia with my connections. She seemed surprised that I wanted to know more about her and appeared amused by some secret jest. My cheeks grew warm at the thought of being the butt of an unknown joke.

Despite my earlier confidence in getting her there, I found myself stumbling over my words during our conversation. Olivia didn't laugh at me outright, and for that, I was grateful. It would have been a serious blow to an eighteen-year-old's ego.

So instead, we spent the evening talking about everything except ourselves. She put me at ease once I stopped trying to come up with corny pickup lines. In return, she spoke to me about life— something no other female friend had ever done. Olivia was genuinely interested in everything I had to say and never interrupted. She didn't ask the typical, trivial questions girls my age often did and offered advice only when I asked for it.

I learned something from her that I had never learned from any girl my age: the value of friendship and mutual respect. Although my crush was real, Olivia wasn't interested, and surprisingly, I was okay with that. She even understood my homesickness and encouraged me to write to my mother or anyone else I cared about. I decided to write to Racquel.

Racquel

"That's it," I told myself. "No more college guys."

Unable to soak in a bath, I took a long shower, letting the hot water cascade over my body. I tried to relax, pushing away the memory of how close I had come to being violated. As I scrubbed my skin, I meticulously washed every spot Gerald had groped, avoiding my sore breast, which I could only soothe with cool water. I wondered how many others he had hurt. Sick bastard, I thought, biting my lip to hold back tears. Climbing out of the shower, I gargled with Listerine for what felt like an eternity. Still shaken, I dressed in pajamas and a plush blue cotton robe, determined to put the night behind me.

Earlier, when I walked in, I had tossed Mr. Syclas's note onto the bed, debating whether or not to open it. I put my letter from Marcus in my bookbag, planning to read it during a class break. As for Mister Syclas's note, curiosity and reawakened anger got the best of me. I snatched it off the bed, more angry with myself, thinking that if I had met with him, I might have avoided the whole situation. Grabbing a pencil to use as a letter opener, I hesitated for a moment before opening the note. After reading the first few words, I set it aside on my dresser, still undecided about how to feel. Telling myself I'd read it later, I slipped under the covers and quickly fell asleep. The next morning, Gracie woke me up bright and early.

"Hey girl, how was everything last night?"

"Meaning?" I replied dryly, determined not to dwell on yesterday's events.

"You know, going out with one of the finest guys on campus, that's what!"

"Do you really have to talk so loud? And to answer your question, nothing happened."

"Racquel, he is so fine."

"I really don't see anything fine about him. Trust me, he's not all that," I said, letting my hand flop dismissively. She had no idea how overrated he was. To me, he was the ugliest of men.

"Don't you have a class or something to attend?"

"Nothing happened?" she asked, still not convinced. "Nothing at all?"

"Nothing," I replied, wanting to keep the details of the date private. I recounted the evening, leaving out the parts I didn't want to share. I let her believe I had a fabulous time and that everything went okay.

"What's this?" she asked, picking up a note from my dresser.

"Do you have to inspect everything on my side of the room?" I snapped, snatching the note from her hands.

"It's from my father," I said.

"Did he send you any more money?"

"Is that all you think about? Money? There are more important things than just that."

"Oh, he's your father now?" she asked with a raised eyebrow. It hadn't occurred to me that I called that man my father. I was just as surprised as she was. Swinging my feet over the bed and slipping into my comfortable flip-flops, I read my father's note to the closest thing I had to a sister.

Over the next few days, I successfully dodged Gerald's calls, which made Grace very suspicious. After a week or so, the calls stopped, and life returned to normal. Unfortunately, I bumped into him while stopping at a water cooler en route to my biology class.

Stopping at a vending machine, I bumped into someone I never wanted to see again.

"What's up? You don't return calls."

"Is there something you want, Gerald?" I shot back.

"You're bugging out," he said, sounding defensive.

"Are you crazy or something?" I whispered, my voice tight with anger. "You tried to rape me and now you're pretending like it never happened."

"Rape you?" he scoffed, as if the idea was absurd. "Girl, please. I can have anyone on this campus I want."

"Well maybe you should date them." Shrugged and I stepped out of his path and walked toward my dorm. But he grabbed my arm and spun me around.

"Rape you," he said as if the thought was incredulous. "Girl pleassse. I can have anyone on this campus I want. You know that. You wanted me, but also want the pressure of saying yes taken off you, so you don't look fuckin' easy. Triflin' hoes like you make me sick; you need guys like me to bring the true freak in you out. So fuck you, dick tease it was a pleasure for you just to be seen with me. You should thank me."

Fear from our unexpected meeting quickly turned into seething anger. "How dare you?" I struggled to keep my voice low. "You think you can justify what you did by blaming me? You're a real weirdo. You're actually sick and need professional help. Stay away from me. If you ever bother me again, I'll press charges. I'll go to Student Affairs, your coach, the dean—try me if you want."

Nodding, I displayed more courage than I actually felt.

"You can't prove a thing," he said, though his voice wavered. "You were drunk in your room. Who would believe you?"

I straightened my shoulders and met his gaze. "Try me," I challenged, keeping my expression unreadable. That was our last conversation. I briefly considered questioning his aversion to women and his sexuality, but I already had the upper hand. There was no need to waste more energy on him. He was still standing in the hallway when I entered my class. Damn tree jumper, I should have kneed him in the balls.

As I grew older and understood more about the dynamics between the sexes, it became clear that men like Gerald harbored an extreme dislike for women. They needed to humiliate them to feel special or powerful—hurting women that was his "bag."

Towards the end of the semester, Gerald was arrested for forcible sexual contact. He had lured another girl out under the pretense of a date and took advantage of her. The day he was arrested and hauled into county jail (for just one night), his parents rushed to get him released. The school held meetings in the dorms—what I called a "town meeting"—with a focus on the topic of date rape.

Girls were encouraged to come forward quietly and were offered both private and group therapy, funded entirely by the college. Despite more girls pressing charges, Gerald vehemently denied any wrongdoing, of course. Many students found it hard to believe the allegations because of his popularity. According to the "unlucky" few who hadn't dated him, he was too attractive for such a thing.

One of his "victims" I met at a group meeting seemed to be a tall, slender, vivacious character, radiating confidence. But after hearing her speak, it was clear that her encounter with the legendary "G" had left an unseen mark. Gerald had been a friend and had promised to take her to the mall as a favor, but they never made it there. Instead, he raped her in the back seat of his car in a deserted area before driving her back to school. He told her it was what she wanted and convinced her to keep quiet.

What lingered in my memory long after the meeting was hearing her tell the group that Gerald had stolen something from her that she could never get back—her sense of security. She frequently replayed that day in her mind, fantasizing about a different outcome. The incident had occurred during her first year of school.

I was personally outraged when the school allowed him to stay. He worked out a community service deal. Not long after hearing the charges against Gerald, Grace cornered me in the dining hall and asked if anything bad had happened on our date. When I told her what occurred, she was visibly shaken and kept repeating that it could have been me.

"Wow, Racquel, thank God you threw up when you did." It was a weird thing to say but she was right.

"I guess the smell of vomit lessened the attraction. Grace, I was drunk, and he took advantage of that. I didn't do it to avoid being raped. I'm not much of a drinker, you know that. I was just scared," I said with a nervous laugh.

"Well, let's just put this behind us, shall we?"

"Don't tell a soul," I warned her. "I know how much you like to gossip."

"Other people's business, yeah, but you are family."

"Almost being assaulted is not the same as being assaulted," I said. "I feel sorry for the girls who were actually violated by him."

The community service deal left a nasty taste in the mouths of die-hard feminists at the college. The real slap in the face was that he continued to play football. Needless to say, quite a few girls transferred out of Morgan. Some sisters reversed their decision to leave, staying only to protest Gerald's stay and the school's obvious support, hoping to make his last year there a living hell. In order to thwart this kind of behavior, it must be discussed.

My fathers letter said it was long overdue that we met. He explained that he only learned of my existence six years ago. He left a contact number, ending the letter by reassuring me that I deserved answers and that we could talk whenever I was ready.

I was planning to relocate to Hunter College in New York City by next fall, under the pretext of expanding my horizons. Maybe I missed the hustle of midtown. Grace didn't understand why I needed to go, but the truth was, I also needed a change from our Batman-and-Robin dynamic. I was tired of always being Robin.

The more I thought about it, the more certain I became—it was time for a change. Besides, I missed New York.

Mr. Scylas's contact number was in Manhattan, New York, at an advertising firm called BBZ&R. I still hadn't forgiven him for abandoning my mother and me, but if I happened to run into trouble

Chapter 6

Marcus

A man's first love isn't necessarily the first woman he sleeps with; it's the first woman he gives his heart to. As it happened, I met my first love in St. Thomas. I'd been on the island for nearly a year and hadn't slept with anyone—that was a record for someone like me. Although Olivia had refused any advances, that didn't mean I had given up on other prospects.

One night, as I walked along the beach thinking of America, a cool breeze blew, and I sat down in the sand to enjoy it. I dug my feet into the crushed white pebbles and made small caverns.

Even though it was 11:00 p.m., the beach was still lively with tourists. I got up and walked two miles down the shore, hoping for solitude away from the crowd. Glancing at my watch, I realized I had been walking for two hours.

Respecting that my grandmother worried tirelessly over me, I decided to head back. As I walked toward my rented moped, I saw a figure walking alone. On this island, it wasn't uncommon for people to walk alone, but this was a coincidence.

As I got closer to my moped, I noticed her and was taken aback by her beauty. She looked as though she had been crying. Who could have made this angel cry? She was dark brown from the warm Caribbean sun, and her hair spoke of her Carib indigenous ancestry. When she finally spoke, her accent sounded more English than Caribbean, revealing her schooling in London.

"I asked her if I could be of any help."

"No," she replied in a whisper.

"Damn," I said, "you sound as if you've lost your whole world." After asking permission, I used the bottom of my shirt to gently wipe her face. "It can't be that bad," I joked. "My name is Marcus."

Her name was Monica Mackenzie, and she lived on the main island of St. Thomas. Monica visited frequently because her grandmother still lived on the island, though the rest of her family resided in England.

I mentioned that it was my first time returning to the island in eleven years. After a bit of coaxing, she revealed that she had broken up with her boyfriend Kenton, a Jamaican guy in England, who turned out to be married with a child.

"That bad, huh? It sounds like you need a drink. On second thought, that might not help the problem." I offered her a ride on my bike, and as we rode, she began to share her life story. Because of her unwillingness to settle down, her boyfriend had been unfaithful, had a child, and then married. Fresh out of high school, I didn't want to show my ignorance by asking her age directly, but she revealed she was twenty, which made things easier.

Monica also told me she was planning to attend New York University and was currently studying at Imperial College of Science and Medicine in England. I mentioned that my father was a doctor and also a professor at NYU. She shared that she wasn't interested in settling down with children because her goal was to become a doctor and teach, just like my dad.

I told her my father always believed that everyone's path in life is unique, and one must follow their own. This bit of advice seemed to cheer her up. We talked the entire night, and by morning, I hadn't gone home. Together, we watched the sunrise with droopy eyes filled with sleep—a moment still vivid in my memory.

That day, I felt like her hero. Three years later, my fiancée was true to her word. On a visa, she came to America to study medicine, vowing to build a life together after school. My mother loved her, though I was not as enthusiastic. I worried about the dynamic between them, fearing that if problems arose, I'd face a conflict of loyalties. Would my mother remain loyal to me, or would she side with Monica?

Although Mom was pleased that my fiancée was in medical school, she still clung to her dream for me to become a doctor. She proudly told her friends there would soon be three doctors in the family. "Mom," I said, "we might be the black power couple, but if I remember correctly, I'm attending Columbia for business."

"I can't do a thing with you."

"No mom, you can't," I say, hugging her.

Monica was two years ahead of me in school, which didn't bother me, but it did concern her. She gently urged me to attend summer classes if necessary to graduate with her. She also criticized my choice of profession, which should have been a warning sign. I was so wrapped up in my mother's dream and so focused on Monica's plans for our future.

We married a year after I graduated from Columbia with a degree in finance. Instead of the small, intimate ceremony we had originally planned at Holy Trinity Baptist, Monica and my mother decided on a grand wedding extravaganza. No expense would be spared. The wedding was to be held in St. Thomas, where we had met. Her aunts, uncles, and cousins were flying in from London, and all I could think was that this was happening too quickly. My entire life seemed to flash before my eyes. It felt like being at an amusement park, riding the Hell Raiser after eating twenty hot dogs and drinking several beers.

The day arrived, and there was no backing out. I spoke to the man whose opinion I always valued: my father.

"Son," he began, "I was nervous just like you, but I knew I loved your mother, and nothing would keep me from her." Embarrassed by his confession, he clapped me on the shoulder and then left. Given that my father was a quiet man who rarely expressed his feelings, I felt honored to hear his admission. Yet, I was certain that my unease had nothing to do with love. I loved Monica, or at least I thought I did, and I hoped that love would be enough to sustain me through a wedding I no longer wanted. For our honeymoon, we traveled to London to meet her relatives, although most had come for the wedding. Monica felt it was important for me to bond with her family. It was my first time in England, and I found the city fascinating—the culture, the people, the museums, and the mix of nationalities all speaking in Queen's Standard English were intriguing.

From the airport, we stopped at the Brown Hotel to rest before heading to the Mackenzies' home in the West End of London. Their house looked like a quaint cottage in the exclusive Bloomsbury area. Her mother, Sophia, was a gem, but her father was a different story. He scrutinized me closely from the moment we met. I couldn't blame him; we were still virtual strangers suddenly thrust into a family relationship. It was clear he wanted me to earn his trust. I confidently smoothed the way by firmly shaking his hand, making direct eye contact, and promising to love his daughter and give one hundred and ten percent to our marriage.

When I made my promise, he seemed somewhat reassured and replied, "Son, marriage is not a game, and only mature people need apply."

"Daddy, Marcus is wonderful to me, so please cut him some slack," Monica interjected.

"Okay," he said with a smile. "It's just my job to check him out," his Caribbean accent blending with his Cockney-turned-aristocrat tone.

My father always emphasized the importance of first impressions, advising me to look people in the eye and shake their hands firmly as a sign of sincerity. Feeling confident that I had won both the battle and the war, I leaned back and hoped that my wife's family's affection for her would extend to me as well. One of the happiest times in our marriage was the trip to London. Little did I know, though, that there would be few more good times to come.

The moment we returned from our honeymoon, everything changed. The person I knew and loved from St. Thomas had transformed. On the very day we got back, she insisted that I immediately apply to graduate school and draft my ten-year plan. She became a nagging tyrant, second only to my mother. My worst fear was coming true. Within months, she altered my dressing habits, my eating habits, and even chose my friends for me. Monica was like a plague of locusts, consuming every aspect of my life. When I didn't comply with her plans, she ranted and raved until she got her way.

She was constantly saying, "Marcus, you need to do this. Marcus, you need to do that." "Marcus, pick up your socks. Marcus, I've asked you a million times to put the bloody seat down." My childhood friend, Mel—a basketball partner and high school gym teacher—disliked her from the start but was discreet about it. Though it was well-known he didn't like her, he never voiced his objections about her looks. On a few occasions, I caught him trying to take in Monica's curves from afar, but since no lines were crossed, I chose to ignore it. Other than my male cousins, whom I barely saw, Mel was the last friend Monica hadn't scared off.

"What kind of name is Mel?" she would say. "You need more productive, affluent friends like yourself." She was always introducing me to doctors, lawyers, and financial advisors from her social circle. After spending all day working with professionals, the last thing I wanted was to come home and mingle with a stockbroker.

In Mel's opinion, I had married Monica far too soon. He claimed to know all about women like her. "The pretty ones like to be in control and have their man on a leash. Just do what I do—

sleep with them, then dump them. Don't marry them," he said emphatically. "A self-made man doesn't need a woman telling him what to do."

"Some of those women you dumped tried to stalk you, chasing after you," I replied. "So, no thanks."

"Marcus, I'm just saying, man, at this point in your life, instead of a wife, you should have women lined up around the corner."

"What about Stephanie?"

"What about Stephanie? She doesn't even know she's part of the lineup. Besides, she knows her place. She doesn't push up on me. She gives me my space. I need to breathe."

"Okay, but don't say I didn't warn you. I'd hate to see you all laid up and hurt."

"Nah, man. Remember Nathan? That's how he ended up. Chasing that same dream."

"Did he catch AIDS?"

"Nah. The brother's got six kids, all by different women. They've all dragged him to court for child support. Now he's working two jobs and always broke."

"Damn," I said, shaking my head. "Can a man catch a break?" I laughed.

One Friday, Monica's shift ended until Tuesday. Instead of spending that time with me, her husband, she joined a group of young investors. I told her it wasn't necessary since, working at Solomon and Smith, I had a portfolio and was entitled to quarterly profit sharing. I offered to help her create her own portfolio, but off she went.

Monica and I had been married for a year, and I couldn't remember the last time we did anything together as a couple. Most marriages are built on partnership, but mine with Monica had become more like a business arrangement. To some extent, all marriages are, but with Monica, it felt like I was leasing her with the option to buy. I began seeing her less and less at home, and the few times we spent together were awkward and problematic.

What I once found attractive about her started to grate on my nerves. From the way she chewed her food to the way she casually insulted everything I took pride in, it all began to irritate me. Her English accent, which I once thought was so appealing, became especially annoying. Though I couldn't pinpoint when it started, in

Chapter 7

Racquel

Leaving Morgan University was easy. Finding a part-time job that paid enough and attending Hunter was another story. More than once, I considered calling Mr. Syclas. "Nope, things aren't that bad," I'd tell myself. The advertising firm he worked for was only fourteen blocks from my school. The more I thought about it, the more I felt I deserved an explanation from my father.

Aunt Lynn wasn't pleased with me making decisions without consulting her, but I gently reminded her that I was growing up. Maryland was too slow-paced for me; I was confident that the hectic energy of New York would pull me out of any rut. I embraced the challenge of surviving in New York completely on my own. With nine thousand dollars in savings, I knew I didn't have a lot, but it was something. So, in my junior year, I transferred my scholarship, found a job, and looked for a one-bedroom apartment—refusing to do the roommate thing. It would be more of a struggle, but it would lead to fewer problems in the end.

I found a place in Brooklyn, right at the beginning of the bridge. It was a former sewing factory that had been used as a sweatshop.

I struck a deal for six hundred dollars a month for two rooms and one small bathroom. The major wiring was still intact, so all I needed to do was gut the place and buy a stove and refrigerator. In three months, between studying and spending two thousand dollars from my savings, the owner was surprised that I managed to make the place habitable. Everything was second-hand, from the stove to the curtains; the only new purchases were my mattress and bed linen.

The thought of lounging in someone else's old, worn-out space didn't sit well with me, so I moved on to purchasing towels and bath accessories. I updated the apartment with white hardwood floors, a plexiglass door, cream-colored curtains, and new bed linens. I splurged a bit, spending two hundred and fifty dollars in total, including an antique lamp and a crystal vase. I painted the walls white with a hint of violet, which made Aunt Lynn's faded burgundy sofa look less out of place. Light pink throw pillows helped brighten it up. My bathroom, the size of a closet, was decorated in lapis and white. Its tiny size made having a shower seem almost miraculous. The hardwood floor, though marred by a few unsightly blotches, was polished rather than carpeted for economic reasons.

My neighborhood was a multicultural delight, with the aromas of halal dishes mixing with herring. In my explorations, I discovered a deli that made mouthwatering hoagies, a diligent dry cleaner, and my favorite spot, an antique shop. I often wander in to browse, careful not to attract the unwanted attention of an over zealous store detective.

On my very first day browsing the antique shop, I bought a lamp and an old painting of flowers done in soft watercolors for eight dollars. Decorating always made me daydream and yearn for my dream job after graduation, and eventually, that dream home or condo. Until then, I planned to be content. With the fourth month of living on my own approaching, I had to stop procrastinating or risk running out of money. I thought finding a job would be much easier.

As I exited Archie's Antiques, I checked my watch, realizing I needed to find the local grocery store.

"Whoa, hold up," a voice commanded. I turned just in time to avoid a collision with a dog and its owner. "Sorry, miss," he said, pausing as if waiting for me to introduce myself. He was a deep, smooth shade of chocolate, the kind that immediately caught my attention. "It seems like you've got your work cut out for you," I replied, deliberately withholding my name. I wasn't much of a dog person, but the golden retriever was so friendly. The owner bent down beside me as I petted the large dog. "He's harmless, just like his owner."

"Hi, I'm Zachary, but my friends call me Zack or Zee," he said, shaking my hand. I decided to keep my personal information guarded for now.

"Hello, my name is Racquel. What's his name?" I asked, motioning to the dog.

"Oh, that's only Killer."

As my first lover, Zack was gentle and patient at first, then intensely passionate and aggressive. He ignited a fire within me that I didn't even know I had. I was so ready that I was soaking wet even before he touched me. The next morning, I woke up aching, but it was worth it. Though I had no one else to compare him to, I felt he was a good lover. I enjoyed it, but I wasn't in love with him—not yet.

Zack's dream in life was to be a comedian, and that was his sole focus. There were no backup plans, which I found difficult to accept as an avid planner myself. I wasn't interested in unnecessary drama. Things between us had become simple: respect my space, and I'll respect yours. A year had passed, and I had been seeing Zack almost every day since that first night he stayed over.

Living with Zack—or rather, not living with him since it was my apartment—I noticed only a few minor habits of his that annoyed me, like not capping the toothpaste or leaving the toilet seat up. His quirks were slightly irritating but manageable.

What really got on my nerves was his public behavior. I remember a time when we went to McDonald's for lunch. No matter the time of day, the girl behind the counter always seemed either disgruntled or indifferent. Zack, however, couldn't help but make a scene. He analyzed the name tag of the cashier, Shwameka, and commented on how she seemed rushed while preparing our order, even though she took her time doing it. "Wait," he said, "I have a joke. Give me a pen and paper." I felt ridiculous but handed over the items. After jotting down his joke, he proceeded to tell it to the customers. It was highly annoying, and I hated being in the spotlight. I let him know afterward.

"Sorry, baby," he said, still grinning at his own joke. I rolled my eyes, feeling like I might have accidentally slurped down some of her spit along with my milkshake. The thought made me queasy, and I threw it out. Zack often stopped to write down jokes, no matter where we were. Despite this, we rarely argued. He kept me laughing and was sweet overall.Seeing him three to four times a week, I eventually gave him a spare key to my apartment. I often wondered about my hasty decision. Coming home from my temp job, I shuffled through the living room on aching feet and went straight to my bedroom.

Sitting on the bed, I took off one shoe, wincing at the pain. Being a "girl Friday" meant saying goodbye to the comfort of my feet. I took off my other black Nine West pump, massaged my toes, and flexed them to relieve the ache. Zack should be here any minute, I thought, glancing at the watch he gave me for Christmas. I counted down the seconds—five, four, three, two, one—before unlocking the door and seeing him walk in. He was so predictable.

"What's up, babe? How was your day?" he asked.

"Tiring," I replied, still sitting on the bed. Zack used his long legs to sit behind me and began massaging my shoulders.

"I know where this is heading, Zack, and I'm tired."

"No, just relax," he said.

Watching Zach massage my shoulders in the side mirror I started to relax

and put my head back against him.

"Mmm that feels good."

"That's right, just relax," he said, unbuttoning my blouse. "I'll do all the work, I promise." Taking a breast in each hand and kneading them softly applying more pressure the more he was aroused. We were watching each other in the mirror by this time. "You don't know how beautiful you are Racquel, this neck was made for kisses, your breast made for my hands." Turning my lips towards his lavish kisses and suckling the imaginary dew from the corners of my mouth. Without turning around I pulled my skirt off and he unbuckled his pants.

Content on letting him do the rest from behind he lifted me on to him without breaking visual contact. Sitting on him from behind looking sideways in the mirror made my body tingle from head to toe. Heat rose to my cheeks, I was completely nude, he was still dressed from the waist up his pants were entangled around his ankles. Movements were slow and sensual. Then the pace changed faster and faster he moved bucking up wildly. Sucking his fingers in and out of my mouth I bit down rather than yell out while I orgasm, he was already too cocksure so I did not feed his ego further. Besides, he was always commanding me to say his name. Holding me tight Zack's face contorted as though in agony he yelled out my name then went limp and asked what's for dinner?

"Take out," I answered.

"I'm only joking Racquel. I have a gig tonight."

"Where?" I asked. "That night club Mattie's?"

Hours later freshly showered. "I can't, have finals and I promised My Aunt Lynn that I was coming to Sunday's service. There will be a guest speaker."

"This night is important to me every time I ask you to come, you come with the bullshit."

"Is that part of your routine? Trust me, I'm not amused."

"Listen, Racquel," he said, moving slightly towards me, "I thought we had

something special here, please come see me tonight." As much as I wanted to say yes, my graduation was too close to mess up.

"No. Zack I said, I can't. After Wednesday I'm all yours," raising my arms I embraced him. But quickly without showering he dressed. "You just don't understand or give a damn," he said, slamming the door behind him.

Zack, who was nearly a decade older than me, still struggled to express himself like an adult. His lack of maturity turned me off— if the sex weren't so good, our non-existent relationship would have ended a long time ago. I took a quick shower and then sat cross-legged on the sofa. Zack's contentment with being a college dropout made him unable to grasp my drive to finish school or my struggle to maintain a 4.0 GPA. I told myself not to let it bother me as I buckled down to study. My eyes burned, but I finally managed to fall asleep around two a.m. The ringing of my phone jolted me awake. My nightstand clock read four a.m. I checked the cold, empty space next to me—Zack must have been calling to apologize.

"Hello," I answered, my voice groggy.

"Yes, hello. Can I speak to Zack?"

"Who is this?" I asked, now fully awake.

"Never mind who I am. Put my husband on the phone."

"Excuse me, but you called my phone. If you don't tell me who you are, no one will be speaking to anyone."

"I'm Solana, his wife, and I want to speak with him."

"Look, the Zack I know isn't married."

"I've dealt with hussies like you before. Now put him on the phone, Ms. High Street. You live near High Street, don't you? Put him on or I'm coming over."

"I told you that you have the wrong person. How did you get my number?" I asked, assuming she had found it in the phone book. "Don't call my mother freakin' house with your psychotic bullshit problems," I said, slamming the phone down. But the insistent woman called right back, undeterred. I turned off my phone, hoping at least one of us could get some sleep that night. Unfortunately, it wasn't me. Awakened from what had started to be a peaceful sleep, I stomped into the bathroom, muttering that if she showed up, I wouldn't hesitate to have her arrested. Zack was at work at the time. I had no choice but to beeped him to find out what was going on. It took him three hours to return my call. He reassured me that one of his ex-girlfriends must have picked up my number from his mother's house, reminding me that they still visit, which is why I hadn't met Ms. Blake.

According to Zack, visiting was Solana's way of keeping a connection with him. "If Solana and other 'friends' still visit, why am I needed in your life?" I asked him.

"You're the only one with the thing that makes a nigga sing," he said, drawing out the last word with a pulpit-like emphasis. That was one of my pet peeves—his habit of referring to himself with that term. I'd let the mysterious phone call slide before but picked it up again two weeks later. It was all the way at the back of my mind, Weeks later the psychotic woman called me back a week before my last final.

"Solana?" I answered. "What do you want this time? It's over—accept it." I felt a fleeting sense of victory until she surprised me by asking to meet for lunch, her treat. "Are you out of your mind?"

"I want to apologize for my behavior," she said. "I've had enough and don't know what to do. Please meet me tomorrow at Blue's. It's in the city near my job, at noon, which is my lunch hour. It's a few blocks from Mattie's." Mention of Mattie's piqued my interest, so I agreed. The next day, I arrived an hour early and settled into the restaurant, observing the patrons and the pedestrians passing by. The place was a classy after-hours spot where jazz was the preferred music. For a twenty-year-old like me, it felt sophisticated just being there. A slim, well-dressed woman entered, her hair stylishly cut, her brown skin indicating she was likely in her mid to late thirties. As she approached, I muttered under my breath, "That can't be her; she's at least five years older than him." Sure enough, she sat down at my table, introducing herself.

"Hello, I'm Solana Wood."

"I'm Racquel Middleton." I nearly fell over. I'd expected someone much younger based on our phone conversations. Her entire attitude had led me to believe she was a younger, more superficial type.

"I know this is awkward for you, but I am Zachary's wife," she said, pulling out a small leather case. With a snap, she revealed a wedding photo of them and a second picture of a child—clearly their child. Zachary was full of surprises. "I'm sorry. I had no idea," I said, needing a drink. I signaled the waitress and asked for something strong. She returned with a gin and tonic.Unaccustomed to hard liquor, I took a few sips before setting the drink down.

"Well, I can honestly say I didn't have a clue."

"Did you ever meet his mother?"

"No," I replied.

"Ever go to his home?"

"No. I assumed he lived with his mother and thought I'd meet her eventually. I know this sounds naive, but I work and I'm a full-time student. Our relationship was…" I trailed off, searching for the right word. "Comfortable," I finally finished, taking a breath.

Since she'd questioned my intelligence, I figured it was only fair to question her self-worth.

"Is this the first time this has happened to you?" I asked, feigning innocence. She looked right through my motive and answered, "No." She also mentioned that "they were soul mates," acknowledging Zack's flaws but insisting he was a good man.

"We love each other, and like any couple, we have problems," she said, as if repeating it a thousand times might convince herself.

"I'm sorry, Solana, but he lied to both of us. I'm too young for this kind of drama. I genuinely didn't know he was married, but after meeting you today, I'm no longer interested in dating him."

"I really must be going," I said, rising from the table, eager to distance myself from the entire situation. I couldn't wait to get home, purge my apartment of Zachary's things, and remove him from my life completely. First order of business was to change my phone number, then change the locks. Aunt Lynn wouldn't mind a visitor for a week, I'm sure.At Holy Trinity Church, there was a guest speaker, and Aunt Lynn asked Grace and me to attend. For me, it was the perfect way to clear my mind of Zack and his trifling ways. It had been eleven months since I'd seen Grace. She hadn't changed much, except her clothes looked more expensive.

After interning at a condominium company called Oak Towers in Washington, D.C., Grace landed a full-time job as an assistant executive after she graduated. Telling her about Zack and me felt awkward; I didn't want her to know how he treated me.

"Uh, no girl, weren't you saved last week?" Grace asked.

"Grace, stop playing. I'm serious. Zack had a wife and a kid." Thank God we were in the last pew, given that our conversation had nothing to do with God.

"See what happens when you try to work with a broke brother. She had all the money, didn't she?" Grace probed.

I hated to admit it, but I answered, "Yup."

"She was old and he was fine."

"Imperfect combination," Grace sang, imitating the original artist. Her smugness was grating.

"Lower your voice," I whispered. "We're in church."

"Please, everyone's too busy acting up to listen." Aunt Lynn proved her wrong by eyeing us and fanning herself, making me feel ten years old again. Whispering, she said, "Have I taught you anything? Leave the struggling brothers alone."

"Grace, I wasn't in love with him," I defended. "I'm just disappointed."

"Anyway," she said unsympathetically, "are we still on for next weekend? You promised you'd come visit. Give the guys where I live a try. Actually, I know someone who would be perfect for you. I've found an okay guy myself."

"I'm definitely coming down, but I might pass on the blind date," I replied.

Given Grace's track record since Steven, she was known for trying out a few guys.

"Racquel, don't be so corny. Let me hook you up," Grace insisted.

"Alright," I agreed. "But Grace, I'm telling you now, do not fix me up with any of your castaways."

"Nah girl, this guy's on the up and up. And if there's one rule I follow, it's never to take work home with me."

In the front row sat all the main performers from the church service. Sister Abigail, seated in the aisle, was so caught up in the spirit that her wig sat askew, and an usher had to search for her glasses in the third aisle. Aunt Lynn declared loudly that the Holy Ghost had come down to anoint, shouting "Hallelujah!" I was so absorbed in my own relationship troubles that I barely heard any words that could impact my life. Once again, the idea of going to church seemed like an afterthought. At the end of the service, during fellowship, I spotted Marcus, his mother, and an unfamiliar woman. Aunt Lynn came up behind me and whispered, "That old battle-axe is even snootier since she bought her way onto the board of trustees."

"Aunt Lynn, she can't be that bad," I said.

"She most certainly is," Aunt Lynn insisted. "And she took Deacon Hallowell's parking spot." I glanced at Marcus, who was pulling at the collar of his shirt, looking bored and uncomfortable. His mother, on the other hand, looked pristine, with her hair pulled into a tight bun and her navy blue outfit perfectly matching.

"Look out, fashion divas," Grace said, approaching with her friend Jackie in tow. We'd known Jackie from Holy Trinity since we were twelve. While we were friendly, sharing details about my marital woes with her was risky. Not only would she lecture me, but she might also put the information in the Holy Trinity 'Times.' I could already hear the headline: "Not sweet little Racquel and somebody's husband—Lord, say it ain't so. I knew that child was troubled, something in her eyes." The elders would have a field day. I had made Grace promise not to say a word.

Jackie Black-Hallowell was married to the deacon of the church, who was twice her age—she was twenty-four, and he was forty-eight. They had two children, Parker, who was three, and Brianna, who was one. Jackie was about two hundred and fifty pounds and seemed to believe that everyone wanted her husband. Together, they weighed half a metric ton. "Is that Marcus's mother?" Grace asked.

"Yes, I believe it is," I replied, trying to sound unaffected by their presence.

"Well, who's that with them? Wait a minute, homegirl's got herself a ring," Grace observed.

I glanced over and saw the pair watching us with curiosity. Marcus was still looking our way as his companion looped an arm through his, leading him toward Reverend Steele.

"Excuse me, looks like someone's getting married, if not already married," Grace said.

Instead of taking Grace's bait, I suggested we get ready for brunch at Maurizio's Café. During our meal, I made the unfortunate mistake of mentioning I needed a new job.

"You know, Racquel, you would have graduated by now if you'd gone straight through the summer and doubled up on classes like I did," Grace's friend Danielle Hodges casually remarked.

"Actually, Danielle, I did take some graduate classes but decided to forgo the graduation," I said, hoping to end the conversation. Although Jackie, Danielle, Grace, and I had taken different paths, we were close friends growing up at Holy Trinity. Or at least as close as women typically get with one another. Danielle had always dominated the conversation when we got together. Jackie knew Danielle had a knack for showing off, even when she didn't have much to flaunt when we were kids. Danielle found a way. Since going to college, she had physically changed, her elevated awareness only slightly. If possible, she seemed even more engrossed in "elevating" others.

"The companies would have snapped you up," Danielle said, smacking on her crepe Suzette. Now I remembered why I didn't always enjoy these get-togethers. The catty behavior sometimes became too much. Everyone at the table knew Danielle's primary reason for going to college was to escape her project life and her crack-addict mother. Despite her drastic appearance change, Danielle's behavior hadn't changed much. She had green contact lenses, a waist-length blonde weave, and nails almost as long as her champagne flute.

The weave made sense—Danielle's hair had never fully recovered from when Grace tried to put a relaxer in it back in the day. Grace felt it was her duty to address Danielle's hair issues, given that her mother was either too cheap to perm or too lazy to comb it. The fact that Danielle had opted for blonde hair and green contacts seemed a bit extra to me, but I figured it was just a form of personal expression.

"Yeah, I should have," I agreed, sipping my mimosa.

"Yes," Danielle continued, "At Howard University, I graduated in the ninety-eighth percentile." She took a sip of her second glass of champagne, and it was only two o'clock.

"I've been offered a job with Philip Morris as an inspector." I couldn't help but wonder if this was the same girl who used to smoke a blunt twice a week when we were teenagers.

Jackie excused herself to go outside for a smoke and mentioned she also needed to call her husband. Aunt Lynn congratulated Danielle, not realizing that Danielle's favorite topic was always Danielle. So my aunt was cornered in a long conversation where Danielle did most of the talking. If it weren't for her occasional acts of unexpected kindness, no one would associate with Danielle.

Two sides of the same coin. Jackie and Danielle were always at odds; Jackie thought Danielle was self-centered and often a French fry short of a Happy Meal. Grace, along with the rest of us, had grown tired of Danielle's non stop bragging and tried to steer the conversation back to Marcus.

"It seems like Marcus brought a piece of 'back home' with him," Grace observed.

Glancing at my watch, I realized it was already three o'clock. I stood up, offering my apologies. "I really have to be going." As I finished my grapefruit mimosa, Grace reminded me that since she was on vacation, we were going to hang out and that I needed to hurry so we could leave that night. Aunt Lynn chimed in, "You haven't packed yet? You girls never change. Always last minute." When I left the restaurant, it was pouring rain. I opened my umbrella, waved goodbye to the group, and hailed a taxi home.

After changing all the locks and packing for three weeks instead of two, I remembered I had handed in my letter of resignation and paid two months' rent in advance. I was ready. My new job started at the beginning of the following month, giving me plenty of time to unwind. Going to Maryland with Grace would be a relaxing escape from the drama with Zack. Grace's apartment was immaculate and well-organized, a stark contrast to the dorm we shared in college. It was one of the condominiums she had sold, spacious and luxurious.

Since Grace was on vacation herself, she wasted no time introducing me to her D.C. friends and setting me up with dates. First up was Khadir Abdul. He was too militant for my taste. What was his issue with white rice and flour? I should have known something was off when he took me to a vegetarian food stand and briefly mentioned his past as a swine-eater before finding Allah. He was one of those light-skinned brothers who overcompensated with ultra-pro-Black attitudes to assert his blackness.

Next was Simon Rutherford III—who wasn't militant enough and was a Republican to boot. This brother was as dark as midnight, and the more he spoke, the more I realized he was uncomfortable in his own skin. Diagnosis: disguised self-hatred. I figured it was only a matter of time before he ended up with a white woman.

Philip Stapleton was too pretty and superficial. He reminded me of Prince. His first mistake was picking me up thirty minutes late without an excuse or apology. He moved, talked, and gestured with such practiced flair that it felt theatrical. His texturizer S-curl was cut low in a fade with carefully styled baby hair, and his manicured nails were immaculate. When he shook my hand, I had to apply more pressure than he did. Philip wore earth tones to complement his complexion and asked me how he looked. But the final straw was when, after dinner, he looked at his reflection in his pocket mirror and smoothed down his mustache twice while we were sitting at the table. Meticulous? More like obsessively self-involved. The only date that made any sense was Darren White—a name I was sure Khadir would have had trouble understanding.

It was only my second week, and I was getting ready for my fourth date. Upon meeting Darren, I found him attractive—down-to-earth and not uptight. The evening flowed like beautifully orchestrated music until he revealed his eight-year stint in jail. He had made the desperate mistake that many impoverished black teenagers make: he sold drugs, which earned him time in Sing Sing. Despite his intelligence, the evening took a downturn.

"How did it go?" Grace asked as I walked into her condo.

"It sucked, I like my men rough around the edges, Grace, just not that rough. I am not desperate," I told her, yawning. "Where are you finding these guys? At the gas station or a five-and-dime?

And what do you tell them about me?" Too tired to shower, I undressed and lay down on the pull-out sofa still wearing my pantyhose.

Imitating her, I said, "I have this cousin who's been played out and can't get a date." Handing me a lightweight quilt, Grace barely looked contrite as I recounted how my evening with Darren had crumbled.

"It's not like that, Racquel. You're hard to fix up. And no, I never knew Darren had been in prison. Not all brothers in jail deserve to be there."

"Hey, I'm not judging him," I defended. "Well, that was your last try," I said as I settled under the covers on the couch.

"Jail doesn't make you a bad person," Grace said, her last words before I fell asleep. I dreamed of Darren White—strong and debonair—holding me, kissing me, touching my hair, and then choking me to death. I woke up hearing my own voice yell for help. Thank God Grace slept like a log and didn't witness or hear that. I was awake at five in the morning, unable to go back to sleep. I walked a few feet to the dining area and made hot chocolate. After downing the last sips I attempted to sleep again.

Chapter 8

Marcus

"Marcus, I have to work a double shift tonight, so please apologize to your mother for me."

"Monica, the dinner is in our honor," I lied. I was confident my mother wanted to show off further, and I didn't want to endure the scrutiny of a dozen busybody women on my own.

"Marcus, I'll make it up to you," I added.

I had expected Monica to want to go; she hardly ever missed a chance to play the "queen" and treat everyone else as her peasants. What was it she said to Reverend Steele? "Thank you for inviting me to your little church; it's so quaint." The reverend was so captivated by Monica that he didn't realize she had insulted the Holy Trinity. It was a trait in her character I couldn't understand— her need to put people down. She was self-centered and required constant attention.After making her apologies Monica proceeded to rub my groin at any other time it would have been pleasurable, but that was her answer for everything.

Every single argument ended with one of us giving in before the orgasm. At first I did not mind, but I started to wonder how we resolved anything. For a woman with a college degree and her diplomacy skills needed work. "Okay," I Agreed to her cancellation, removing her hand from inside my zipper. "I Thought you had to work." At my vague interest in her attempts to seduce me,she left with a baffled look, promising to call me if she was coming home later than expected.

I called my mother, hating the thought of disappointing her, but I wasn't interested in being dissected by her church friends.My mom was understanding. I feigned a headache and gave a flimsy excuse about Monica, which I was sure she saw right through.

I swapped my monkey suit for sweatpants and the previous day's socks and shirt. Finding my favorite chair, I slouched into it, one hand on the remote and the other tucked inside my underwear. I flipped through the channels, desperately searching for a sports station. Hours later, hunger pangs began to set in, so I walked to the fridge. There wasn't much to see, so I grabbed a beer and closed the door. I knew how to cook, and well, thanks to my grandmother's insistence that girls couldn't "run style" on me, as she put it. Since marrying Monica, I had taken on cooking and cleaning duties, sometimes feeling like our roles were reversed.

She would come home and ask what was for dinner. I was uncomfortable in that role but hesitant to admit it, as admitting such feelings seemed male chauvinistic. Just last week, I had run our clothes to the Laundromat while Monica was home due to a break in her schedule.

My Neanderthal understanding was that women were trained from birth to nurture, placate, cook, and clean, essentially training to become someone's wife. Men, on the other hand, were not trained to be husbands or family men, but if guided correctly, they learned to provide when necessary. Seeing how my mother was a good housewife and my father, whom I loved dearly, maintained his own things and that was it, I had almost forgotten it was my bright idea to share household chores—a decision I now regretted.

Although I prided myself on being a twentieth-century kind of man, I found that my pampered upbringing meant I only coped with cooking and cleaning under pressure. Instead of calling my mother to ask for cooking tips, I ordered China Palace's number seven and Singapore noodles.

At ten o'clock, Monica called to say her shift was over and she'd be home in half an hour. As I hung up, I thought of Racquel. She still looked attractive but seemed as self-absorbed as ever. I remembered the one time I had written to her years ago. She never replied or called. Bitterly and filled with slight jealousy, I imagined her faceless boyfriends and wondered if she ever thought about me. These thoughts felt selfish and borderline adulterous. Pushing

Racquel out of my mind, I focused on planning for work on Monday.

At 12:15 Monica arrived; if she was having an affair it would take the pressure off me, and made obtaining a divorce much easier.

"Darling, I'm home." I turned off the blaring television in our bedroom feigning sleep.

"Do you mind I have to work tomorrow," I answered grumpily.

"Sorry," she whispered. Then took off all her clothes and slid into bed naked. After she kissed my back I turned over, undaunted Monica stuffed my penis into her mouth. After laying still for five minutes and enjoying her services. She climbed on, only for me to push her off. It was as if a bucket of ice water was thrown on, leaving me flaccid. I was feeling ill-tempered and unsatisfied.

"What the bloody hell is wrong with you? It's like you don't want to fuckin' touch me." Her voice had become shrill in her anger. "Look, I just want to sleep." She wanted to play games, but I was the master. If I took the time to analyze the situation, it wasn't so much Monica's lack of complete honesty that bothered me. It was seeing Racquel and being unable to acknowledge her due to Monica's shielding presence.

By morning, I was in a better mood. My mother had called us at five, as was her habit, to make sure we were awake. Monica left the house at a quarter past seven on days when she was on schedule, and at ten on her days off. I left at seven thirty, allowing myself an extra fifteen minutes of sleep. By the time of Mom's second call and the blaring alarm clock, I was already up. Mom started her day at six.

Her life as a housewife and board member of Holy Trinity, ensuring all church functions went off with style and fluidity, was hard work. Asking her about her day could lead to an hour-long one-sided dialogue about which colors the ushers should wear. Many times, I'd overhear my father saying, "For God's sake, Gloria, just tell me the price."

Monday mornings held an unexpected dread for some people. I, for one, enjoyed my job crunching numbers. I always looked for idealistic ways to help the company save money without resorting to their old, unpleasant methods—like issuing pink slips. My contentment with just that was an enigma to Monica. I invested wisely and had a balanced return on all stock. Monica's fixation on margin calls, IBOs, and profit-sharing was curious, especially since I thought her first love was medicine. My wife's love of money and anything related scared me. I wanted to provide the best, but we were still newlyweds—just two years of marriage. I hoped to start a family in a few years, but Monica had other plans.

She surrounded herself with stock traders and encouraged me to do the same. After working hard all day, all I wanted was a beer and some breathing room.

It had been exactly two years, seven months, and eleven days since we got married. Our joint savings amounted to eight thousand, forty-two dollars, and ninety cents after buying the condo and her Mercedes. She was only a third-year resident at the hospital. The fact that she knew little to nothing about investing and wanted to sink our savings into the latest hot investments was downright frightening. I strongly advised her against it and even offered to withdraw my $7,000 and add it to my personal account, leaving her with her share. A man couldn't be too careful. But despite my warnings, she continued buying and spending recklessly.

It wasn't until her recent stock venture took a nosedive, taking $7,000 of my money with it, and her refusal to tell me who her adviser was, that I became furious. All she would reveal was that her adviser was a white guy named William Hardaway. Discovering that she had her portfolio managed by a competing company she met at one of her networking lunches only made me angrier. The fact that I could have lost my job for insider trading— a job I love— seemed irrelevant to her. I was so enraged I wanted to shake her senseless, but the thought of possibly injuring her stopped me.

My father always said: never let a woman interfere with your ability to provide for yourself. His second rule was the same as his first: dedication and education are the keys to any master lock.

The day I realized Monica's so-called investments had failed was not when she told me, but when my check card was declined at Men's Warehouse while trying to buy a few business suits. I thought it must have been a mistake, so I called to clarify. When I came home, confused and furious, I had to fight to keep my voice down, struggling to believe that this bright, beautiful woman could be so reckless or selfish. I caught Monica just before she left for work.

"Marcus, what on earth is the problem?" she asked, hearing the front door slam.

"Just when were you going to tell me you spent $7,000? Whatever it is, it's going back. You didn't consult with me."

"I don't need to ask for your permission. It's as much mine as it is yours."

"You damn right you need to ask me when $7,000 out of $8,042.90 is mine." Imagine if he put more in.

Hearing her story didn't make me feel any better, even though she claimed she did it for us. That was the final straw for me, especially when she escalated the argument. Monica slapped me and called me a loser, and in the heat of the moment, I called her a bitch. While I don't think she didn't deserve some of the blame, I was raised not to disrespect women, and hitting a woman was strictly off-limits. She dared me to hit her back and then threatened to call the police if I did. That was the breaking point.

"Monica," I said as I walked toward the door, "a woman—no, a girl like you—needs a man to hit her to force her to respect him. It just won't be me." I left without looking back and never regretted the decision.

Racquel

Before I was set to leave Maryland, Grace and I decided to hit the clubs. We each picked a place: a jazz spot called Panache and a hip-hop venue named Tim's Red Lounge. It's probably clear who chose which. Grace wanted to start with her pick. At that time, go-go music was all the rage. Grace was decked out in a tight, dark blue leather dress that screamed "I'm available," while I wore my black leather pantsuit—hey, it was leather night. We were ready to dance.

When a song came on, Grace threw her arms up and shouted, "This is my jam," letting the rhythm take over. Even Danielle had opted out of joining us.

"Come on, Racquel, let your hair down," Grace urged. A few familiar faces greeted her with, "What's up?" It was clear she was a regular here.

"How often do you come here?" I finally asked.

"Not too often," she replied. "But I have a few friends on my 'Let's Party Together' mailing list. We hit up whatever club is the hottest at the moment."

"How do you manage that?"

"Manage what?"

"Change so completely from the business attire and unshakeable demeanor this morning to this hood rat vibe I see before me now."

"Forget you," she said, rolling her neck. "That's what I do for a living, but you know I like to party. That hasn't changed."

"I'm getting a drink. Want anything?"

"No, thanks," I replied. I wasn't much of a drinker.

"Girl, I'm bringing you back a drink to loosen you up," Grace said with a look that reminded me of Aunt Lynn's no-nonsense stare. "Lord, please let this not be how she found my dates," I thought.

A few minutes later, I spotted Simon on the dance floor. He was wearing a flashy silk shirt, black slacks, and a neck chain that said 'SEXY' shaking his neck like an ostrich caught in a headlock. He was dancing, sweating profusely, and stepping not once, not twice, but three times on the young lady's foot he was with. "Grace, I could kill you."

I never imagined Republican Simon Rutherford III would party with us mere Negroes. Yet, there he was, dancing slightly offbeat and giving nerds everywhere something to cheer about.Trying to duck behind a couple, I was still spotted, and Simon, along with his date, made their way over to where I was standing.

"Hello, Racquel," Simon greeted me. "This is my friend Anne." Anne didn't look too thrilled to be called just a friend, but I didn't give him away. "Hello, Anne," I said politely, not wanting to cause any trouble.

"Are you here by yourself?" Simon asked, as if that would change the fact that he wasn't my type, especially with Anne standing just five inches away. "No, my cousin Grace is here," I replied, secretly hoping she was on her way back from the bar.

Right on cue, Grace arrived with drinks sloshing in her hands.

"Hey, Simon, what are you doing here?" she asked.

"Hanging out. I wanted to party with the people tonight, you know, come down to the hood."

Grace and I exchanged glances, struggling not to laugh. "Come on, Simon," Anne interjected, "I'm thirsty." She led him away before he could say anything else. "Goodbye, nice meeting you," I said as they left.

Grace and I stayed at Tim's Red Lounge until 2:00 a.m. before heading to club number two: Panache, a cool jazz spot Darren had introduced me to. I loved it—just a few drinks and some music to unwind. In the dimly lit club, smoke curled through the air, but I didn't mind—I was in my element. The saxophone, accompanied by the horn, made love to my ears, caressing my back, gliding over my face, and easing away my anxiety. Whether it was the champagne or the music, I couldn't tell—maybe it was both. I didn't want to meet anyone that night; I was content to sit, thinking and dreaming about my future, lost in the music.

Grace kept insisting that a man at the bar was watching me, urging me to check him out. My cousin seemed to believe it was necessary to meet someone every time she went out. I just wanted to chill. After my last margarita, and with our sentences starting to slur, we decided to leave. We'd both had a little too much to drink, so the bartender called a cab. The man at the bar helped us in, even slipping the driver a twenty to ensure our safe delivery. It was five in the morning, and like nocturnal creatures avoiding the dawn, we hurried inside, closing the door against the coming daylight.

I stumbled into the apartment and collapsed on the couch, one arm still caught in my leather jacket, fully dressed. Grace was on the floor next to her bed, where she sat, too tired to move.

We woke up that midmorning, groggy, only to discover both of our purses were gone. My first thought was, *That son of a bitch robbed us.* After contacting the police, I canceled my bank card and American Express. I was ready to go home but decided to stay longer to file a report. The thief had made off with one hundred and sixty dollars, along with our debit and credit cards.

The police station was on Waverly Road, and when we arrived, we waited for half the morning before anyone would take our statements. After growing indignant, we were finally directed to the second floor.

Detective Thomas Cambrian was assigned to our case. He listened attentively to our story, though I could tell he wasn't entirely convinced we'd been robbed—he seemed to think we might have just been forgetful due to our inebriated state.

"Did you know the suspect?" "Uh-huh, and what was he wearing?" "How many drinks did you have?" "Can you describe the perp?" "What exactly was in your bag?" "What time did you leave the club, and what were you wearing?"

He asked all the usual, asinine questions. He might have been attractive if he wasn't acting so detached and unapproachable.

"Thank you, officer. He could have done more than just take our bags that night," Grace said, her hand clasping her throat.

"Laying it on a bit thick," I muttered as the detective walked away to type up the report. His superior attitude annoyed me, but Grace found his anal-retentive behavior cute.

Returning to New York for the second time was necessary, it was my dream to work in advertising there was no better place to be. In July of that year, I interned at Freedman's Journey, a division of my father's private company, Robert Scylas. It was a small, Black-owned advertising firm still trying to get off the ground. Founded a few years before I started there, it seemed organized and was gradually gaining influence in the advertising community.

Mrs. Alorton, a close friend of one of the office executives, Mrs. Fields, had helped me secure the internship. On the day of my appointment to meet Mrs. Fields, I arrived early, carrying my résumé in the leather briefcase Aunt Lynn had given me as a graduation gift. Dressed in standard black and white, I had considered adding a splash of red to show some spunk but decided against it. I sat down and waited until the exact time of my appointment.

When the secretary approached me and said Mrs. Fields would see me now, I felt prepared. I had drilled myself on the company's history, just in case she was interested.

Mrs. Fields, a Black woman in her mid-fifties, welcomed me into her office with a brief smile and a firm handshake. Her brown eyes were deep-set, framed by bushy eyebrows. Her long, curved nose gave her a somewhat hawk-like appearance. Her hair was cropped close to her scalp—a style not easily pulled off in corporate America, but she must have been there for decades to do so. She scrutinized me as closely as I did her.

Once I sat down, she began firing off questions in rapid succession: Where did I see myself with the company? How could I contribute to its growth? Et cetera, et cetera. After gathering enough information to suit her needs, Mrs. Fields began laying down the law of the land.

"I see you working here, Miss Middleton. Now, here's the catch." She held up a finger, pausing as if sensing my unease. I pressed forward, but her constant, direct gaze was unnerving. "You can either succeed in this business or fail. It's that simple," she said, revealing teeth stained—probably from too much coffee or cigarettes. "I've survived twenty years in this industry, and my first piece of advice is free: CYOA—cover your own ass."

Standing up, she moved to sit on the edge of the desk. "Next on my list, there's no such thing as ass-kissing or individualism. In this creative field, you must use a balanced mix of both, and timing is everything. You'll need to use your own good judgment for that." Succeeding didn't seem so difficult, I thought, based on that criterion. But this was what I wanted, so I was determined to stick with it.

"And… I want you to pay close attention to everything and hang in there," Mrs. Fields encouraged.

Chapter 9

Marcus

The day I left Monica, I was grateful we didn't have children together—that would have been disastrous, not to mention giving her a bargaining tool. My mother cried when I finally told her we had separated. She couldn't understand it. She insisted that all we needed was a marriage counselor, but I wanted out and had refused. She kept asking what the church would think about us being separated, nearly whispering the word as if she was afraid to say it aloud. But since I didn't feel the need to live up to the standards of strangers, it didn't bother me one bit. Monica's father hated me, but her mother understood, so she continued to send Christmas and birthday cards, and occasionally gifts.

I was a bachelor again. I let Monica keep the condo and moved into a smaller apartment. My mother handled all the particulars, even down to the design and decorating. But I put my foot down on any fuchsia, pink, or peach—opting instead for grays, beige, black, and if necessary, white. These were the colors that represented my emancipation. Once a week, my mother even came over to do laundry and housekeeping. I asked her not to, but she told me that's what mothers are for. Using her spare key, she would come and go, sometimes leaving dinner or a few coconut rolls. I knew my mother wanted to fill up her time fussing over me, and to tell the truth, her home-cooked meals were better than a China Palace special any day.

I walked around in my boxers, left the toilet seat up, drank the juice, and left the empty carton in the fridge—without anyone standing over my shoulder to nag me. My clothes lay wherever I dropped them, and I only cleaned if I had guests. *Yeah, I'm gonna like this,* I thought.

Some women were drawn to married or recently divorced men, especially if they weren't looking for too much commitment. Since I no longer wanted a relationship, I had no problems. The furthest my commitments went was showing up on time for a booty call.

Racquel

The turning point. I guess every woman has one. It's when you decide what you're worth, what you want, and that just any man won't do. My self-imposed celibacy began after my last lover, Miguelito—a muscular, fine-as-hell Hispanic UPS driver. We had nothing in common, and after a while, we bored each other silly. His lack of education had nothing to do with it.

After that, I remained celibate for sixteen months and fourteen days. I counted each and every day like a horny little toad. I was often tempted to break it, but sex toys were never an option for me—they could never replace a living, breathing, responsive man. The moisture on my lonely sheets at night and moments of wakefulness drove me half crazy. The wetness I felt after a flirtatious smile or a professional handshake... It was like every fine brother within a five-mile radius whom I would normally be attracted to suddenly approached me in all flavors, shapes, and sizes. It was interesting what a sista' notices when she's not getting any. Brothers were beautiful.

While tempted, I stayed strong. I learned to love myself. Fine arts and music, family and friends occupied my time. I threw myself into my work, gaining the respect of my employer. I even extended the olive branch to Robert Scylas, also known as Daddy Missing in Action. What I realized about myself was that I wasn't immune to feelings of rejection.

At the end of the meeting I initiated, I sat down next to the stranger who was my father, crying so hard I was hiccupping. The old feelings came pouring out—the loneliness, the little girl in me revealing herself. I realized that I had missed having a doting, concerned father. Children all over the world go without parents and eventually cope with their abandonment, but the desire to have both mother and father around never truly dissipates.

It was only then that I understood why I had pushed myself so hard in college. I wanted to be successful so that if I ever met Mr.

Scylas, he would be proud to acknowledge me as his daughter. The decision to forgive him helped me heal old wounds.

The experience changed me profoundly and was one of the most emotional of my life. He spoke of a young, carefree Susan Middleton—my mother. He confessed that he had fallen in love, but also admitted he was young and unprepared for children or marriage. My mother became pregnant during his first year of undergrad and never told him. She feared that forcing him to take responsibility would make him hate us.

I began to view relationships differently, learning to accept both the good and the messy parts of a person and understanding that things don't always go according to plan. As our relationship grew, we started calling each other once a week for advice and meeting for lunch or dinner once a month. My father had married a few years after graduating college, and I discovered I had siblings—something I had longed for as a child. However, with Grace around, I was hardly lonely, so I wasn't pressed to meet them. I was content with getting to know my father and being his friend.

I found many similarities between us, such as the way he woke up early to drink chocolate and his religious routines and weekly plans. Judging Robert Scylas now, he seemed okay, far from the villain I had initially thought him to be. Our awkward meetings gradually became as normal as could be for two related strangers.

Grace was happy when I told her I had forgiven my father and encouraged me to focus on the positive aspects of him, hoping to erase some of the old negative feelings. Initially, she thought I was crazy but later commended my decision to stay celibate for a while. She admitted she couldn't do the same, given her "must-have-it-once-a-week rule."

Chapter 10

Marcus

Our divorce lawyers met in a conference room at New York Methodist Hospital, a neutral ground for our negotiations. Monica's lawyer, Ms. Corbinstein, was a white female with blond hair and graying temples. Her face was creased with years of other people's aggravation. She wore a white shirt buttoned to the top, and black horn-rimmed glasses perched high on the bridge of her nose. Her whole demeanor screamed angry feminist.

My lawyer, Mr. Charles Maxton, fit the profile of an angry Black man to a tee. His no-nonsense attitude, especially towards women, made him a top choice for men seeking divorce lawyers.

As we sat at the conference table, Ms. Corbinstein presented Monica's list of demands. I played it cool, willing to give in, eager to end what should have never begun. My lawyer and I reviewed the document. Monica wanted the condo—fine, it's hers. She also wanted the car I had bought for her—she could have that too. But she was asking for alimony—three thousand dollars a month— despite earning as much as I did. That was too much. I wasn't going to waste any more of my money.

I maintained a serene expression as I instructed my lawyer to pull out our joint bank statement, revealing a balance of just five hundred dollars. I also produced a fake bankruptcy application and a list of her credit cards, which I might agree to pay off if she dropped the alimony claim. Additionally, I showed her car's title, which was registered in my name.

The negotiations began. The final deal: no alimony, she keeps the car and the condo, and that was it. I was determined to get this over with. Papers signed, negotiations complete—I won.

My mother never forgave me or Monica for divorcing. To her, it was unforgivable. The idea that I no longer loved Monica was inconceivable. Nevermind that they weren't that close. I never intended to persuade my mother to see things my way; perhaps she never would. According to our mutual friends, Monica started dating an investment banker at Solomon Brothers. I was relieved she was out of my hair, especially since Monica had my mother's full support until that point.

Dating in the nineties felt like a test of wills. Who would give in first? Would I take her out to dinner, or would it even be necessary? Would my car or where I slept influence the outcome? It often felt like a matter of time before the results were the same.

Some women required more patience and effort than others, and I found that I enjoyed and respected them more. The dating scene was new to me, so I frequently had to change my number and occasionally found myself caught between two very angry women. My mother guilted me into going to church, hoping it would reform me. I knew I should have hired help for the apartment, but little did she know that some of the women I dated I met right there in church—or sometimes through work.

"Marcus, if you want to find a nice girl, come to church," she'd say.

I thought to myself, comically, that I already had them. My last serious girlfriend from Holy Trinity even slashed my tires. As my tastes evolved, I realized it was important to pursue stable women and make use of my cell phone. I wanted women with their own apartments, cars, and money. Despite this, I still paid for most of our dates, called intermittently, and occasionally gave cards and teddy bears. I wasn't a complete jerk.

One Friday, as I stared unfocused at my computer screen saver, I reminded myself that I had a date with Jacqueline later that evening. Strangely, I wasn't looking forward to it. I had met her in the grocery store line. She started the conversation by commenting on the great articles in Sports Illustrated, although we both admitted that wasn't the only reason men bought it.

Jacqueline was a legal secretary working her way through school at night. She was attractive, intelligent, and ambitious— good qualities for a girlfriend. However, I wasn't looking for that, and I made no secret of it. I was always upfront about my intentions.

An hour into our first date, I realized Jacqueline wasn't just ambitious—she was self-centered, much like Monica. I wasn't naïve enough to think all ambitious Black women were self-centered, but when the conversation began and ended with me, it was a clear sign. Nevertheless, the first date was successful. We ended up back at my place, her legs in the air.

Was there really any reason for a second date? Then it hit me—absolutely not. She was clearly looking for a relationship, and I could tell. Jacqueline dangled her resume in front of me: "I graduated from here... I worked there... There aren't enough strong Black couples..." She had all the right qualifications, but like a dial tone, there was no real connection. I figured I'd come up with some excuse. With that settled, work became easier to focus on.

As much as I thought of Racquel (as a married man), I didn't think of her often as a bachelor. The thrill of wanting her and knowing I couldn't have her—that haunted me. Childish as it was, it lingered. I never once sought her out in the congregation during the rare times I went to church, and according to my mother, she attended even less than I did. My life seemed to be on track, with everything falling into place—except for my personal life. I had dated so many women that I lost count, but the emptiness of those fleeting encounters began to wear on me.

They lacked the intimacy, companionship, and mystery that drew people together in the first place. Instead, my relationships had become more like quick, hollow exchanges: "wham, bam, I'm too busy, goodbye." I grew jaded and realized I could no longer blame Monica for it. Reforming from such a doggish lifestyle wasn't going to be easy; it would take some serious adjustment. I often found myself wondering, What can I do? How can I change? And will I ever meet a woman worth changing for?

Chapter 11

Racquel

"I now pronounce you man and wife. You may kiss the bride." The reverend smiled as the happy couple sealed their vows with a kiss. It was a beautiful day for a wedding ceremony, I thought, even as I stood there noticing the cream-colored roses tied with sheer gold ribbons starting to wilt, and feeling my high-heeled shoes pinching my right toe.

I hugged Grace and congratulated her. At first, I thought she'd hit her head when she told me she was dating Detective Thomas Cambrian. Then I thought she'd gone crazy when she said they were getting married. "But Grace," I argued, "he's not even your type. He's too uptight." Grace assured me that it was just an act for his job and that he was really down-to-earth. With no other choice, I wished her well.

To me, it all happened so fast. I had only been back in New York for a few months when Grace told me she was getting married. "To who?" I asked, trying to remember her last boyfriend's name—was it Bill, Bob, or Bernard, something like that. When she told me that it was Detective Thomas from the robbery case who had proposed, I was surprised, to say the least. But there they were, man and wife, both looking extremely happy.

Throughout the ceremony, I convinced myself that my celibacy was a good thing and believed that, one day, I'd have a husband of my own. Hopefully.

But why was it that at every wedding, there seemed to be a handful of snakes that slithered out from under their rocks to attend? They all seemed to think women came to weddings hot and bothered.

Sitting at the bridal party table, playing with my limp salad, I noticed one of the wedding "snakes" slithering up to sit down next to me.

"Hey, good looking, smile," he said.I gave a half-hearted grin.

"There you go, there you go," he encouraged, extending his hand. "I'm Reginald Cambrian, Thomas's cousin."

"Hello, I'm Racquel," I replied, shaking his slightly damp hand.

"You were the maid of honor, right? The bride is your cousin, just like the groom is mine. I saw you sitting out here alone and wondered if you'd like to dance." I hesitated, prompting him to add, "A pretty girl like you shouldn't be sitting here all by herself."

Standing, he offered his hand. Only when I stood up did I notice that he was about five foot two, barely reaching my chest. With my heels on, I was a towering six feet tall. Dancing with me, he looked like a messy child, his tuxedo shirt decorated with remnants of his dinner—splattered steak juice, salad dressing, fruit punch, and wedding cake crumbs all encrusted on his suit. His buttons strained against his bulging belly, and he scratched at what looked like a six-month-old stomach. I almost asked him when he was due.

"Beauty must run in the family," he remarked, staring up at me. I looked down and murmured, "Thank you."

"I like things like this," he continued, nodding his head. "But sometimes weddings drag on forever and can get too noisy. You see that car over there?" He pointed to a black Camaro. "That's mine. I bought it a few days ago. The only thing is," he paused, waiting for a response, "I haven't tested its limits yet. I need to know what a car can do before I can truly appreciate it." Eye-level with my chest, he spoke more to my thirty-four C's than to my face, glancing up only occasionally. Then he asked the absurd. "Would you like to test drive it?"

"We can sneak off. Who's going to miss us?"

"I really can't," I said, biting the inside of my mouth to keep from laughing.

Caressing my hand with his index finger, he shrugged his chunky shoulders and insisted, "We'll be gone for just a second."

"Single ladies, it's time to catch the bouquet!" the coordinator announced.

"I've got to go," I said, wasting no time to end the dance with Reginald.

"I'll be over here if you need me," he said, gesturing with his eyes and hands toward the car.

As I walked over to the crowd of women gathering on the dance floor, I couldn't help but think, "That ridiculous little man. Grace, girl, what kind of strange hillbilly family have you married into?"

I stood off to the side as the front became congested with women eager to catch the bouquet and tie the knot. Grace looked at me, then deliberately aimed the flowers in my direction. I reached out but missed. A sister, who must have been a former gymnast, leaped up and caught them just before they landed in my hands, executing a full split in mid-air. I let her have it—I wasn't in the mood to fall out on the floor fighting over a bouquet. The last thing I needed was a photo of me with my dress over my head, sitting on the floor clutching flowers.

As Thomas took his place on the floor, a few brothers out of the one hundred and fifty-nine guests—who were clearly in committed relationships—made half-hearted, fraudulent attempts to catch the garter. That was my signal that the party was winding down. I found Grace and told her I was leaving.

"Bye, girl. Love you. I'm so happy for you,"

"Don't worry; it'll be you next. Bye, cuz," she replied.

It was time to leave. As I sat in my car, I noticed Reginald making eye contact with me. I started the engine, sped past him, and headed straight for I-95.

Marcus

I was not born an African-American, yet I was still a black man living in the

United States, raised with the benefit of two parents and blessed with a father

that provided financial stability. As a child I have experienced racism to a subtle degree. Blatant racism escaped me and my parents, since we arrived in the early seventies though the remnants of it still existed. That was why I crossed my T's and dotted my I's. Five years on the job this year, and I held on. Work was hectic to stay on top and visible, I arrived early and worked late a few times a week.

And, since, I stopped sleeping with my assistants—help was consistent.

My mother gave up matching me up but continued to help at the apartment. Monica still called, even though our divorce was final, wanting to catch up. She only called when her short lived relationships caved in. She thought I'd be her backup plan but, surprise, I had no time for her. That part of my life was over. My personal life was not perfect, a few disillusioned sisters wanted to marry, settle down. Not me. My last "friend" hung around one month, which I had to end. During the first week of meeting and after spending the night, she marked her territory by leaving her purse. The next week it was a blouse and extra pair of panties.

The week after that she wanted to come clean up. I had informed her that my mother came over to help me. But insistent she brought over a mop and bucket and put them in my utility closet. Avoiding damaging her sensitive feelings I thanked her and told her that I would put it to use. The less time I started to have for her, the more she wanted to see me. Without being offensive, I hinted that there was someone else. She eventually got the message and stopped pursuing me. I wasn't involved with anyone else; I just detested being chased.After locking up my office and saying goodnight to building security, I drove home to Brooklyn. With my signal on, I turned right onto Cranberry Street.

That's when I saw her—crossing the street with those shapely legs, her hair still reaching the middle of her back. The outfit she wore suggested she had just come from work, and her walk showed she was tired. I wondered where she worked; it was ten o'clock at night. Not wanting to scare her, I drove ahead and parked.

Stepping out of my Lexus coupe, I took out a napkin and wiped imaginary dust from the hood. From where I stood, I glanced to the left—she was watching. I kept wiping the car, giving her time to reach me. I was nervous and did not know why. I turned around the second time she called my name.

"Marcus, is that you?" she called out incredulously.

"Hey, Racquel," I replied, turning to face her. How could anyone with eyes miss her? She was beautiful.

"Long time no see! Do you live in this neighborhood? Imagine bumping into each other on the street," I said, surprised.

"I know," she replied. "What are you up to?" she asked, eyeing the car. Before I could answer, she added, "You haven't changed—you look the same."

"Please, I look terrible," she responded with feigned modesty.

"If you're not too far, I can drop you home," I offered. She declined, explaining that her apartment was only a block away. I insisted, and she eventually agreed. Our meeting was ending too soon, so I asked if she'd like to come over for a drink. Wrong move, but it was too late.

She gave me a wary look and turned me down. Trying to make amends, I handed her my business card as we stopped in front of her apartment building. "Thank you," she said curtly.

As she opened her door, I took one last shot. "If you're not busy, how about lunch next week?" I asked, hoping to show her that I hadn't meant to suggest anything inappropriate earlier.

"Call me, okay? I really hope you do," I said, giving her a kiss on the cheek.

She paused, looked at me thoughtfully, then got out of the car and went inside without saying a word.

Racquel

Days later, After collecting my mail from the box, I took off my shoes and winced as I walked up three flights to my apartment. I placed my toe killers in a neat row beside the door. Despite having a decent job, I wasn't ready to give up my small, affordable apartment—I hadn't made the kind of money I wanted yet.

Thinking about my cousin and wondering when we last spoke, I decided to give her a call. Grace's husband, Thomas, answered.

"Hi, Thomas. Is Grace around?"

"Hey, Racquel. Hold on a second," he replied, his voice sounding as though he had Mono. I never quite understood what Grace saw in him.

"Hi, Racquel," Grace answered, her tone chipper—everything Thomas wasn't.

"Guess what," I said.

"What's up?"

"I saw Marcus. Girl, he's divorced."

"And still fine?"

"Girl, yes. He's driving a nice car, so he must be doing okay."

"Girl, all it means is that he has a car note," Grace said dismissively.

"Anyway, he looks good," I replied.

"Well, what have you been up to, Racquel?" she asked before I could respond. "Guess what, I think I'm pregnant."

"Grace, you just got married a few months ago."

"I know, but Thomas wants to start a family right away."

"Is that what you want?" Her pause answered the question for me.

"Later, much later."

"Well… tell him."

"I will," she said noncommittally. "How's the job?"

"More money, more responsibilities, but I love the challenge."

I decided not to mention my graduate classes. "Keep me posted about the pregnancy," I told her as I hung up. Grace was married, Danielle was engaged, and even Jackie had someone. Norman, the quirky guy at work, was starting to look more appealing. That was until I bumped into Marcus. Thank you, Marcus.

"I am alone, not lonely," I repeated my mantra aloud as I prepared for bed. It didn't have its usual effect, and I fell asleep thinking about that fine, tall, cocoa-brown brother with the Lexus coupe.I waited a week before calling Marcus. After dialing the number he gave me, he answered on the second ring.

"Hello, Racquel," he said after I identified myself. "I almost gave up on you calling."

"How are you, Marcus?" I asked. He looked the same—just taller. At six feet tall, with broad shoulders and arms, he must work out at least four times a week, I assumed. The suit he wore last time looked expensive, and his pants fit his trim waist, but unfortunately, didn't reveal what he had downstairs. He pulled me back to the conversation by asking about my cousin.

"Racquel, you haven't changed a bit. How's your sister— I mean, your cousin Grace?"

"She's fine. She's married now."

"That's cool. Listen, I'm swamped at work. Why don't you call me before you get off?"

"Okay," I said, disappointed that he was so busy. He didn't call, and I forgot to write down his number. He later called me at home well after ten to apologize.

"Sorry for not calling back. I had to take care of a few things at work."

"No problem. No one understands the pressures of work better than I do," I said.

I was fully aware that he didn't have to call, but I was glad he did. We talked briefly about nothing in particular. I recognized this stage—it was the "nice talking to you, but this is awkward" stage. In our short conversation, I noticed his voice had a deep, resonant quality as I fiddled with the belt on my night robe. We ended the call with a goodnight.

The next day was Thursday, and I had to pitch an idea for an important project. Unable to sleep, I finished typing up my proposal well into the night, struggling with a bout of insomnia. I stopped at the fifteenth page at three in the morning.

Needing something to wear for the next day, I walked over to my closet. Professional but sexy was the goal, just in case I ran into Marcus again. After going through my entire wardrobe, I narrowed it down to two outfits: a black dress with red accents or a navy pantsuit with a light gray collar and cuffs. After a few minutes of deliberation, I chose the pantsuit. I had the perfect color suede shoes to match. Walking towards the bathroom, I muttered to myself, "Okay, should I wear my hair up or down?" I asked my reflection in the mirror. I pulled my hair up and searched for the decorative Chinese sticks.

By four in the morning, I finally nestled into bed. It seemed like only moments later that I was half awake, searching blindly for my alarm clock. I grabbed it and placed it under the pillow on the empty right side of my bed to muffle its loud sound. My left wrist still wore the watch I habitually kept on even while sleeping. The time was seven o'clock. I showered, dressed, and did my hair in twenty minutes flat. By seven-thirty, I was downstairs, warming up my car.

By a quarter to eight, I was driving towards the city, aiming to arrive at work by eight-thirty.

"Hello," my assistant Rita greeted me. We quickly got organized for the day. I handled most of the research and statistics, while Rita took care of the proofreading and retyping. Together, we were an unstoppable team.

Throughout the day, I kept glancing at my watch, but Marcus hadn't called. I ordered lunch and stayed in the office to eat. The day seemed to fly by, and before I knew it, it was time to go home. My supervisor had to postpone reading my proposal due to a personal emergency, despite the late hours I had put into it. I drove home, resigned to starting the process all over again for Friday.

I knew I needed to get out more. On Sunday, I planned to join Aunt Lynn at Holy Trinity. Saturday was reserved for my hair appointment. I splurged on a French manicure and pedicure, then went over to Sun and Moon Salon for a facial. By Sunday, I was ready to go.

The church was a restful place when your mind was racing at eighty miles per minute. That day, I felt a bit guilty—some sisters came to church not just for the word but to stave off loneliness. I sat in the pew next to Aunt Lynn and Uncle Herbert, relaxing and pretending to enjoy the sermon. It was my habit to say my own prayers while partially listening to the preaching, but that day was different. Reverend Steele was in a frenzy.

On the dais behind the animated reverend sat Deacon Hallowell, his girth squeezed into his velvet chair. I couldn't help but think, "Who's going to help him out?" I felt a chuckle coming on but stifled it with a sneeze. Jackie Hallowell sat in the first pew near the aisle, eyeing the congregation. Her snack-indulged frame was crammed into a dress.

"You should have bought the bigger size, girl," Aunt Lynn leaned over and whispered to me. I looked at her, trying to admonish her while suppressing my laughter to avoid embarrassing us both.

The reverend had the church jumping and rocking with catchphrases like, "Somebody needs an anointing tonight," "Ain't no party like a Holy Ghost party," and "This time is the right time." People were jumping up, and "spirits" were coming down. The place was electric. An old woman who had come in with a cane dropped it as she danced on one good leg. A man bent over, waving his arms in surrender to the unseen power.

As an observer rather than a participant, I struggled to understand it all. After years of attending Sunday services, my understanding was that the true miracle was in living like Jesus. Nowhere in the scriptures did it say that Jesus or his apostles jumped around catching the spirit. He was the most blessed and spiritual of us all. I was content simply to stand and clap in the aisle. When the reverend collected the tithes, church service finally came to a close. Members who weren't lingering to fellowship or gossip filed out in twos. Mrs. Collin and her vainglorious group were at the front, leading the others out.

Aunt Lynn, who refused to call Mrs. Collin "Sister Dr. Collin," tapped her politely on the shoulder.

"Excuse me, Sister Collin, do you remember my niece, Racquel?"

"Oh yes, I recall the face. How are you?" Mrs. Collin asked.

"Fine," I answered, shaking her hand.

"These children grow up so fast. It was good seeing you, dear. Take care." I thanked the more affable Mrs. Collin for her good wishes and then joined the throngs leaving church for the evening. As I made my exit, I looked up and walked into a familiar face— it was Marcus.

"This must be some coincidence running into you again," he said.

"Well, I decided to pay old Trinity a visit today."

"I see. Well, I'm here to pick up my mother. Have you seen her?"

"I believe she's on her way out. I saw her just a moment ago."

"I'm double-parked outside." I hugged Aunt Lynn and Uncle Herbert and then walked with Marcus back outside. He looked adorable with his hands shoved deep into his pockets and his baseball cap turned backward. This casual look was as much of a turn-on as his suit and tie.

"Marcus. Marcus," his mother called. "There you are."

"Hi, Mom," he greeted her with a kiss on her upturned cheek.

"Let's go. I have to catch your father before he makes his rounds at the hospital."

"Racquel, how about tomorrow? I'll pick you up. Call me around four in the afternoon."

"Sure," I agreed, nervous that I was making myself too accessible. Marcus jumped into the driver's seat while I walked to my jeep, parked around the corner.

The next day, Marcus left work early to pick me up at six o'clock. He mentioned that he usually stayed until seven or eight. I left my car overnight in the company's parking lot and gave Orphe, the attendant, extra money to keep an eye on it. When

Marcus arrived, I settled into his car, feeling the cool leather interior against my skin—quite a contrast to the fabric interior of my own car. Elements of Love by Earth, Wind & Fire played softly; it was one of my old favorites. Marcus reached behind his seat and placed three yellow roses in my lap.

"How nice of you. Thanks," I said, smelling the blossoms.

"You like them too?" he asked, referring to his choice of music.

"My father kind of dug them."

"But enough of them," he said, popping out the compact disc and replacing it with Kenny Lattimore.

"Are you hungry?" he asked while shifting gears. I was lost in his deep, bedroom eyes for a moment until he broke our trance to watch the road.

"Yes, for food"

"What are you in the mood for? Caribbean, soul food, or Italian? I know the best places for all three," he assured me. "But if you choose the first one, I'll have to cook for you."

"You can cook?" I asked.

"Yeah, I learned when I visited St. Thomas. My grandmother taught me. Have you decided?"

I opted for neutral Italian. Shifting gears and changing directions, he drove to Tribeca in Greenwich Village. The restaurant was a ritzy downtown hole-in-the-wall with two stone lions perched outside the entrance. Linen curtains covered part of the windows for patrons' privacy. Nice, I thought, wondering how he found this place. He was too fascinating, posing a serious temptation.

Over dinner, we caught up on old times and laughed about our childhood disagreements. I almost forgot how irritating he used to be.

He turned the conversation to whether there was anyone special in my life. "At the moment, I'm single," I told him, unwilling to mention my decision to stay celibate. I worried he might see me as a conquest, and I knew I'd have to keep my distance—my thoughts had already begun to stray.

I asked about any women in his life. He admitted he had friends but nothing serious. He briefly mentioned his ex-wife, but discussing her seemed to make him uneasy, so I redirected the conversation.

Leaving the restaurant, Marcus paid the attendant. On the drive home, at a stoplight, he played with my hand. His knuckles brushed mine with the briefest of touches, and his caresses were so soft they felt almost imaginary. His steady, warm hand sent shivers through a place long neglected.

As he parked in front of my house, I hesitated to invite him in. I wasn't sure if that was what I wanted. My look, however, conveyed that he could leave at any time. My hand traveled up my arm and past my neck, and I buried my fingers in his hair. Crooking my finger, I beckoned him closer. Leaning forward, I said, "Stop staring and kiss me."

His tongue was warm and slightly salty as he slowly dipped in and out of my mouth. He lingered, his gentle assault on my lips making me think, if only this weren't the first date.

Chapter 12

Marcus

I rushed to finish all of that day's work. Instead of staying until eight, I left at six. I picked her up from work. The building doorman called up, and she came down. "Hi," she said, kissing my cheek. The fading scent of her perfume, a mix of flowers and citrus, was subtly appealing. She was one of those women who needed very little makeup, if any. Smiling at my appreciative glance, we walked to my car.

"Do you drive, Racquel?"

"Yeah, but I'd rather use yours. I have a Suzuki 4Runner for now. Sometimes I take the train to work—parking is a nightmare."

I had never heard her curse before, even when we were teenagers. It didn't suit her, and I didn't like it.

We decided to go for Italian. I had the perfect place in mind. I pulled up alongside the restaurant and opened her door. The valet parked the car. Tribeca was crowded and had only a sprinkling of Black patrons inside. The waiter arrived ten minutes after we sat down. We placed our orders. I chose my usual: seafood lasagna.

"What's that?" she asked, curious.

"It's shrimp, clams, squid, and dried tomatoes cooked in a wine sauce, topped with pasta and mozzarella cheese."

I showcased my knowledge of Italian food, having frequented nearly every restaurant around my job. Italian cuisine was high on my list. I coaxed her to try my seafood and wine cream sauce lasagna. I held out the fork teasingly, but she hesitated and placed a portion on her plate next to the shrimp scampi. We both ordered red wine.

The evening went well. She asked if I was dating, but without prying. I let her know that although I wasn't seeing anyone seriously, I did go out from time to time. She admitted that she hadn't been on a date in a while and could hardly recall when the last one was. I found it hard to believe and suspected she might be stretching the truth.

I drove her straight home since we both had to get up early. Besides, it would have been futile to invite her over; I knew she wasn't ready to take things further. I gave her a long peck on the cheek and said good night. Oddly content, I then drove back home. Willing to go at her pace, which was atypical for me, I waited a week before calling her again. I'd always wanted to see *Miss Saigon* and hoped she would join me.

Chapter 13

Racquel

The first time we made love, it was unexpected. We had just spent the evening at dinner and a play—Miss Saigon. The singing and romance of the story lingered with me long after the final scene. As we walked to my car, I commented on the beautiful weather and, before I forgot, thanked him for a wonderful night. He invited me back to his place, saying he had something to show me. The look on my face made him laugh.

"You can stop giving me that *What-do-you-take-me-for* look. Besides, we're both adults here."

"Whatever," I replied, smiling.

"I'm not trying anything. I just have something to show you."

We drove back to his place in my Jeep. He lived in one of the new condominiums on Spring Street. It had just been built. I parked in the lot, and the doorman let us in. I was impressed. His place had an Art Deco vibe, with beige and black dominating the decor. I'm sure he considered these colors "safe"—manly.

My intention was to leave after seeing whatever it was he wanted to show me. The feelings between us were too strong to be cheapened by meaningless sex.

But when we stepped into Marcus's apartment, the air felt thick with unspoken words. All thoughts of talking vanished. His unspoken question, asked with his eyes, was answered with a kiss. Marcus had a kiss that felt timeless, as though he worshiped my mouth. My tongue explored what I had stared at during dinner.

His mouth was beautifully formed, with clean, neat teeth. My hair was raised from my shoulders as he kissed me, his tender fingers massaging the back of my neck. He made me feel safe, silently letting me know that I could refuse at any time. His hands were unrushed, his movements slow yet firm. We slowly unbuttoned each other's shirts. Despite my experience, I felt nervous, unsure of how to begin. I was caught in the midst of deep like and love.

Making love to someone you're falling in love with sheds a different light on past lovers. The difference is so significant that it can be felt deeply, without the need for outside stimulation. When I tried to unbutton his trousers, his hands stopped me, gently lowering mine to my sides. Without a word, he stepped away, leaving me feeling exposed, and it had nothing to do with the absence of clothes. Confusion and the fear of rejection ran rampant in my mind.

A chill spread across my arms from the absence of his solid, velvet body next to mine. The lights were dimmed, and soft music played from his Bose radio system. When Marcus reentered the living room, he finally spoke. "I've waited for this day, Racquel. I'm in no rush." He brushed his hips against mine, back and forth, then led me to the couch. As he kissed me, he paused at intervals, undressing me with the reverence of a man handling a prized, fragile possession. I wanted him so much. His hands became my clothes, exploring paths on my skin—up, down, across, and inside of me.

I wanted to return the favor and undress him, but Marcus shook his head no. He was content with looking and touching. His silent perusal made me self-conscious. There wasn't a place he didn't touch, taste, or kiss. With the ball of his thumb, he circled my core as his greedy tongue lapped at my breast. I felt electricity travel wherever he touched. His fingers invaded every part of me. A wave as deep as an ocean overtook me. The hypnotizing notes of Kenny G faded; so secluded was our lovemaking that everything disappeared. Time was suspended.

His clothes seemed to peel off. Then, with his arms under my legs, he carried me to his room and gently laid me down on his massive bed. As I looked at his body, I marveled at his wide shoulders, lean stomach, strong legs, and the most beautifully formed penis. I was excited and nervous. He never bragged about being a great lover—we never had those conversations. He didn't need to promise me anything; he showed me the difference. He studied me, watched for my responses, learned, and controlled me. He took and gave back all he could. I tensed, held him tight, and surrendered to my orgasm. Nearly drowned by the ocean, our souls touched. I was breathless.

The experience was so real, so special, that tears slipped out from the corner of my eyes.

The experience felt so real, so special, that tears slipped from the corners of my eyes. I was sure his orgasm had been just as explosive. It's not every day that a woman can make love to a man who is both handsome and a great lover—Marcus was both, a true pro.

After napping, I woke to find him still watching me. With one eye open, I caught him observing the rhythm of my breathing, the way my chest rose and fell. When I opened both eyes, I saw the pearly gray predawn light suffusing the room. The white sheets had taken on a light blue hue, and his velvety, cocoa-brown skin looked almost blue-black in the soft light. The red numbers on his alarm clock, resting on the nightstand, read 5:25. His face held a tender expression, but his dark eyes were unreadable. I wiped the lower part of my face, but it was dry. I smiled and asked, "What do you want to show me?"

"Oh!" he said, shrugging his shoulders. "My apartment."

"Just kidding," he added with a grin, then jumped up and threw on his discarded sweatpants.

After pulling out an old box containing a stack of pictures, he said, "I saved these, hoping to show them to you one day." He turned on a lamp at the far end of the room and brought the box closer. I flipped through old prom pictures, stunned that he had kept them.

"How did you get these?"

"I made copies of the pictures we took that night."

I looked ridiculous and tried to cover my face. The upswept hairstyle and dress didn't suit my small frame—they were too mature, not the sophisticated look I once thought they were. Marcus looked just as silly with his eighties fade.

"Tell me, Racquel, why did you stop coming to Holy Trinity?" Marcus asked.

"I'm not into organized religion right now. Besides, I was forced to go so much as a child that now I can only handle church in small doses."

"You sound like you're talking about coffee," he teased, imitating me in a falsetto voice. "I'm having a light church, no artificial sweeteners, please and thank you."

I smiled but then stopped as fear crept in. I wanted so much from him in that instant, but I knew he might not want to give it. I commented on how late it was, hugged him, thanked him for a truly beautiful night, and told him that tomorrow was an errand day for me.

"Today is tomorrow," he reminded me, concerned and somewhat baffled. "Is something wrong?"

"No. I just have some running around to do." There's nothing wrong with leaving, I told myself. Men do it all the time, just for different reasons. I gathered my clothes and quickly changed, washing my face, arranging my hair in his bathroom mirror, and reapplying lipstick. While in the bathroom, I discreetly placed last night's underwear in my purse. When I returned to the room, I noticed his disturbed look. He swaggered over to help me button my clothes.

"I'll call you later," I said, kissing him quickly. It was a good idea that we took my car, I reflected as I made my escape in his elevator.

Things moved a bit fast. Jumping into bed with someone wasn't my usual behavior—it was a very rare thing. But the feelings were too incredible to regret. I had waited long enough. I convinced myself that I'd call him the next day. I certainly didn't want him thinking I was too eager or crowding his space.

As it happened, I did have things to do. Number one on my list was taking a shower. Number two was calling Yvonne's salon to see if she could fit me into her schedule. Lastly, number three was reflecting on how I might have ruined a good night by overthinking it.

When I got home, the first thing I did was check my messages. My dad and Norman Maynard—the weirdo from my job—had called. Norman needed information on the Seaman's project and claimed my file was incomplete. He was always calling.

Why did I give him my number? Since he got it, he's called for every work-related reason imaginable. Ever since I started at Willard Advertising, that short, strange little man has been following me around, always asking, "Can I be of any assistance?" and offering to help, but he never actually did. It finally dawned on me that he might not have been talking about work at all. And I didn't care what Mr. Maynard said; there's no way the office could have an emergency every week that only Racquel was capable of handling. I put work out of my mind—they'd have to manage without me, I reasoned. I tuned my radio to CD 101.9. Music always puts me in a relaxing mood.

My apartment was my haven, and I was glad to be in it. I decorated it with splashes of light colors against white walls and hardwood floors, with personal touches of affordable art here and there. In my bedroom, I used more imagination, choosing vibrant colors that coincided with the season. I'm not an interior decorator, but I did a damn good job if I do say so myself. Decorating relaxed my mind and gave me something creative to do. Since it was May, my colors of the moment were light blues, vivid greens, violet, with little splashes of pink. Throw pillows and floor-length curtains added to the effect. Believing in aromatherapy, I also had various bowls of potpourri scattered around the room.

After a long, hot shower and getting under the covers, I finally said to the empty space, "What a night." I replayed the events of last night in my mind, a smile lingering on my lips. I briefly reminisced over the delicious feelings and the night I spent with Marcus. I sat up and thumbed through my daily planner, deciding it was time to get motivated. Picking up the phone, I called my hairdresser, hoping the timing was right.

"Hello. Yvonne's," the receptionist answered.

"Hi, Angie. How's it looking in there today?"

"It's Saturday, girl, so it's kind of busy, but I know Yvonne will see a loyal customer. You can come in, but be prepared for at least an hour's wait."

While waiting for a stylist, I called Gracie, who was in Washington D.C. She was still the closest thing I had to a sister. "Girl, guess what?" I said, trying my best not to be overheard. I whispered, "I slept with Marcus last night," not waiting for her to ask what. I felt so juvenile telling her, but it was that good, and she was miles away. I didn't give her all the details, just enough to get by. I told her the essentials—he was big, and he knew how to work it. How I went straight to sleep. All the basics. "That… good?"

"Girl, I can't even begin to explain."

"Well," she said, "it sounds like he can handle a woman in bed, but how does he handle things out of bed?" There she goes, raining on my parade with her dose of reality.

"Look, I'm the rational, mature one. Don't hit me with something I'd normally tell you. And yes, to answer your question, I really like him as a person. It's not just the dick."

I looked around for eavesdroppers. One nosy older woman leaned closer, trying to listen in. "I'm in the salon, girl. Let me call you back," I told Gracie, watching the curious sister straighten her posture while she continued to flip through her Essence magazine.

The following day, I was sure that day three was the best day to call him. Then it dawned on me—he hadn't called me. When it comes to these things, it's always best if the man calls first.

A week passed, and Marcus still didn't call. Only pride and sheer will prevented me from dialing his number. I used that time to immerse myself in work. I put up a wrought iron chandelier in my living room and reorganized my entire apartment. I was in overdrive. On the eighth day, I regained some of my composure. It was Monday. I woke up, turned the radio on, and glided into the shower.

I spritzed on perfume, curled my hair, and wore my new work suit with the matching shoes I'd bought that Saturday. Feeling pumped, I hopped into my Jeep and drove into the city, ready to groove all the way to work, high on a positive feeling and the pep talk I gave myself—"Don't stress over dick, 'cause it doesn't stress over you." I turned on the radio. Mary J. was on one station, and the melancholy croon of Toni Braxton was on another. Damn them, I thought, and turned the radio off.

At work, I was grumpy, sending my assistant off almost in tears after making her redo all the old file codes for the second time. I told her that this time, I wanted them entered into the computer by state and, in addition, wanted companies in alphabetical order, doing away with the old biggest-account-first system. If I had called Gracie, she would've said, "I told you so."

Why did I have to be so stubborn? I wanted to call him, so I should just do it. The problem was, if he wanted to talk to me, he would have called already. By the time I got home that evening, I resolved not to give a damn.

Arriving late on Tuesday morning, my assistant, Rita, reported that my father had called, and a Mr. Collin needed to meet with me around one-thirty.

"I can't make it, so cancel for me, Rita. Thanks."

"He figured that," Rita said, "so he sent these bright pink roses." She smiled, finally realizing the cause of my recent bitchy mood. Along with the dozen roses was a card that read: *I know you might try and cancel, but have a heart and see me anyway.*

Arrogant bastard, I thought, but he sure had a way about him."On second thought, Rita, call Mr. Collin and make arrangements for Grenade's on Sixth."

Thank God I had worn my power suit to work. Initially, it was meant to help me negotiate a new contract and a raise from my boss that afternoon. I looked good. The pinstripe pantsuit said I meant business. It wasn't that I hadn't missed him—because I had—but after making me wait nearly two weeks before calling, he now wanted to meet. Well, I was ready for him. At one o'clock, I left the office, arriving at Grenade's at one-thirty sharp.

Every sister meets one brother in her life who makes her climb the walls. For me, that man was Marcus. The brother could tickle a spine. In the weeks that I didn't see him, I remodeled, reorganized, and reshelved the shelves to take my mind off him. But at night, while relaxing in the tub, I wished he was there. Six foot one, cocoa-brown skin, straight white teeth. Sexy dark brown eyes, full soft lips, a tongue that tasted lightly sweet and salty. He smelled like warm rain, cedar, and fading cologne. His black hair was soft to the touch, with broad shoulders, a six-pack stomach, long slim legs, and a butt that had "pushing power" written all over it.

Yes, as Grace had said, a sister was sprung. I couldn't deny it, but I didn't ring his phone off the hook, either. In fact, I didn't call him at all. I wanted him to make the first move, and when he didn't, my feelings were hurt. But when he left roses at the office, I was as giddy as a schoolgirl and took my time deciding whether I wanted to see him or not. In the end, I went ahead—against the good sense the Lord blessed me with—and called to meet with him anyway.

Chapter 14

Marcus

Every time I try to figure out a woman, it feels like I don't know a damn thing. Racquel and I have been hanging out for a few weeks now after bumping into each other in Brooklyn. I decided to play it cool, like I didn't even remember her. How could I not remember? She looked the same and was still as attractive as ever, even after all these years. My divorce was final. I was a free man. Truth be told, I'd been a free man since I left my ex-wife. Maybe I should have called Racquel sooner, but I needed to make sure I was doing it for the right reasons. I didn't want us to waste our time on misunderstandings.

I wasn't interested in any serious relationships—maybe "good" friends, but that was it. But Racquel was different. I liked her a lot. After having some of the best sex I've ever had, why does she make me feel like I've done something wrong? My intentions were good. I wasn't trying to set her up. I know that's what she was thinking, but I'm positive she enjoyed it as much as I did. My feelings for Racquel are strong, but I'm just not willing to explore them any further right now. But if I'd told her that last night, would she have stayed? I doubt it. She would've let me take her fine ass out again and again. This would have gone on for a while, but how long before the complications of love began?

We've been playing this game for too long. If I had to do last night over, maybe I would've been upfront, although I know better. Racquel was never just a conquest. After experiencing the most intimate relationship possible with a woman—marriage—and watching it fail, it's hard to deal with a woman who wants those things. Racquel would never outright mention wanting to settle down, but it's in the way she asks certain questions. It's in the way she points out adorable children. The way she talks about her job feels like she's marketing herself. I could see all the signs. Racquel isn't a slouch by any means—she's intelligent, beautiful, ambitious, and responsible, especially in a time when being promiscuous and sexually free is more accepted. As she gets older, it's clear she desires more. She makes good money, and any man would be proud to have her as a wife. As for me, I don't plan on getting married, not now, and certainly not ever again.

Racquel

I arrived at the restaurant on time and then waited in the car, fixing my makeup, checking for stray strands of hair, and spritzing on a little perfume. I wondered whether I should stroll in casually or be upfront for a change. Grace was right—I must've been whipped. I gathered my purse from the passenger seat and handed my keys to the parking attendant. He smiled and said, "You are a very attractive lady, if you don't mind me saying."

"Not at all," I replied, hoping the compliment might earn me a discount. Parking in Manhattan was expensive. With my blue ticket in hand, I headed towards Marcus, who was only half a block away.

The restaurant was classy and air-conditioned, one of the more expensive ones, but I felt I deserved it. Slightly flustered, I made my way to the table. It was difficult to act normal when you were both angry and attracted to someone. If I had just taken him to any restaurant and ordered the lobster, he would have seen right through it.

"Hello Marcus, good to see you," I said, giving him my cheek.

"Hello, Racquel. You look well."

"Thank you."

After the initial greeting and seating, we both seemed at a loss for words.

"Let's order lunch," he suggested. He chose a rare steak, salad, and red wine.

I ordered the most expensive wine on the list, an appetizer, and the priciest entrée—curried cabbage, raisins, and shrimp. For dessert, I went for strawberry and raspberry ice cream topped with caramel.

"That angry?" he asked.

"More," I countered.

" Racquel, I'm sorry. I assumed you didn't want to be bothered. You could have called me at any time."

"I shouldn't be angry with you, Marcus, but I am. Even though you made no promises."

"I thought about you every day," he replied, as though that would lessen the sting.

Soon after, our waiter arrived to serve lunch. I felt embarrassed by my childish behavior but was too stubborn to cancel the appetizer and dessert. We ate in silence, with me mostly picking at my plate. Silence can offer protection; it minimizes the risk of offense when no one speaks. I was the first to break it.

"Thank you for lunch. But I must be going." As I stood to leave, Marcus placed his hand on mine. The brief contact sent shivers through me. I told myself it was the air conditioner that made me shiver and rubbed my arms up and down, looking around. We both ended up grinning despite my pretense.

"Look, Racquel, I like you. I'm sorry I didn't call you earlier. I've missed you. I'm not into playing games—I actually hate them."

"Yes, honesty and maturity work," I agreed, shaking my head. The problem was that it was all so complex. Sometimes you ask for the truth but don't really want to hear it. A part of me would have preferred if he had lied. If he'd said he lost my number or was falling in love with me, I would have known it was a lie, forgiven him, and—heaven help me—gone back to him again and again.

"Well, Marcus, I like you too," I finally admitted after a pause.

"Racquel, I'd like to start being your friend again, maybe go out sometime."

"I'll call you, Marcus, but I really have to go."

"Don't be so hard on me, Racquel. Give me a chance."

"I don't know, Marcus. We'll talk about this another time. I'm running late, so I'll call you."

I returned to the office half an hour late, postponing my talk with my boss for another day—one where my best work would be recognized. My friend and coworker Catherine Maritzio, the only other woman in the sales department who worked as hard as I did, was five years my senior. If she had been in the promotions department, we might not have stayed friends.

Catherine was what I called a workaholic. After a brief run-in, we talked and managed to iron out our differences. Her blunder had been suggesting I grab lunch at the nearest Popeyes. When I then asked if her godfather knew of any places where I could find a discount audio system, she got the message, stopped making assumptions about me, and peace was restored.

"What's up, Racquel?"

"Hello, Cathy."

"Are you just coming back to work?"

"Yeah," I replied, unwilling to offer more details.

"Listen, I'll catch up with you later." I headed to my small office down the hall. I didn't share that I planned to ask for a raise; that was my business.

Marcus

I had put myself on the line asking Racquel to lunch, and she wouldn't even attempt to resolve our misunderstanding. I could rationalize it as cowardice or a misunderstanding, but either way, I had tried. The ball was in her court now.

When I arrived at the hallway, my mother was mopping. "You usually don't come here on Thursdays," I said, feeling a mix of pleasure and annoyance.

"I thought you might like me to cook for you today," she replied.

"Mom, I can cook. Gran' taught me."

"Your father's mother?"

"The very same," I said, untying my stifling necktie.

"Do you remember Racquel Middleton from church?" I asked.

"No, I don't recall."

"Mom, her mother died when we were kids. Remember?"

"Oh, the homeless girl?"

"Yeah, I shouldn't have called her that. She's never forgiven me," then shook my head.

"What about her?" my mother asked, curious.

"I ran into her a month ago. She works in the city now."

My mother watched me suspiciously. "How is she doing? It's a terrible thing to lose a mother so young. Are you two dating now?"My mother didn't mince words.

"Not really," I answered, then changed the subject. "What about Dad?"

"He's fine. His arthritis has been acting up lately. You should come over and visit," she said. The truth was, I was afraid to face him. I hadn't seen him since my divorce and didn't want to see his disappointment in me. I had always admired my father and felt that, after my disastrous marriage, I had let him down. Visiting him wasn't on my agenda at the moment. My father and I were so similar in thought; I assumed he understood.

"Mom, I'm stepping out and need to get ready. I'll eat later." I dressed for the gym and headed out to meet my friend Mel. Since my divorce from Monica, I had been spending extra days at the gym. I stopped by the store for my usual Gatorade, essential after a workout, and ran into Cheryl, a former friend.

"Hello, Marcus," she said with a hint of mock attitude.

"What's up, Cheryl?" I greeted, noting that nothing had changed—her artificial multi-colored hair and pounds of makeup were still the same. I wondered what I had been thinking when I took her home back then.

"Where have you been hiding?" she asked.

"Nowhere," I replied uneasily. "I'm on my way to the gym."

"Hey, that's where I'm headed too. Can you give me a lift?"

"Oh… I don't work out at Eastern Athletic anymore," I lied. She wasn't dressed for a workout anyway. "I'm going to Gold's Gym now."

"Well, it was nice seeing you," she said. As we parted ways, she hinted that she would like to see more of me. I could have reconnected with her if I wanted to; Racquel and I weren't in an exclusive relationship. But with something promising on the horizon, why settle for something empty?

As expected, Cheryl wasn't at the gym when I arrived—she had no intention of working out. I spent three hours at the gym with Mel and his friend Travis before calling it a night. I gave each of them a pound and left.

Normally, I stayed later, checked out a few prospects, and had some drinks, but not that night. I was hoping to hear from Racquel. Once home, I took a much-needed shower; the gym had left me smelling less than fresh.

I checked my messages. Cheryl had called to say she had just left Gold's Gym and was sorry she missed me. "Sorry, babe, you had your chance," I said to the machine as I sipped on Evian. My mother had also called, asking if I would be attending the surprise birthday party she was planning for my father. It was months away—I'd call her later. My assistant had called for my computer password. "No, for the umpteenth time," I said to the machine.

Then I heard Racquel's message and called her back immediately.

"Hello," she answered, her voice soft with interrupted sleep.

"I apologize for waking you."

"Not a problem," she replied, as though she had been expecting my call.

All my energy renewed, I no longer felt worn out. I wanted to invite her over.

"You want to come over?" she asked before I could extend the invitation.

"I'll be there in twenty minutes," I said, and we hung up. We spent the evening walking, talking, and eventually returned to her place, where we explored each other's bodies with slow, loving intimacy.

~197~

Chapter 15

Racquel

After eight months of seeing Marcus, things were going so smoothly that there was a noticeable change in my mood at work.

"What's got you so chipper this morning?" my co-worker Cathy Maritzio asked.

"No reason," I responded with a smirk. "It's just a beautiful day."

"But it's raining outside. Oh boy! Have you been bitten?"

"By what?" I asked, puzzled.

"By the love bug."

"Impossible," I thought to myself. Marcus and I had only reconnected recently. But damn, she was right. I was falling in love with him.

"Nothing like that," I told her. She would want details.

"Ms. Middleton, you have a call on line two."

"Janice, please transfer it to my office."

"Thanks, Janice. Hello, Racquel Middleton."

"So professional. How's my girl?"

"Daddy?" I said, caught off guard, expecting it to be Marcus.

"Did I call at a bad time?"

"No, Dad," I reassured him.

"Are we still on for dinner tonight?"

"Of course," I said, though I thought Marcus would understand if I needed to cancel.

"So how's everything at work, Dad?"

"It's fine. Same time and same place."

"Okay, Dad. That's a date then." Marcus called toward the end of my workday.

"Hey babe, what's up? I'll pick you up later tonight?"

"Sorry, Marcus, I can't. I have plans I can't break."

"Oh," he replied.

"I'll call you when I get in."

"Alright," he said, then hung up. I planned to tell him about my father later; it was too complex to explain over the phone.

At exactly seven, I met my father at his favorite soul food restaurant in Harlem.

"Hey, Dad," I said, hugging him. I had long since stopped calling him Mr. Scylas. It was what we both wanted—me fulfilling the desire to have a father, him wanting to reclaim his long-lost daughter.

"How's everything?" he asked, always appearing completely absorbed in whatever I told him.

"The raise I asked for was turned down."

"That's a pity. You could branch out and look for other employment."

"I've put a lot of time into my job, but I'll keep that as an option."

"You may find a company willing to pay you what you're worth. But, of course, I respect your decision to stay." My dad was flexible.

"Racquel, I have a favor to ask of you. Please think about it before deciding." His interest piqued, I listened intently. "I've told my wife Martha and my other children about you. They would love to meet you. Please consider it."

"I see how important this is to you, so I will definitely think about it. The only problem is that I'll be nervous."

"Understood. But don't worry, it won't be an uncomfortable experience. We've been anticipating this."

The evening ended with my father dropping me home in his Lincoln Town Car. "Thanks, Dad. I'll call you to set up a time to meet your family." Once inside, I checked my messages. Marcus, Grace, and that lunatic Norman had called. After settling in, I called Aunt Lynn and told her about my father's request. She was happy to hear things were progressing so well.

Marcus didn't call until after midnight. I was too tired and engrossed in my thoughts to see him, so I declined his offer. Instead, I asked him to the movies that weekend. After my Saturday ritual of getting my hair done and a manicure and pedicure (he appreciated well-groomed feet), I planned a trip to the mall with an old school chum, Shelly. I found a casual dress and matching shoes. Once home, I placed unlit candles in my bedroom, just in case he came over to my place instead of his. Marcus picked me up at half past eight, and his behavior was subdued, not his usual self.

"What's wrong," I asked.

"You tell me," was his answer.

Taken aback by his abrupt reply I remained quiet. Then before asking, am I missing something? Are we having a problem that I'm not aware of?" I asked, suddenly defensive.

"Let's walk," he said, strained.

Parking the car and turning the ignition off, we walked to Central Park.

Marcus' hands were jammed in his pockets. He was ahead of me, putting distance between us.

"Racquel, I'm serious about you. Since, Monica, you are the only woman who has captured my attention past a month, hell past a week. If there was anyone else you'd tell me right?" He was being vulnerable and it must've been because he cared.

"Marcus, of course I would," I said, eager to share about my father and hoping he wouldn't judge me based on my parents' choices.

Giddy that he was serious about me and feeling a tinge of jealousy, I told him about Robert Scylas in detail, hoping he would understand my background. Marcus's family life was pretty normal, and being the only child of a doctor, he had been spoiled rotten.

When I explained that I was having dinner with my father once a month and not seeing another man, Marcus seemed relieved and told me so.

"Close your eyes and open your hand," he said.

I obeyed, and he placed something cold and metallic in my palm. It was too heavy to be an engagement ring, and I closed my hand around it to discover they were keys.

"I want you to move in with me, Racquel."

"This is a big step, Marcus. What if we don't get along?"

"I'll kick you out," he said, amused.

"I'm serious."

"Well, just think about it." He stopped me from handing the keys back, wanting me to keep them. Remembering how he had been a notorious ladies' man before we started dating, I held onto the keys.

Marcus

Asking Racquel to move in with me took some deliberation. We were spending so much time together anyway. The more I thought about it, the more it seemed like the right move. We were together every day, hardly ever argued, and she was neat and cooked for me at her place. In a way, she was like a girlfriend slash wife—better than a wife in many respects. And in my mind, we could turn this relationship off anytime we wanted, but right now, it was definitely on.

At first, I worried that she might be seeing someone else behind my back. But she reassured me that wasn't the case; it was just her father she saw once a month. The thought of her being with someone else was unbearable, and I couldn't sleep, realizing that I cared for Racquel more than I had ever cared for any other woman.

My feelings for Monica could not compare. And I had been married to her,and I still paid for bills she ran up while we were married. Because her sneaky ass still charged accounts as Mrs. Collin I canceled every single last credit card in my name. She made good money, but always mismanaged her shit. She was in debt trying to live above her means. I was not about to let her silly behind ruin my credit. Racquel and I did not share credit cards and accounts nor did I intend to, therefore, eradicate that problem.

Within a few weeks my father would be celebrating his sixty-seventh birthday and I'd invited a few close friends from the job. Melbourne and his date. I also invited Racquel in order to reintroduce her to my parents, as well as my cousins Michael, Glen and Lashawn after all they at one time also attended Holy Trinity. I had not seen them since childhood. It was an important day for my dad; so I wanted it to be perfect. No expense was spared. My mother invited a few of my father's colleagues and close members of Holy Trinity along with Reverend Steele. I had no idea my mother was inviting Monica. If I had known, she would have been uninvited.On the day of the party my mother and Monica were there early to receive the guests.

The plan was to surprise him after everyone arrived. I set it up by pretending to take him out. He was caught off guard then made a joke out of it. He pretended to take his belt off for scaring him half to death. Monica, of course, swept around the hall as if we were still married.She had the nerve to wear her old wedding ring. She stopped to talk to people she normally would not speak with. She spoke to Mel briefly and met his date, playing the gracious hostess to a tee. I was not fooled. I had introduced

Racquel to my father's family and I also was reacquainted with Reverend

Steele. Everyone was under the impression that Monica and I were still married, by the way she carried on, and I had to dispel them of that notion with the constant introduction of Racquel. I cornered my mother and asked why Monica was invited. She never liked Monica, she only liked the idea of her. My mother: Her excuse; She did not tell anyone that we were divorced. I was heated because of the situation that she put me in. After spotting Racquel Monica made her way to her but—I intercepted her.

"Where the hell do you think you're going?" I asked, grabbing Monica's arm and guiding her outside.

"What games are you playing tonight, Monica? When my mother invited you, why didn't you just decline? This party is for my father, and I don't want it ruined by your nonsense."

Undeterred by my irritation, Monica continued her charade. "Hi, darling. I was hoping to meet your friend."

"Forget about her and she is more than a friend," I clarified. "She's busy meeting my family."

"Marcus," Monica said, feigning hurt, "why waste your time? I know you miss me." She let her hands creep up my suit jacket.

"Don't flatter yourself," I said, pushing her away. Her arrogance was infuriating. Disgusted, I walked back inside, with Monica following me.

As I reentered, I saw Racquel chatting with Mel's date, Stephanie. She looked up, smiled, and waved me over. Monica saw this as an opportunity and linked her arm with mine. It was fortunate the venue was crowded, as I didn't shake her off to avoid making a scene. From where I stood, I saw Racquel excusing herself to join me.

"Monica, I'll speak to you later," I said, but she stubbornly continued walking with me.

I stopped her by introducing her using her maiden name to one of my coworkers. "Gary Weston, I'd like you to meet my ex-wife, Monica McKenzie."

After the introductions, I excused myself, claiming I needed some fresh air. I took Racquel for a drive to cool down, with Monica trailing behind and continuing to irritate me.

"It's a really nice dinner party," Racquel commented. "Your mother knows quite a few people."

"Did you enjoy yourself?" I asked.

"Yes, I did," she replied.

"Who was that other woman serving everyone?"

"She was one of the hostesses my mother hired," I lied.

"She seemed well-acquainted with everyone," Racquel noted.

"Yes, she's quite popular," I replied sourly.

At least Racquel hadn't seen Monica enough to recognize her, I thought. After spending a half-hour outside with Racquel, I headed back to my father's party. My mother greeted me at the entrance. "Monica has been looking all over for you," she said, much to my annoyance. "And we're about to cut the cake."

At the cake table, the photographer rushed to snap pictures of my dad cutting the cake and of us standing together. My father hugged and kissed me, and Racquel managed to capture that moment in a photo. She said she would treasure it. As the evening came to a close, I did not see Monica again. According to Mel she had left with Gary. I reminded myself to thank him on Monday morning.

"Yes, she's quite popular," I replied sourly

Chapter 16

Racquel

Exhausted from another night of making love to Marcus, I decided to take a rare day off from work. I called in sick, using a voice I had perfected in the mirror to sound like I was on death's door. My assistant, Rita, was convinced. "Gosh, you sound terrible," she said. I couldn't help but laugh after hanging up.

Lounging around in Marcus's nightshirt, I eventually made my way to the kitchen—mentally planning the remodel I'd tackle before fully moving in. I opened the stainless-steel Whirlpool fridge, the only thing I intended to keep after the remodel, and pulled out some butter pecan ice cream. "Breakfast of champions," I joked to myself.

The catalogs I'd gathered for the remodel were scattered across the table. "I'll look at them later," I muttered, procrastinating. Instead, I decided to call Grace. She was in her second year of marriage and actually pregnant this time.

"What's up, Prego?" I greeted her when she answered.

"Hey girl, what are you doing at home?" she asked.

"Stealing a day, what else?"

"How have you been feeling?"

"Tired," she replied, "but wonderful." She then launched into the details of the miracle growing inside her. I couldn't quite imagine something moving and swirling inside me, and the thought made me shiver unconsciously.

We talked for hours, catching up, knowing it might be a while before we'd have time to chat again. She had a husband, and I stayed busy. "Wait, I've got to get going if I'm going out," I told her. We promised to visit each other soon before ending the call.

Keys turned in the door, and I assumed Marcus had left work midday to spend time with me. I tiptoed into the shower, eager to get fresh for him. After pinning up my hair, I showered and perfumed my body.

Stepping out, I realized I'd forgotten to bring a towel, and there weren't any clean ones since it was laundry day. "Well," I murmured, glancing over my body, "this is nothing he hasn't seen before." Applying a bit of blush and lip gloss, I tousled my hair and prepared to greet him.

After a hard morning of work, I knew I was exactly what Marcus needed. I waltzed out of the bathroom toward the hall, but to my disappointment and unholy horror, it wasn't Marcus—it was his mother, Mrs. Collin.

"What are you doing here?" she asked, nearly outraged. "Does Marcus know you're here? Don't you have a job or something?"

The hell? "Mrs. Collin, I… I…" Fuming and sputtering, I could only squirm naked in place."Mrs. Collin," I stammered, "I had no idea you would be here." Sputtering for more to say. I backed up and grabbed Marcus' wet shirt from the floor, quickly slipping it on.

"Don't you have a place of your own? A job? Somewhere you need to be?" she asked, her tone indignant.

"Yes, I do, I mean I have a place and I was ill so….." I replied, feeling like a naughty schoolgirl caught in the act.

"Umm hmm. Well, I should have known Marcus had sleepover dates. They usually leave in the morning. It is now twelve o'clock," she remarked, adjusting her watch. She peered at Anne Klein, then back at me, her spectacles perched on the bridge of her nose.

"Marcus knows I'm here," I said, determined to set her straight, anger simmering at her scrutiny and mention of Marcus' prior sleepover dates.

Waving her hand dismissively in front of her face, she asked, "What is that smell?" She coughed, clearly disapproving of my choice of perfume.

"It's a gift from Marcus," I countered.

"He always liked women who wore too much makeup and perfume."

Heat began to rise from my ears at her implication.

"And look at this mess in the bathroom."

"I'll clean it, Mrs. Collin," I offered.

"Don't you worry your sweet little head about it," she replied, lacing each word with sarcasm.

"If you'll excuse me, I have to go," I said, pivoting on my heel and marching to Marcus' room to get dressed. As I put on my clothes, I felt more self-assured and ready to face the old dragon. She was leaving at the same time I was—whether by coincidence or because she didn't trust me not to steal something, I figured it was the latter.

"Marcus, you are dead for not telling the tyrant we live together," I fumed inwardly. After enduring her barbs all day, I walked to the elevator, subdued.

During the elevator ride, I should have guessed she'd bring up Monica, his ex.

"Marcus and Monica had a lovely condominium. She has such style; it's decorated so beautifully," she pointedly remarked. "Poor Marcus was so brokenhearted after they separated. He left all the decorating to me—couldn't bear to do it alone, you know, too many memories."

My mother, God rest her soul, always taught me to kill obstinate people with kindness. It just wasn't working.

"And you did a wonderful job, Mrs. Collin," I replied.

"Thank you, child," she said, trying to smile. I thought the attack was over until she mentioned church. "When was the last time you attended a service at Holy Trinity? The choir sings like a group of angels. You must come. In fact, I believe there will be a special service in two weeks," she added, as if she could scarcely recall. "The church keeps me so busy."

The elevator took forever to reach the garage, but I thanked heaven when it finally did.

"Have a nice day, Mrs. Collin."

"Excuse me—oh, you too, my dear."

She walked to her car, and I walked to mine. She could test the patience of a saint. How does her husband deal with her? I wondered. Once I reached my apartment—yes, my own apartment—I tried to take my mind off Mrs. Collin. It was a good thing I let her lock up to avoid further prying. I changed my clothes and thought it was a smart move not to give up my apartment. I couldn't help but wonder why Marcus didn't warn his mother I'd be there.

It was only one o'clock in the afternoon, and I had so much to do, but I couldn't resist calling Grace. She, of course, burst into laughter and begged me to stop telling her more or she might go into labor. We had to stop clowning around on the phone. I told her I had a bundle of things to do before I went home—excuse me, to 'Marcus' house.' We cracked up at that again.

I picked up the items Aunt Lynn needed to plan Grace's baby shower, and I also headed to the grocery store to grab things to cook for Marcus when he got home. "Look at me, I'm all domesticated," I mused. Heading back to Marcus's place, I surveyed the garage area, half-expecting his mother to jump out at me. Extracting the gift Marcus had given me from the bottom of my black suede bag, I located the keys.

I unlocked the first lock and pushed the door. Then came the second. It wouldn't budge. She had locked all three goddamn locks. I only had keys for two. Arms heavily laden with groceries, I stormed back to my car and threw the bags—cheesecake and all—into the back seat. By a quarter to four, I was back home, stewing and trying to find the right words to tell Marcus just how furious I was.

How could I explain to him that his mother had intentionally driven me crazy that day? It might backfire, making him defensive and protective of her, so I decided not to bother. I regained my composure after pacing around, and calmly cooked my soul spaghetti surprise at home, as intended. Marcus and I ended up having dinner at my place. But it wasn't until we joined his mother for church that the simmering pot began to boil.

Marcus

One Sunday morning, Racquel dragged me to Holy Trinity Baptist, keeping me from my Sunday football special. I complied when she told me she had promised my mother. After we sat down, the reverend began his sermon for the day. The topic was the wages of sin. Then his voice boomed through the church.

"The wages of sin is death. Y'all don't hear me this morning. I said the wages of sin is death. Adultery, living in sin—it's all sin. Coveting thy neighbor's things, lying, stealing, and killing, are all under the same thing: SIN," the reverend declared, full of emotion.

"Hallelujah," my mother said, turning around to thank us for coming, smiling pleasantly at Racquel. Reverend Steele continued his fervent sermon on sin. Racquel looked angry—at what, I couldn't say—but she remained tight-lipped.

Probably a women's issue, I assumed. The reverend, intoxicated with the power of absolving sinners, continued. "If y'all don't have Jesus in your lives," he warned, shaking his head, "then it's time to get to know Him."

Reverend Steele went on for an hour, though it felt much longer. I leaned closer to Racquel and whispered, "You made me give up football for this."

"Trust me," she replied, "I had no idea," and she glanced pointedly at my mother.

After the service, Racquel excused herself and rushed off to find her aunt and cousin Grace, who was expecting, as they were planning her baby shower. I rejoined Racquel, who was standing stoically with her Aunt Lynn and cousin Grace.

"Congratulations," I said, hugging Grace and shaking her husband's hand. My mom breezed up next to me. "Hello, everyone. The pastor was filled with the spirit today."

"Why, hello there, Grace, is that you?" my mother said, as though seeing her for the first time ever. "That can't be little Grace, all grown up now," she exclaimed. "Expecting a baby? How exciting. And a husband, good girl—no living in sin for you. Well, I'm off. Marcus, are you coming? I cooked all of your favorites."

"Mom, I'll be over later. I have a few things to do," I said, leaning over to kiss her goodbye.

On the drive to Racquel's apartment, she was quiet, barely uttering a sound. When we stopped in front of her building, she finally spoke. "Marcus, I really don't think your mother approves of us dating. In her mind, you belong with Monica."

"My mother doesn't really like Monica anymore. To be honest they only got along *after* the divorce," I told her. "You two will probably need to get acquainted. I'm sure she'll enjoy your company as much as I do." I leaned over to give her a kiss and patted her inner thigh. "Courage, remember you're a people person," I added with another kiss.

"You're probably right. I'd invite her over for dinner one day," she replied.

That wasn't exactly what I had in mind, I thought to myself, not happy with where the conversation was heading. "I have to meet my dad at his place at six," she reminded me. As she leaned over to kiss me goodbye, I asked if she needed me to come along, sensing her unease about the awkward meeting with Mr. Scylas's wife and children.

"No, I'll be fine. But I really want you to meet him," she said. "Next time, I promise."

Chapter 17

Racquel

At the end of the month, Aunt Lynn and I hosted a baby shower for Grace at Marcus's apartment. I extended an invitation to his mom, but she had other plans. Marcus typically made himself scarce at such gatherings, opting to play ball instead. Danielle, who was also expecting and getting married, helped with the decorations. Her small, rounded stomach reminded me once again of life's wonders.

The party was attended by forty women and one guy—Grace's husband, Thomas. Thomas looked around as if he regretted not accepting Marcus's offer to hang out. We played the usual games, making Thomas uncomfortable with some of the sexual jokes. We indulged in junk food and cake. Grace received a lot of beautiful green and yellow baby clothes, along with other gifts.

Jackie Hallowell complained that no one followed her registry instructions and bought from the list. Danielle argued that people should buy what they could afford, angrily flicking her black micro braids over her shoulder. Her hair was no longer platinum. Despite the disagreements, everyone had a good time. As Thomas packed the last of the gifts into his car, I decided to get another perspective on the situation.

Aunt Lynn looked at me. "Alright," she said, "you're next."

"Next for what?" I asked.

"It's your turn—to get married. I didn't raise my only sister's child to just play house."

"Marcus was married before," I defended. "He's not ready to get married again."

"First of all, when that boy was married to what's-her-name, he was a child himself," Aunt Lynn said.

"Monica," I supplied.

"What are you going to do, Racquel? Live in sin forever? And what does he get out of it? Lovin' when he wants a full-time maid?"

"Aunt Lynn, you too?" I said, feeling overwhelmed by everyone's opinions about my life.

"What are you talking about, child?" I then gave a brief summary of my conversation with Mrs. Collin.

"If you have any sense, Racquel, you'll stay clear of that whole situation," Grace volunteered.

"Trust me," Aunt Lynn added. I reflected on this, having come home hours ago from church.

"And yes, one day I want to get married," I admitted.

"If he gets too comfortable with this situation," Aunt Lynn warned, waving her finger back and forth, "y'all will never get married." I was in love with Marcus, and I felt that he loved me too, though he had never said it out loud. I kept that to myself.

"Thomas's mother was a trip too," Grace couldn't help adding. "Before we were married, she would lay out his clothes every night and even put toothpaste on his toothbrush. Once we were married, she came over once a month. I called it inspection time, though she claimed it was a visit. But the real change didn't happen until I got pregnant. Only then did she start treating me like family instead of an adversary."

"Why doesn't she like me?" I bemoaned. "I'm a nice person. I have a job. I have a degree—hell, I have two."

"As I told you before, it's not just you. Millions of women go through this," Aunt Lynn advised.

"It's more like a reversed Oedipus Complex," Grace added.

"Do not let that woman get under your skin," Grace advised. "And if this Monica person was so wonderful, Marcus would never have divorced her."

"That's true, Aunt Lynn," I agreed.

I told them I needed all the self-control I could muster after overhearing Reverend Steele thanking Mrs. Collin for her input on his sermon.

"I heard that Mrs. Collin is vying for Deacon Hallo's position," Aunt Lynn said, rotating her neck.

"You know, Jackie's pissed," Grace added.

"Lord, save us," I replied dryly.

"You know, fault-finding hypocrites live in church," Grace said with a hint of humor, trying to lighten the mood.

I thanked them for their advice and for letting me vent. I really appreciated it. The party was officially over now that Marcus and his friends had arrived, sweaty and smelly from the gym.

"Bye, cuz," I said, hugging Grace. "Someone better call me as soon as labor starts."

"If I can reach the phone, I'll call," she laughed. "Come on, Grace, I need to go check my numbers. I had a dream, I hit it."

Grace rolled her eyes as she heaved herself out of the recliner. "Bye, Aunt Lynn."

"Bye, child. Remember what I told you."

At eleven that night, Marcus's friends Mel and Brian finally went home. I cleaned the living room and went to bed, exhausted but unable to sleep. I reflected on what my aunt had said.

For a man who wasn't ready to marry again, Marcus certainly acted like it was a possibility. He said all the right things and did much of what I asked, but he never said those three special words I longed to hear. From his last real relationship, it seemed saying "I love you" wasn't necessary. For me, it was a need.

I had broken my celibacy with him, and he wanted us to move in together. What was holding him back? I guessed it was fear. He cared enough to keep me around but not enough to open up and risk his feelings. His arrogance and toughness felt like an act. How else could I have gotten this far?

Mrs. Collin's constant references to his former wife, Monica, didn't concern me anymore. In time, it wouldn't matter. I was his choice, for however long that would last.

I chose to focus on what we had and work around her unjustified opposition. I was content with whatever he was emotionally willing to give.

Until I decided that it wasn't enough. Although I sought permanence in his life, I didn't push and went with the flow. With that thought in mind, sleep became attainable.

However, I hadn't anticipated the flow lasting over a year.

Holidays came and went. We had been together for two years now. The following year, I would be turning twenty-nine, with no children, no husband, and no talk of having a husband. I was starting to feel a bit anxious.

The relationship had started to strain on my end. Marcus's aversion to marriage, stemming from his failed relationship with Monica, made me question why she was considered marriage material and not me. My silence and moodiness around the house were often softened by Marcus's infectious laughter and humor, which prevented me from staying angry for long. Consequently, I had put my own desires for marriage and children on the back burner.

When Grace finally went into labor, I was at work. Thomas called me in tears, his voice filled with joy. "It's a girl. It's a girl." I was moved by his happiness and excitement. I half-expected that after a few days, his enthusiasm would wane, and the baby would become just another source of noise. "What's that crying? Oh, it's the baby," I imagined he might say once the novelty wore off.

"Well, congratulations! How's Grace?"

"She's fine, just tired."

"How many hours was the labor?"

"Twelve," he replied. At that point, any fleeting thoughts I had about having a baby myself were momentarily extinguished.

I managed to convince Marcus to drive me down for a visit. We spent two days at Grace's home, taking many pictures and enjoying the time there. By the time we returned home on Sunday night, Grace's daughter was eleven months old, and I hadn't seen her since her birth. I was surprised that Grace, whom I had known all my life, chose to prioritize home life over returning to the corporate world.

I took my vacation in the middle of the year without Marcus. I wanted to reconnect with family and enjoy some quality alone time. So, I drove down to Maryland for a visit. Marcus wanted to come along, but I thought a little distance might be beneficial. Things had become somewhat tense between us, and I needed to reassess our relationship. Monotony had set in, and my patience was wearing thin.

Eight pounds, two ounces, Grace finally gave birth to a beautiful baby girl."I am so glad you came," Grace exclaimed, holding her daughter Taylor. She carefully passed the sleeping child over to Thomas, who held their daughter with a look of pure pride. His gaze was gentle, filled with wonder at the life they had created together. Taylor was an adorable child, with light brown skin like Thomas and dimples reminiscent of Grace.

As Grace helped me into their two-story home, I couldn't help but imagine how handsome Marcus would look holding our child.

Grace led me to the room where I would be staying and then proceeded to give me a tour of her new home. Taylor's room, which Grace had decorated herself, was charming. Three walls were painted white, while the fourth featured a mural of pastel butterflies fluttering against a soft blue sky. It was a sweet and serene space, reflecting Grace's careful attention to detail and love for her daughter.

Lilies adorned the room, and a border of lightly colored butterflies lined the top of the mural. Thomas handed me their creation, and as I held her, I was overwhelmed by her baby smell. At that moment, I realized I wanted one of my own.

With the baby settled for the night and Thomas heading off to work, Grace and I had a chance to discuss both Marcus and Thomas, uninterrupted.

"Thomas looks like fatherhood agrees with him," I remarked.

"I must admit, I have no complaints," Grace replied. "He's attentive and so involved with Taylor. I know you had doubts when I married him, but Racquel, I couldn't be happier."

"Now spill it. What's going on between you and Marcus?"

"I don't know how, Grace, but Marcus and I have slipped into this routine. It's as if we're already married, and he hasn't even asked."

"And if he gets too comfortable, he might never ask," Grace added. "Spice up your love life. Take him on a trip. Show him why he can't lose someone like you."

"Marcus can't be forced into anything," I told her.

"Who said anything about force? Persuade. You coming here without him is a start. He'll be so glad to see you when you get back. Trust me, you might just come home to a marriage proposal."

I floated on that thought throughout the remainder of my visit, and I only called home once.

Marcus

Marcus seems to be struggling with a lot of frustration and confusion in his relationship with Racquel. It's clear he feels he's put in significant effort and made sacrifices, but he's not seeing the appreciation or understanding he hoped for in return. His father's advice seems to be echoing in his mind, adding to his sense of helplessness.

Marcus sat in the quiet of his apartment, surrounded by the evidence of how Racquel had made it her own. His closet space, now crammed with her clothes, and the bathroom, cluttered with her cosmetics, were stark reminders of the changes she brought into his life. He tried to ignore the feeling of being displaced in his own home, but it gnawed at him.

He recalled his father's words: "All women are hard to please." It felt like an unfair blanket statement, but lately, it seemed to fit his situation all too well. No matter what he did, it felt like nothing was enough. He paid the bills, gave Racquel her space, and tried to be supportive. Yet, she had the nerve to say he was taking her for granted.

Marcus felt like he was at his breaking point. He had moved Racquel in, an act he had never done with anyone else. He had hoped this gesture would show her his commitment, but instead, it seemed to exacerbate the issues between them.

He needed to address this with Racquel, but he wasn't sure how to start. He felt like he had exhausted every avenue of communication without resolving anything. His frustration was mounting, and he knew that continuing to internalize it would only make things worse.

The next time Racquel came home, Marcus decided to sit down with her for a serious conversation. He wanted to express his feelings honestly but also listen to her perspective.

"Racquel, we need to talk," he began, his tone serious but calm. "I've been feeling really overwhelmed. I thought moving you in would be a step forward for us, but instead, it feels like I'm losing a part of myself. I pay most of the bills, and I try to support you, but I feel like my efforts are going unnoticed."

He paused, taking a deep breath. "I know we've talked about marriage before, and I thought we were on the same page. But it seems like we're stuck in a routine, and it's not what I envisioned. I need to understand what you want from me and what you need.

And I want to make sure that we're both feeling valued and heard in this relationship."

Marcus hoped that by opening up about his feelings, he could pave the way for a more constructive dialogue. He wanted to move past the frustration and find a path forward that acknowledged both of their needs and concerns.

Racquel went to see Thomas and Grace's new baby, Taylor. I was positive, by the time she came home, she would be on a let's have a baby kick. Well I was not ready, not all the nagging in the world will not change that. Racquel was gone for a week and the house seemed empty without her. All of what I told myself on Sunday, by Thursday I had missed bumping into her as we both prepared for work.

"If she would have waited we could have gone together," I grumbled.

Unwilling to admit that maybe I had begun to take her for granted. Friday night rolled around and it was payday. My boy Melbourne called me up to hit the clubs that night. I approved and it was time to get out.

"I almost thought you'd stay home, any other time you can't because you're

locked down."

"It was not a lock down, it's called quality time," I corrected him. "Hell's yeah let's go," I gave up the pretense. We picked an old hang out spot, The Studio. I dressed Italian down, it was not everyday I clubbed, so I took my time getting dressed. A little Fahrenheit after shave, along with Racquel's deodorant, Secret's, summer breeze. What did they put in the stuff; it worked better than any men's deodorant on the market. With a fresh new cut I was ready to hang with my boys. I looked good, Ismelled good. I was ready.

I was enticing temptation, and bound to bump into a former friend. Mel and I sat at the bar having a few drinks. Mel did most of the flirting since, out of us two, he still considered himself the single one. He caught a few numbers which I knew Stephanie would fish out of his pockets, come morning. He leaned over to me as he winked at a girl from across the bar, "I'm not buying her ass anything."

"Women make a whole lot more now-a-days."

"Man you are crazy," I said, polishing off my amaretto sour.

"Hey, they have no one else to blame, but the women's suffrage movement,"

he said, very serious then ruined it by laughing at his own joke.

The club was packed, and as usual, an argument broke out on the dance floor between two young men. I remembered why I usually stayed home. The tension escalated quickly, and then someone screamed, "He's got a gun!" Panic surged through the crowd as everyone rushed towards the exits.

In the chaos, I lost sight of Melbourne. I pushed through the frantic crowd, my heart racing, and made my way outside. I waited near the garage where we had parked, hoping Melbourne would find his way out safely.

A few minutes later, Melbourne appeared, looking shaken but unharmed.

"Yo, man, it's crazy," he said, catching his breath. "These kids are actually shooting at each other over a bump on the dance floor."

"I told you before," I replied, shaking my head, "we're too old for this crowd."

Melbourne nodded, the gravity of the situation sinking in. The night out, meant to be a temporary escape, had ended in a reminder of why I preferred the quieter side of life. We both knew that we'd dodged a bullet—literally—and the thrill of the club scene now seemed more hollow than ever.

As we drove back, I found myself reflecting on the night's events. The violence and chaos at the club had jolted me back to reality, underscoring the unresolved issues waiting at home. I realized that my temporary escape had done little to change the core problems with Racquel. It was time to face them head-on. As

I dropped Melbourne off, I spotted Beverly walking with her friends. I remembered dating her briefly—just two weeks—but couldn't recall why I ended it. Then it came back to me: she had three children she rarely saw because of her demanding job. Most of her free time was spent in the clubs, and I suspected she was looking for someone to share the financial burdens with.

I drove past, turning my face away. I didn't want to be seen by her or her friends. Since I started seeing Racquel, no other woman had even sat in my car, not that I couldn't have had others. I just hadn't been interested, and tonight wasn't the right time for any social encounters.

As I drove home, the thought of calling Racquel crossed my mind. But it was three a.m., and I decided against it. We had spent only two hours at the club—twenty dollars wasted on the cover charge and another thirty-six on drinks. It felt like a waste of time.Funny how you can get used to someone being around. Racquel had become a part of my daily life, so much so that she felt like a piece of furniture until six days ago. That realization hit me hard tonight. I knew what I needed to do.

I had to confront the issues between us, not just brush them aside or hope they'd resolve themselves. I needed to have an honest conversation with Racquel, to address our concerns and figure out how we could move forward. It was time to face the problems head-on and make a decision about where our relationship was going.

Racquel

Marcus should have missed me enough to fall on his knees as soon as I walked through the door. That's how I had envisioned it as I drove back from Grace's. In my fantasy, he'd be on his knees, begging for forgiveness and pleading for another chance. Instead, Marcus had a different plan.

He greeted me with a warm kiss and then took me out to Miakoto, the Japanese restaurant I had been wanting to try. The setting was lovely, but my mind was preoccupied.

"Ugh! What's this green stuff?" Marcus asked, holding up a spring roll.

"Fusion cuisine. It's a cilantro lime sauce. It's sushi. Try it," I said, trying to sound enthusiastic.

"Oh okay," Marcus sniffed the food before popping it in his mouth.

"So, did you miss me?"

"You know the answer to that," he replied with a smile. He then pulled out a white box. "I thought you might like this."

My heart skipped a beat. Grace's words echoed in my mind: "You must play the game if you want to get married." I was bracing myself for a grand gesture, but instead, I opened the box to find pearl and diamond earrings.

"Oh, thank you, Marcus. They're beautiful," I said, trying to mask my disappointment. I slipped them on, my small gold hoops now replaced.

"They look gorgeous on you, baby," he said, his eyes lighting up.

"Thanks," I replied, feeling my appetite slip away. I forced a smile and made small talk, but my mind was racing. Despite his gesture, I felt a pang of frustration. The earrings were lovely, but they weren't the grand romantic gesture I had envisioned.

As we finished dinner, I couldn't shake the feeling that something was missing. Marcus's attempt to make things right was genuine, but it didn't quite hit the mark for me. I remembered Grace's advice and resolved to play along, to keep up appearances and navigate this relationship in a way that would eventually lead to the commitment I started to crave "Marcus, can you leave work early next Wednesday? I have something special planned for us," I said, trying to keep the mystery alive.

"What's that?" he asked, curiosity piqued.

"It's a secret," I replied, enjoying the suspense. It was time to put the (N.I.T.M.M) campaign into action—Negro, It's Time to Marry Me.

The first step of my plan was to spend less time with him. I busied myself with meetings and clubs, filling my schedule to keep him guessing. The second step was to limit our intimacy. I started complaining of frequent headaches. But Marcus, being perceptive as always, seemed to sense the change. Before I could even properly fake a headache, he'd be at my side, initiating affection. He'd start with my ankles or kiss the back of my neck, making me question what I expected him to do—ask if I was in the mood?

Despite my efforts, his persistence left me struggling to maintain my resolve. More often than not, his advances ended with me having two or three orgasms, and by the time I wanted to discuss marriage, he'd be sound asleep, exhausted.

Determined, I resolved that every night was the last night, and in two days, I'd escalate my plan. I convinced myself I wasn't being conniving; Marcus just needed encouragement.

Wednesday arrived, and the evening was set. Lionel Richie was performing a free concert in Central Park, followed by dinner at Over The Streets Café. Marcus and I shared a love for old songs, so I knew he'd be excited. I had planned the night meticulously. After the concert and dinner at one of our favorite spots, the evening would conclude at the Cedar Inn. Earlier, I had prepared the room with plump strawberries, champagne, and lavender-scented candles—the works.

As we left the concert, Marcus was in high spirits, smiling and singing along to one of Lionel Richie's classics. I watched him, thinking how much I loved him—his rugged beauty and the way his face lit up with every note he sang.

The restaurant was within walking distance, and we strolled hand in hand, our fingers interlocking. The crisp air was refreshing, and although it was chilly, it gave us a reason to draw closer together.

"What are you looking at?" Marcus asked with a grin, catching me eyeing him.

"Nothing," I replied, maintaining my mysterious demeanor. We chatted about Lionel Richie and how incredible it was that he could still draw such a huge crowd, even after all these years.

As we walked, I handed Marcus a piece of paper. His expression shifted to puzzlement as he looked at the address.

"What's this?" he asked.

"Come and find out," I said with a playful smile. I left him there, seated with empty plates and a look of curiosity on his face.

Hurrying back to the Cedar Inn, I was eager to set the stage. I had already showered and prepared everything earlier in the day. The room was adorned with plump strawberries, chilled champagne, and lavender-scented candles flickering softly, casting a warm glow.

I checked everything one last time, making sure everything was perfect. The stage was set for the night I hoped would bring the conversation we needed. As I waited for Marcus, my heart raced with a mix of excitement and nervous anticipation. I was ready to see if my plans would spark the commitment I had been hoping for.

When he finally arrived, I greeted him with a smile, hoping that the evening would unfold as I had imagined.

The following week I took a trip to the lingerie Red leather cowboy hat, freaky Fredrick's cut out panties, garter, nylon's and

high heeled shoes stayed on, took the bra off. Marcus salivated as he walked in.

"Now this is a pleasant….."

"Shh," I whispered. It was not all the time I played a sex kitten. I wanted to do it to the fullest. I laid him down then told him to close his eyes. After handcuffing him I undressed him, being in charge felt exhilarating. I touched myself and then his body just to get things started. Slowly kissed and nipped at his sides and shoulders, to tease. I climbed on with the intention of leaving an impression. With the dips, jerk, twist, slow grind and fast gyrations. I marked my territory; another woman can't touch this I told myself. This body was made for him. Like his body was made for mine. After he convulsed deep inside me. I thanked him for his services, breathing heavily I dipped my hat, and in a Midwestern accent I said;

"Howdy, much obliged, much obliged."

"You have to do this more often," Marcus said, holding me close as I slid next to him, uncuffed from the evening's earlier play.

"Marcus, I love you," I said softly.

"I know you do," he replied, accepting my words. He kissed me, as if to silence my next words. But I pressed on, feeling the urgency of the moment.

"We can be like this for the rest of our lives. Honey, don't you want that?"

"I know what you want, Racquel," he said, his tone gentle but firm. "The only thing I can say right now is maybe one day, in the future."

His words pierced me, the way he said it felt like a cold reality check. I couldn't help but think that by the time he was ready, I might be past my prime for starting a family. We made love again later that night, this time without any handcuffs. With every twist and sway of my hips, I prayed he would change his mind, that my love and the evening would sway him to my way of thinking. Yet, Marcus remained resolute. I found myself grappling with a decision: Should I 1) destroy what we have by making incessant demands, or 2) give patience one last try? I also recognized that if he did eventually give in, I might question his motives. If he really wanted to be with me or would he put a shut up ring on my finger.

As I lay there, contemplating our future, I felt the weight of my dilemma. My love for Marcus was deep, but the red flags concerning his mother were flagging.

Chapter 18

Marcus

"Racquel, Racquel you should never handcuff a black man."

"Unless you do what you did the last time," I said, sucking her fingertips.

"Don't blush, it's too late to act shy now, cowgirl," I teased her, unable to resist.

Earlier at work, I couldn't help but recall the night we made love last week—or rather, the night she dominated me. I was handcuffed while she waltzed over in sexy red cowboy attire, wearing cut-away satin panties. It was a night to remember, but she almost ruined it by bringing up the topic of settling down. I told her I wasn't ready, and I finally had to admit to myself that I loved her. I had denied it for too long. But things weren't that simple.

I even thought that one day, maybe, I would marry her. But I knew I had to be ready, and no amount of badgering, mind games, or satisfaction would change that. I hated to disappoint her, but in this, I had to move at my own pace. I'm the man, and I've been married before.

I took her out to lunch on Tuesday to tell her that I'd loved her for quite some time. I also asked her to respect that her man loves her and needs to take his time. The next time I marry, I want it to last. Over the next few weeks, Racquel's noticeable manipulations stopped. She seemed to go along with my way of thinking. The funny thing about women is that you can never really tell.

As it happened, Melbourne and Stephanie became engaged. I never thought in a million years he would ever marry. He assured me it was a "get off my damn back" ring, not an engagement ring. But in my mind, it was only a matter of time before Stephanie started planning their wedding. They invited us out for drinks and dinner. I should have known there'd be repercussions. Throughout dinner, Stephanie babbled non-stop, frequently gesturing with her left hand. Racquel had a fixed smile on her face the entire night, looking almost deranged. Melbourne appeared exasperated, and I was uncomfortable, thinking, *I'm in for it later*.

"Sorry, Racquel. Stephanie was showing off. If I'd known, we could've stayed home."

"It's okay, Marcus. She was just happy, that's all."

I searched her face for any sign of deceit but found none. She was being straightforward. Good, I thought—no more schemes. I never considered that what I offered might no longer be enough. I apologized and kissed her goodnight. We lay in bed, content to hold one another. I didn't attempt to make love that night; I could tell she was lost in thought.

Being honest with yourself should be easy, but lying to yourself is easier. I'd convinced myself that I needed no one, that I'd be happy if things always stayed the same. But that, in itself, is a lie. Things always change, whether you want them to or not. Was I being fair to Racquel—the woman I know and respect? No. Throughout dinner, Stephanie babbled non-stop, frequently gesturing with her left hand. Racquel had a fixed smile on her face the entire night, looking almost deranged. Melbourne appeared exasperated, and I was uncomfortable, thinking, *I'm in for it later*.

Racquel

Judging by the voices in the apartment, I assumed Marcus's mother was visiting. After digging through my bag for what seemed like an eternity, I finally found my keys and whispered, "I finally found you," holding them in my hand. I wasn't sure if Marcus had told her that I'd moved in. Even after nearly two years, we still sneaked around. I couldn't wait to tell Marcus the good news about meeting the CEO of Kraft Incorporated and landing the advertising account. I smelled an upcoming promotion.

I slipped the jingling keys back into my pocket, deciding to act like a visitor instead. Ringing the bell, I waited but received no answer. "The hell with it," I muttered under my breath. His mother would have to know eventually. Opening the door, I was greeted by angry voices. Marcus's voice was unmistakable.

"That's all I have to say about this!"

Another voice responded, sounding much younger than Mrs. Collins's unique, raspy, cultured tone. It had a slightly elongated vowel sound and a distinct, though unidentifiable, non-American accent.

"Listen, Marcus, you have it all wrong as usual. That's not the way it happened."

I pushed the door ajar with one hand and saw a woman, about my age, stylish and put-together, standing alone with Marcus, who was draped in nothing but a towel. She looked somewhat familiar, though I couldn't place her. Marcus's body was wet and steaming, likely from a recent shower. Heat rose to my face, and I felt even hotter once I was spotted. My presence was now known.

"Did I come at a bad time, Marcus?"

"Racquel, please come in. Monica was just leaving."

Clicking her leather briefcase closed, the elegant woman walked across the room toward the door.

"I'll call you about this matter later, Marcus."

On her way out, she had the audacity to turn to me and smile, adding, "He's a handful, isn't he?" She licked her lips, looking like the cat that swallowed the canary, and slowly wiped her bottom lip.

Stunned, I had no comeback. I let the barb fly right over my head.

"Sorry about that, Racquel. She can be a real pain in the ass."

"Pain in the ass isn't the word that comes to mind. More like brazen hussy. Now, do you mind telling me what's going on? Why did I come home to find you half-dressed in the living room with Monica?"

I broke one of my own dating rules—rule number three: don't crowd your man's space, and no matter how tempted, don't badger him with questions. It'll only make him run like the wind. But as I interrogated him, he dodged my questions like a running back zigzagging to the end zone.

"Yes, I know who she is—your ex."

Fed up with his evasiveness, I asked outright, "What was she doing here, Marcus?"

"Oh, hell no, Racquel. I will not be interrogated."

"Marcus, are you still seeing her?" I pressed.

"Well, if you're going to accuse me of something, then there's really not much to say."

"Fine."

"I'm not in the mood for any of this today. You can leave."

"Okay, Marcus. Maybe I should," I said, hurt to the core.

Saying all that could be said, I walked to the bedroom, took out my duffle bag, and packed. Tears stung my eyes, and my heart felt heavy as I placed his key on the table. I walked out, down the hall, and pressed the elevator button. I tested the strength of our relationship and prayed that when the elevator arrived, he would be there too.

My prayer was answered, he did not want me to leave. The weight in my left hand was gone—Marcus held my bag. "Look, baby, I'm sorry I snapped at you. It's not what you think. Please, come back in and I'll explain."

Marcus

The tinkling of champagne glasses and the laughter in the restaurant only heightened the tension between Racquel and me. She didn't say a single word or believe anything I said throughout dinner. "Maybe this was a mistake," she finally said. "Maybe I should go home. I'm sorry I didn't tell you about Monica, but I didn't think it was that important."

"Not important? She's your wife."

"Ex-wife."

"Listen, I have something special planned, and you're ruining it."

"Then maybe I should leave," she said, attempting to stand up.

"No, wait, please sit down." I reached out to stop her. "Racquel, I was married to Monica, but no matter what she or my mother told you, it's been over for a while now."

Reaching into my pocket, I pulled out a small black velvet box and placed it on the table—my trump card. This wasn't how I wanted to do this, but I wanted to ask her to marry me. "I loved Monica, but that was a long time ago. You give me what she never could."

"Yeah? And what's that?" Racquel asked, her eyes shifting between mine and the box. Her voice was low, but the anger in it was unmistakable.

"Racquel, you give me realness and sanity. Yes, sanity. The difference between you and my ex-wife is that every day with you is a joy. You wake up with optimism, ready to take on the world. You have an open and kind nature. You're aggressive when you need to be and gentle when you should be. You focus on controlling your destiny, not me. Monica was manipulative and controlling. She didn't respect me as a man. I need that respect. I love my parents, and for whatever reason, their marriage works, but Monica is too much like my mother."

"And what about your mother? She can't stop singing Monica's praises whenever she sees me."

"My mother loved Monica as my wife, but I stopped loving her a long time ago. Anyway, you'll be marrying me, not Mrs. Gloria Collins."

As I opened the box, I briefly glanced down to ensure I had it the right way up. "Share with me. Share my future. I honestly and truly love you. I'm asking you to be my wife."

Tears slid down her cheeks before she nodded yes. The sound of applause reminded us that we had an audience—our intimate moment had become a public spectacle.

Her body language softened as she uncrossed her legs and unfolded her arms. I placed the two-carat pear-shaped diamond on her finger. She leaned over to kiss me and whispered, "Thank you, baby. Yes, I will marry you. And I promise to thank you later until you're tired."

"As you were saying," I teased.

"Oh, never mind. I love you, Marcus. Thank you, it's beautiful." Her face was flushed from crying, and in an effort to keep from tearing up again, she added, "Marcus, I promise to love you for the rest of our lives. It may sound corny, but I will."

I paid the tab and said, "Come on, let's get out of here," eager for the fulfillment of her first promise.

Later that evening, as we lay entwined in the sheets, Racquel shook her head. "That scandalous, trifling nobody—I can't believe she's still ordering credit cards in your name as Mrs. Collins. So, what does your mother think of her now? And what are you going to do about it, Marcus?"

"Whoa, too many questions. Truth be told, I had no idea Monica would pull half the stunts she did. But don't worry, I'm taking care of it," I stated firmly. "Right now, can we not think about her and just enjoy each other?" She agreed and snuggled closer into my embrace.

Chapter 19

Racquel

"You're engaged?" Marcus's mother exclaimed, her surprise sounding more disturbed than delighted. The distaste for our decision to marry was evident in the downward tilt of her mouth, her smile defeated by her truer feelings.

"When did this happen?" she asked, her eyes examining the pear-shaped diamond solitaire on my left hand. The only word she muttered was, "Expensive."

"A few days ago," Marcus replied, a hint of annoyance in his voice. "Are you going to congratulate us?" he asked.

"Of course," his mother said, standing up and hugging us as if recovering from some kind of shock. "Only my son would remarry after divorcing." Although I smiled and appeared calm, my teeth were set on edge. Her unhappiness couldn't have been more obvious.

Mr. Collin, however, warmly embraced me. "Welcome to the family."

"Thank you, Mr. Collin."

"Come on, call me Father Collin, Trevor, or Mr. T—just not Mr. Collin," he joked. Marcus's father was typically quiet, I gathered, except when it came to making someone feel comfortable.

"Sit, sit," he urged us. "Gloria, break out a bottle of wine—it's time to celebrate. It's in the china cabinet under those old *JAMA* magazines." Mrs. Collin withdrew from our group to retrieve the wine and glasses. As she reentered, she finally addressed me directly.

"Racquel, have you picked a date yet?"

"No, not yet. We wanted to wait."

"Good decision," she commended. I added that we'd decided on a small wedding with only family and close friends. "I can help you plan it; after all, I did organize his first wedding." The woman was completely unbearable.

Marcus changed the subject, something he always did when he didn't know how to fix a situation. His best form of escapism was to ignore it. Not to be outdone by the wonderful Monica, I insisted that something small and tasteful was exactly what Marcus had in mind. Sensing a brewing storm, Marcus announced that we had to leave.

"Did you really have to insult my mother?" he asked as I sat in the car. "She was only trying to help."

I was dying to say, 'Oh, she wanted to help, alright.' Instead, I calmly replied, "What? I never insulted her. I wasn't trying to insult her," I defended myself. Inwardly, I rolled my eyes. "I'm just so tired of hearing about the great Monica, that's all. Anyway, this is our wedding, and Aunt Lynn already offered to help."

"When did you speak to her?"

"Right before going to your mother's," I answered. He didn't need to know that I needed to hear a positive response before Mrs. Collins's predicted negative one.

"Look, I'll try harder. She doesn't make it easy. Every chance she gets, she starts espousing the miraculous wonders of your ex-wife."

"Racquel, I already told you Monica is not an issue."

"Baby, I believe you. And as I said, this wedding is about you and me," I reassured him, punctuating each word with a kiss.

I then completely kissed away his frustration, and he drove us to our next destination—my Aunt Lynn's.

"Congratulations! I'm so happy for you both." Her reaction was entirely different from Mrs. Collins's. We sat down, and she started giving us marriage advice early. Marcus took it in stride. "You both had me worried for a minute. So when is the big day?" Marcus started to get antsy, which was my cue. "Aunt Lynn, thanks, but we can't stay. We're having dinner with my dad." If I didn't bug him for a day, why should she?

My father stood up to shake Marcus's hand, and as I greeted his wife, I felt like crying—they genuinely liked each other. They approved of one another. We were at my dad's favorite soul food restaurant, Jezebel's. It was Marcus's first time there, but he seemed to enjoy himself.

They made small talk while I spoke with my dad's wife, Deloris. She reminded me of my mom in both style and behavior.

She made me feel at ease and not at all insecure about the relationship that developed between me and my father. Deloris actually encouraged it after we met. She mentioned knowing a wedding coordinator and invited me to call for advice anytime. I told her that since this was Marcus's second wedding, we both agreed to keep it simple. "Not a problem," she said, "if that's what you want," she emphasized. "Outdoor or indoor wedding? I know you haven't set a date, but we can talk about it."

I smiled. "I'd like an outdoor wedding or to get married at our church. Lots of flowers—white and burgundy will be my colors."

"So you have thought about it."

"Just a little. We've only been engaged since Friday," I said, sipping my margarita.

"I'm excited for you," she said once again as we left the restaurant. On the drive home to enjoy the rest of the evening together, Marcus mentioned how cool my dad and his wife were. I only wish I could say the same for the good Sister Gloria.

Marcus

"Thank God he blessed me by making me a man!" I exclaimed, sinking a three-pointer. I should have played for the Sixers. With all the catfighting going on around me, I was grateful for this hammer and these two nuts. I passed the ball to Mel, laid my hand on my claim to fame, and threw my hands up in triumph. "We haven't even set a date for the wedding, and Racquel and my mother have been going at it."

"I'm actually thinking about eloping," I confided.

"Hey, that's what you should do, man—knock out the wedding and honeymoon in one shot," he said, scoring a two-pointer. Here we are, less than a month into our engagement, and they're at each other's throats. They're disagreeing about everything, from the colors to who should usher in the guests. I'm tired of it. On one hand, I understand why my mother isn't thrilled about the idea. She doesn't believe in divorce and, for whatever reason, bonded with Monica. On the other hand, this puts Racquel in an uncomfortable position, especially when my mother brings up Monica every chance she gets.

"Monica came by my job and caused a potential scene in my office," I said. "I had to ask her to leave and not come back."

I need to stay away from her. That was the second time I wanted to slap the taste out of her mouth. Once she found out about my upcoming marriage, it didn't take a genius to figure out who told her. I wasted no time calling my mother to explain what happened at work and why we divorced in the first place.

"I told you about the pretty ones, man," he began, counting them off. "They all lack self-control, are demanding, and need their egos fed twenty-four hours a day."

"Racquel is not like that, thankfully."

I spoke too soon. Later that night, as we relaxed together, Racquel asked, "Marcus, am I as pretty as Monica?"

"Here we go," I said, shaking my head. "Yes, Racquel, damn." I stomped off to the bathroom and stayed on the toilet for an hour, reading *Sports Illustrated* to avoid any more questions. A knock disturbed the peace of mind I was trying to achieve.

"Honey, I'm sorry. Come out."

"Okay, but only if you don't mention you-know-who."

"Alright, alright, I won't. Now come out."

It was impossible to stay angry with Racquel for long. She had a way of making me laugh or smile even in the heat of an argument, making the conflicts seem childish and unnecessary. Unlike Monica, where sex was the remedy, talking with Racquel was what truly resolved things. "Marcus, I'd really like to start making plans for the wedding," Racquel said. "I know you wanted to take your time, but I think we should decide now."

Her reasoning hit me hard. I decided to let her take charge of the plans and set the wedding date for exactly six weeks away. With such a short timeline, there was no way she could leave me broke. "Marcus," she began, "that leaves me no time to plan."

"Exactly," I thought. "We're keeping things simple." I reminded her of that as the phone rang, halting our conversation.

"Hey Dad, what's up?" I answered. From the tone of my father's voice, I knew something was very wrong. Instinctively, I knew it was about my mother.

"I'm coming," I said.

"Marcus, what's wrong?"

"Racquel, I'll have to step out. I'll call you later."

"Is it your mother? Let me come. I can help."

I seriously doubted that, given the recent friction between them. "No, it's okay. I'll be back later," I said, grabbing my jeans and car keys from the coffee table. I dashed out, hoping to explain things to her later.

I sped down the highway, weaving through traffic, and reached Queens in less than twenty-five minutes. Bursting into my dad's house, I didn't slow down until I reached my mother's bedroom. My father sat beside the bed, looking grim. My mother lay prostrate under the covers, moaning in pain.

"Mommy, what's wrong?" I asked, kneeling by her side. My father had examined her and diagnosed abdominal pain but ruled out appendicitis as a possibility. He'd called an ambulance to be safe, just in case he was wrong. I was shaking uncontrollably. Gloria Collin, sick—never. Confusion and fear overwhelmed me. My father was more composed than I was, dismissing anything more severe than gas pains. The ambulance arrived shortly after I did. My father showed his hospital identification and explained the situation as they helped her downstairs.

At the hospital, my father took over. He was now part of the staff, ordering x-rays, suggesting specific blood tests, and monitoring her pain levels. I stayed in my mother's room, feeling helpless. Racquel called my cell phone twice, but I had no information to give her because, even I, didn't know what was happening. All I knew was that my mother was in pain, and I was powerless to stop it.

The night dragged on with no definite answers, which should have soothed me but only deepened my dread. My mother was advised to go home and rest. As daylight broke at five a.m., I drove back home to rest. My father, having the foresight to take my mother to work with him for more tests, felt better with her under his care than alone at home. However, she pleaded to stay home, and grudgingly, my father relented. I went home to shower and change.

When I walked into the apartment, I found Racquel sleeping on the couch, fully dressed. She must have tried to stay awake for me but had fallen asleep, exhausted. Careful not to wake her, I scribbled a note. Having eaten nothing and slept even less, I traveled back to Queens.

I knew Racquel's exclusion would hurt her feelings, but I also knew my mother to be a proud woman with a dignity that could endure anything. She would not accept help from someone she saw as a rival.

I unlocked the door to an eerie silence. The usual cooking and soap operas were absent. Reaching my mother's room, I found her sleeping on her back, her stomach slightly bloated. Sensing my presence, she opened her eyes and greeted me weakly.

"Hello, son," she said, her voice tinged with pain. "Why are you here? I'm fine."

Her hair, usually in its normal coil, had unraveled. Sweat beads formed on her ashen face. At that moment, I understood she was more ill than she admitted. Despite my protests, she struggled to get up and move around her room, trying to show me she was capable. I wasn't fooled. I spent the rest of the day taking care of her, just as she had once cared for me. The same woman who cleaned my scraped knees and wiped my snotty nose now had me by her side, comforting a mother who had always been there for me.

Chapter 20

Racquel

At first, I thought it might be some sort of ploy on his mother's part. But Marcus's growing concern affected me deeply. Her illness seemed very similar to my mother's. Marcus didn't invite me to help as he visited his mother's house every day. My feelings were hurt, but I understood he had his reasons, so I left it at that.

After a week of suspense, Marcus finally told me that it was a gastrointestinal issue and that his mother would be back on her feet soon.

"I can help," I offered.

"No, Racquel, that's okay."

"Marcus, I really don't mind," I pressed, hoping to be involved.

"Monica visits her all the time. You wouldn't feel comfortable."

"That's why you're there all the time without me," I retorted.

"Racquel, you're being ridiculous."

He left without the customary kiss. My frustration simmered. I thought bitterly that there was probably nothing wrong with his mother. Monica was either sick or desperate, using his mother's supposed illness to stay close to him. I had to put that aside; I grabbed my car keys and rushed off to meet Reverend Steele at five and then to the florist. There were wedding details that needed my attention.

Week three of the wedding countdown was here. I crossed off each day in my planner, getting closer to the big day. I checked and rechecked with the florist, caterer, and the hall. Two weeks before the wedding, I hosted a dinner inviting Marcus's parents, my Aunt Lynn, my father, and his wife.

Since Mrs. Collin was feeling better, I thought it would be a good idea for his parents to meet my father. The dinner, originally scheduled to take place at my home, was moved to Marcus's parents' house after Mrs. Collin decided to cook. The guest list included us, Marcus's cousin Milford and his wife Denise, and my father, who came alone as Delores had a prior engagement.

Denise and Milford were both amiable, and I was relieved that my father and Denise had met before, so no introductions were necessary. The dinner Mrs. Collin prepared was outstanding, though she was quick to downplay the compliments, saying, "Thank you, it was nothing."

I thought maybe we could get along after all, but I was mistaken.

"Racquel, I must teach you how to make this for Marcus. It's his favorite. He's not used to fast food, collard greens, and things like that," she said, clearly expecting me to take notes. My father cleared his throat. Aunt Lynn harrumphed in response. Marcus jumped in to say that his grandmother had taught him to cook, which felt like a small victory for me. I silently thanked him with a glance. Denise, with a sly grin, remarked, "This is the same meal Trevor's mother taught me to make."

I saw that Mrs. Collin remained silent, a subtle sign of the same tension she experienced with *her* own mother-in-law. Mr. Collin noted the resemblance between my father and me, which I took as a compliment.

"I would have liked to have had a daughter, but Marcus was our only child," Mr. Collin said. "But now I'll have a daughter-in-law to spoil." My father responded with appreciation, "Your son looks a lot like you. I'm proud of him for finding such a nice girl."

Mr. Collin's praise seemed to shift Mrs. Collin's attitude for the rest of the evening. She watched her words more carefully, helping Denise clear the table with a more subdued demeanor.

Marcus

I started to visit my mother often but so did my ex-wife. The situation was too serious for her to get under my new finance's skin.

"Monica. Why are you here?" I asked, my voice tinged with irritation.

"Your mother asked me to come. Don't forget, I'm also a doctor," she replied with a hint of defensiveness.

"I haven't forgotten," I said. "I just want to make sure that's the only reason you're here. During our marriage, you barely spent any time with my mother, and now it seems like you two are inseparable."

"Do you object to your mother's friendship with me, Marcus? After all, I am your first wife," Monica said, her tone slightly accusatory.

"Not at all," I responded, "as long as this friendship doesn't interfere with my relationship with my new wife."

With that out of the way, I asked for Monica's professional opinion about my mother's health. Monica refused to share any specifics, only summarizing what I already knew. My mother was up and about by mid-afternoon, her prescribed painkillers having taken effect. Monica stayed to help her around the house, displaying an unusual level of unselfishness. While I was skeptical about her motives, I chose not to question her further. My mother seemed to appreciate the company and the help, so I decided to leave. To unwind, I called Melbourne's cell for some company at the gym. We started on the treadmill to warm up.

"Ex-wife back on the scene," he joked.

"It's not like that," I replied. "She's just visiting my mother."

Melbourne raised an eyebrow and did his best Spock impression. "Interesting concept. Jim." His Spock impression was spot on.

"Very funny." We spent an hour warming up and then moved on to the rowing machine. I decided to get him back by asking, "When's the wedding for you?"

"Next year," he said with a grin.

"Yours?" I asked.

"Next month," he answered.

We both shook our heads and laughed. They got us, we joked. Melbourne put his hands behind his back, as if locked down. But deep down, we both knew the truth. Despite the jokes, we were secretly happy about it. The myth of staying a player for life was just that—a myth. No man is an island. If I had any sisters, I'd warn them about guys like Mel and me. Every man wants to be caught by the right woman, and if he says otherwise, he's lying. Even with all the disagreements I was having with Racquel lately, I never doubted my decision to marry her.

After exercising for an hour and lifting weights for two, I felt exhausted but determined to take Racquel out. The goal was to take her mind off the wedding plans and her growing obsession with

Monica. We laughed, we talked—it was like old times. It was exactly what we both needed. I was worried about my mother's health and staying on top of things at work. A slip-up today could mean unemployment tomorrow.

When we got home, it was late. Instead of heading straight to bed, Racquel opened a bottle of Merlot and put on her Nina Simone CD. She patted the seat next to her on the couch, and I joined her.

She shared her decision to have Robert walk her down the aisle. I thought it was kind of her to forgive him and include him in the ceremony. We all make mistakes, after all. Then she showed me her plans for the wedding.

The plans were simple, just as I'd asked. The thought of planning a wedding while my mother was in and out of the hospital felt surreal. I made an effort to show interest as we flipped through colors and arrangements, knowing it would make her happy to have me involved in the decisions. Despite my attempts to stay engaged, my mind kept drifting back to the worry that my mother might have more than just stomach issues.

Chapter 21

Racquel

In the short time we had to plan the wedding, it turned out to be a success. I respected Marcus's wish to keep things simple. The only change was moving the ceremony indoors due to the unpredictable spring weather. The church was decorated with pink, white, and burgundy, accented with touches of greenery. It was a beautiful wedding, especially considering how quickly it was organized.

Everyone who mattered was there. My father walked me down the aisle, gave Marcus a heartfelt hug, and shook his hand at the altar. Grace was my maid of honor, and Aunt Lynn served as my matron of honor. My father's wife was honored to attend, and Jackie Hallowell and her husband were present, though they gave Mrs. Collin disapproving looks throughout the ceremony for her choice of seating.

It was a small but lovely ceremony. I wore a simple yet stylish eggshell gown adorned with seed pearls around the neckline and woven through my curls. Marcus looked incredibly handsome in his black tuxedo. We exchanged our own vows, slipped on the rings, and sealed it with a kiss. A photographer from my job graciously took the pictures as a wedding gift. The reception at Le Bistro was elegant, though my new mother-in-law didn't miss the opportunity to critique every detail. Instead of the salmon and crawfish mousse baked in phyllo dough, she believed we should have served lobster.

Mrs. Collin criticized the main course, insisting that honey-glazed duck would have been preferable to chicken. She also thought we should have had butter cream instead of the strawberry torte decorated with white chocolate shavings. The only decision she agreed with was serving fresh fruit.

As my guests passed through the receiving line, Mrs. Collin remarked that she had forgotten her allergy pills for the flowers in the chapel. Overhearing this as a new and nervous bride, it was enough to drive me batty.

After some dancing and a few drinks, Marcus and I headed to a Bed and Breakfast in Cape Cod. Neither of us had been there before, so we explored the area, visiting local pubs and getting used to the strong Irish accent. For four days, we spent most of our time on the beach and relaxing at the Inn. On the last day, I discovered an antique store and admired a unique silver and pearl pin. Marcus surprised me by buying it as a wedding present while I was in another store.

Our honeymoon lasted four days. Although I loved the vacation, I persuaded Marcus to cut it short. I couldn't shake the feeling that something was amiss with his mother's health.

"If it was serious, Racquel, my father would have called me. He did finish medical school, you know," Marcus said, trying to reassure me.

I couldn't quite explain why I felt uneasy, but I suspected there was more to her illness than they were letting on.

After the wedding, Mrs. Collin's antics diminished somewhat. Still, Marcus wanted us to bond, so I decided to extend another olive branch. This time, I joined a charity function sponsored by Holy Trinity Baptist Church at Hale House in Harlem, a home for drug-addicted babies. Since I liked children, I thought it would be a piece of cake.

The visit to Hale House was more intense than I expected. The babies, all craving a substance beyond basic sustenance, cried constantly. Mrs. Collin took charge, ensuring all volunteers handled the babies correctly.

The baby I was assigned, Andrew, had been abandoned at a hospital just two days after birth. At five months old, he was active and cried non-stop. I struggled to console him, my efforts only making things worse. Mrs. Collin rushed over and said, "Racquel, watch how you hold him. With his jerking and your unsteadiness, you might drop him. Let me," she said, holding out her arms. She gently rocked and cooed to Andrew, who quickly fell asleep. One for Mrs. Collin, zero for Racquel.

"I'm sorry, Mrs. Collin," I whispered, not wanting to undermine her efforts. "In my line of work, we really don't deal with many babies," I said.

"You'll have to learn sometime if you want any," Mrs. Collin whispered back.

Two for Mrs. Collin, zero for Racquel. "Advertising is very demanding," I replied.

"Oh, is that what you do? I had wondered," she responded with her usual condescension.

Trying to keep things pleasant, I asked if I could have my company's photographers take pictures during the next visit.

"Why?" she asked, her tone uninterested but suspicious.

"Oh, we're running a good nutrition campaign this month. Since seeing Hale House in newspapers and on TV years ago, I thought it would be nice to feature the benefits of a drug-addicted child living here. You know, highlight the good deeds of the home, the love, and the nutrition the babies receive—basic needs for all children."

"Well," she said, looking at me with renewed interest. "What about donations to the organization and mentioning the Holy Trinity Church?"

"I'm sure my company can arrange that," I said confidently. "I'll handle my end, and since you know the director, you can handle yours."

"Okay," she agreed. "This sounds interesting."

Now, if only I could pitch this idea to my boss.

Riding the wave of confidence, I wrote a twenty-page proposal to persuade Mr. Crawford. I walked into his office, bypassing his secretary, and placed one copy on his desk and handed him the other. He briefly skimmed the document, deep in thought.

"No, Racquel, it's out of the question," he said firmly.

"What if I write another proposal? What about those poor babies?" I tried to use pity as a last resort.

"The only way I'd agree," Mr. Crawford said, "is if a cow was set right in the middle of the place."

Would threatening to quit make him take me seriously? My mind was racing.

"No, Mrs. Middleton-Collin, and that's my final answer."

Did I really invite this man to my wedding and do the Soul Train line dance with him?

"If it means anything," he began softly, "I really would like to help, but my hands are tied." In business jargon, this meant, stop asking already. Defeated, I called Mrs. Collin, and gave her the bad news. My husband always said that business and family don't mix. I should have listened.

"I knew it was too good to be true. You are a liar!" Gloria's voice blared over the phone accusingly.

"I didn't lie, Mrs. Collin. At the last minute, the company decided to advertise cows in the Midwest as a source of good nutrition," I explained.

"You can't blame me for that," I added.

"My name is on the line, and so is the church's. And I might add, a church that you also attend," she snapped.

"Look, Mrs. Collin," I said, starting to lose my patience, "the children can still be featured to help the Hale organization, but it will have to be pro bono for now. You know, for exposure."

"The original deal you had me set up had nothing to do with pro bono anything," she retorted, her frustration evident. She slammed the receiver down, leaving me nearly in tears.

Later, I explained the situation to Marcus over dinner. Since he was a businessman himself, he understood the predicament I was in.

"Don't worry, I'll talk to her," Marcus promised.

"But I warned you that she was impeccable with her word when she made a promise. She keeps it," I said miserably.

"Yes, you did mention that," he replied.

"If you weren't sure, why did you suggest it anyway?" he asked.

"It's not my fault; they went with Opie and his heifers from the Midwest," I whined.

I trailed behind him towards the bathroom. He kissed me on the nose and then redirected me. "Believe me, you don't want to come in here," he said, turning me towards the sitting room where a newspaper lay.

That night, I spoke with Aunt Lynn, who persuaded me to attend church the following Sunday. She was being honored for her efforts in bringing at least sixty new parishioners into the fold. Deacon Hallowell and Deacon Mrs. Dr. Collin were also among the honorees. On Saturday, Grace was coming to New York and bringing Taylor. We planned to spend the whole day shopping at the Paramus Mall in New Jersey.

We met at Aunt Lynn's house. Grace drove, and Taylor babbled happily in the backseat. "She's growing so fast," I remarked, looking back at Taylor as she tried to unfasten her seatbelt. One day, I thought to myself.

We shopped until we dropped at the mall, taking a much-needed break for lunch. As we were eating, I spotted the familiar fedora hat and black scarf. It was none other than Gloria Collin, flanked by two Holy Trinity parishioners. She noticed me sitting there and decided to give me the snub. Determined not to make a scene, I deliberately turned my body the other way.

Aunt Lynn, noticing the situation, decided to intervene. "Hello, Deacon Collin, Sister Bettie, Sister Abigail. How are you today?"

Her attention was drawn long enough to return a response. Mrs. Collin acknowledged Aunt Lynn with a formal greeting.

"Hello, Sister Baker. How are you?" Mrs. Collin said.

"Fine, thank you."

"Wonderful passage you read last Sunday. It was really uplifting. The church made a sound judgment in making you a deacon, and it was long overdue. We need more women like you in church, letting that Christ light shine through."

Her companions nodded in agreement. Aunt Lynn briefly commented on Mrs. Collin's Christ-like nature, and her praise seemed genuine. Appropriately set down, Mrs. Collin was momentarily speechless. "Thank you," she stammered. "Ah, Racquel, I have spoken to the director. Let's make arrangements."

"Call me Monday morning to discuss the details. And please have my son give me a call tonight."

"No problem. I will tell him, and I'll give you a call Monday by nine. Have a good evening."

It was that easy, that simple. Compliments were her weakness.

"Aunt Lynn, you need a medal."

"Girl, you've got your hands full. Stay off her bad side and don't worry. God deals with all the works in progress. If that leopard doesn't change her spots, she'll be dealt with, and better with us than with the Father."

I wasn't familiar with Aunt Lynn's take on the situation or her religious perspective. All I knew was Mrs. Collin was petulant. We couldn't find common ground on anything. If this was a glimpse into the life I would have with Marcus, I had my hands full. As the evening drew to a close, I hugged Taylor goodbye and told Grace and Aunt Lynn I'd see them at church.

I stayed briefly to watch Aunt Lynn being honored, then rushed back to cook dinner for Marcus. He had made reservations at Café Collin, where his mother had demanded his presence the night before. After spending two hours in a hot kitchen with a nervous stomach, I put the dinner away in the freezer, ate crackers, and drank some tea. Next, I called my father to schedule our usual meeting.

"Hello?"

"Hello, Delores, it's me, Racquel. How are you, Dana, and William?"

"Fine, everyone is fine. Dana asks about you often. I can't wait for you both to meet. Racquel, you have perfect timing. I was just asking your father about you. How is Marcus, that husband of yours?"

"He's fine. He is out visiting his mother right now."

"How is Mrs. Collin, is she feeling better?"

"Yes, she is. She went to church today."

"That's good. Tell them both I said hello. Well, alright. Here is your father. It

was nice talking to you."

"Hi, dad. Hey sweetheart, how are you?"

"Fine, dad," I answered.

"I was wondering instead of going to dinner I have tickets to an upcoming

basketball game, next week and was wondering if I invited Delores and

Marcus with us." "Dad, that is a wonderful idea, I will ask him tonight." I hung

up the phone and wondered if Marcus would mind, they seemed to get along.

I had hoped he'd say yes.

Later on that evening after Marcus showered I asked if he was would come

to watch a basketball game with me and my dad.

"Who's playing?" he asked while fixing the towel around his waist.

"I think he said the Knicks and the Pistons or Pacers. Does it matter? Are you coming or not?" I asked, my hand on my hip as I enjoyed the view of his muscular, bare chest. His workouts had definitely paid off.

"It does matter because if it were the Bulls, I'd have to say no," he replied.

"Why? Should that matter?"

"The Bulls beat the Knicks so badly one year that I promised myself I'd never watch them slaughter us again. The score was 116 to 69. We got our asses kicked. I couldn't stand watching it up close. But of course, I'm coming," he said, pulling me closer and wrapping his arms around my waist. "And your father makes dough, so I know we'll have good seats. I'll show you what to look for so you can enjoy your first game at Madison Square Garden. Come here, let me teach you about one of the greatest sports in this country."

I sat down with my chin resting in my hand as I listened to Marcus explain the intricacies of basketball.

"The team players are announced one by one. At the start of the game, the referee stands in the middle of the court and throws the ball into the air. Whoever grabs it first gets the first chance to score. It's called a tip-off." Marcus mimicked the movements, dribbling an imaginary ball up, down, and around the kitchen. His actions made his back and arm muscles flex and extend, moving with the sleekness of a panther. He then switched positions. "Then it's the other team's job to stop them by blocking the shot. And whoever makes the most points by the end of the game wins. Now come here."

He led me to the bedroom, dropping his towel on the floor. "I want you to come…with me," he said with a playful grin.

Chapter 22

Marcus

On Sunday, we sat with my parents. Surprisingly, no sparks flew, no twisted lips, no slick comments. Everything ran smoothly for that one day. I hugged them both, savoring their ceasefire. "It's so nice to see my two favorite ladies together," I commented. Both my mother and Racquel looked like they'd swallowed soapy water. Whatever their issues were, they'd have to work them out between themselves from now on. We were family now, and I was confident that once my mother got to know Racquel better, she would come to love her as much as I did. Likewise, once Racquel realized that my mother wasn't as pragmatic as she seemed, they'd get along.

Married life was turning out to be more enjoyable than I had anticipated. If I had known it would be this easy, I would have married Racquel sooner. Nothing much had changed; if anything, we had grown even closer. My father approved of our marriage, and I enjoyed getting to know her father. After church, we went to dinner at my parents' home, where we briefly discussed the topic of children. Even my mother chimed in during dinner, remarking on whether or not we should start a family.

Racquel listened with a smile, though I could tell steam was rising from her ears.

"Don't wait too long to have children, Racquel. That's why God instituted the sanctity of marriage—so that we could have children," my mother said.

The conversation was innocent enough, but I knew Racquel would interpret it differently. With our first Christmas as a married couple approaching in a few weeks, I didn't want to stir up any arguments. I decided to end my mother's line of questioning by stating that we married because I loved her, not specifically to have children.

"When you were married to Monica, she told me you couldn't stop talking about having children," my mother said.

With that statement, we all continued to eat dinner in painful silence. My father shot my mother annoyed glances, likely planning to address her later in the privacy of their bedroom. The evening ended quietly, with Racquel, as predicted, taking my mother's comment to heart. She was so sensitive.

Racquel

That unbearable witch likes to drive me crazy, I stewed. Having children with my husband is personal. She overstepped her boundaries at dinner. I had only agreed to go to dinner knowing it would be unfair not to, then requested Marcus join me and my father. Next, she'll probably comment on whether or not I'm even fit to be a parent, I imagined as I threw my bag down. We were getting ready for the dinner and basketball game my father invited us to.

"Anything wrong?" Marcus asked.

"Nothing," I said, picking up my purse and putting the diva's comments aside, determined to push her latest dig out of my mind.

"Honey, are we having dinner at our house for Christmas?"

"Yeah," he said, dressing.

"Good, because I'd like to send out invitations." My father and his wife, Aunt Lynn, Uncle Herbert, Grace and her family, Stephanie and Melbourne—the list went on.

"Wow, that's a lot to plan."

"Why don't we give out the presents over dinner? We bought something for everyone we invited," Marcus suggested.

"That's a good idea," I thought, planning to give the book to someone else and choose a gift more suited to my mother-in-law's taste. "Let's go, or we'll be late," I said, rushing him.

The winter wind blew as we walked hand in hand, clutching the top of my jacket and second-guessing my decision not to wear a scarf. We had parked a block away. At least I had enough sense to wear a hat in the thirty-five-degree weather. Marcus, however, wore his Knicks knit hat, sweatshirt, and pants, topped with a goose-down leather coat. The New York Knicks and the Indiana Pacers were displayed in bright lights on the overhead screen.

My father and Delores waited at the information desk. "Good to see you, man," my father said when he saw Marcus. They gave each other a pound.

"Come on, my father," Marcus urged. "Lead the way; let's get to this game."

We sat in the eleventh row, right in the center. Marcus was impressed with our seats. He had a clear view of the players' elongated bodies, close enough to hear their grunts and the trash talk between them. The smirks, smiles, head shakes, and signals they exchanged were all vividly visible. I could almost make out Dale Davis's shoe size, which I estimated to be a size fifteen. Although I rarely cared about basketball on television, the experience of attending the game was very different.

"Who is that irate man? He's screaming his head off," I asked, pointing to a passionate fan in the stands.

"Who is that irate man? He's screaming his head off," I asked.

"That's the other team's coach, Larry Bird. He used to play; now he coaches," Marcus explained.

"No, the other one is down in front."

"Oh, that's Spike Lee. He has courtside seats—he can afford them," Marcus said, rubbing his thumb and middle finger together.

"He's practically purple; if he doesn't stop, the paramedics will have to carry him out," I said. Marcus couldn't hear me; my father was pointing at Reggie Miller and Allan Houston, who were in a heated exchange. Marcus stood up, shouting, "That was a flagrant foul!" The basketball game had momentarily turned into a boxing match, but after the first punch was thrown, their teammates quickly separated them.

"Will they be kicked out of the game?"

"No, but they have to sit on the bench and cool off," Marcus replied.

"Are you having a good time?" I asked.

"Hell, yeah. These are perfect seats. I can't wait to tell Mel; he's bound to be jealous," Marcus said with a smooch, then refocused on the game. At halftime, Delores and I went to the refreshment stand.

"Does my father always take you to the games with him?" I asked.

"Sometimes me, sometimes William. It's different from watching at home, right?"

"Somewhat."

"I'm glad Marcus and your father get along," I told her, referring to the rapport between Marcus and my father. I wondered why it couldn't be that effortless for me and Mrs. Collin to get along.

"I think the game is starting again," Delores said. "I always leave before the cheerleaders come out."

As we resettled in our seats, the crowd chanted, "Defense, clap, clap, clap; defense, clap, clap, clap." I joined in, shouting, "Yeah, defense, defense!" The Knicks tried their best but lost in the fourth quarter. The Pistons won by three points. Despite his team's loss, Marcus was still in high spirits.

"Damn good game," my father said.

"If Houston had maintained his cool, he would have won the game for the team," Marcus said.

"That was part of the game plan," my father replied decisively.

At Delores's suggestion, we stopped at a diner before heading home. I was famished, and I was sure Marcus was too. Driving separate cars, we met them at a place called Steak' Urns.

"You both are coming to our Christmas dinner, right?" I asked as we placed our orders.

"Of course," my father answered.

It was getting cold outside, so we ordered to go and decided to head home, where the temperature was set at sixty-eight degrees. Before leaving, I thanked my father and hugged him, saying we had a great time. In my mind, Marcus needed to see that in-laws don't always have to be in conflict.

Three days before Christmas, everything was ready except the tree. I kept the decorations simple: white lights, a long red ribbon wrapped around the tree, and the wreath was up with holly and mistletoe placed in every doorway. The shopping for dinner was done, most of the cooking was completed the day before, and presents were wrapped and placed under a natural spruce pine tree. It was the first Christmas I had looked forward to since my mother's passing.

Marcus stocked the house with rum and brandy, and his mother had made apple wine and something similar to eggnog mixed with rum. It was as if our disagreement had never happened. Aunt Lynn decided to forget the doctor's orders and made ham with pineapple and maple syrup. Not to be outdone, Marcus's mother made chicken and dumpling soup. I prepared four game hens and a beef brisket with all the fixings, along with sweet potato pie, banana pudding, and chocolate cake. I also placed scented pine cones around the house and lit cinnamon-scented candles. On the day of the dinner, Aunt Lynn arrived early to help.

Guests started to arrive at seven o'clock, and the table was decorated in green and red. Nearly everyone was there, so I served dinner at eight-thirty. Dr. and Mrs. Collin arrived fashionably late. Father Collin was dressed casually in corduroys and a sweater, while Gloria was dressed up in a red satin blouse and red leather pants. She always dressed impeccably, I admitted grudgingly, though I didn't want to give her that credit.

"Humph," Aunt Lynn said, noticing Gloria's attire. The house was packed.

"You guys need a bigger place for the next party," Danielle volunteered, mentioning that her fiancé Andre was looking for a home in Long Island for them. She was actually doing the looking herself—Andre was a hospital mail clerk, and she earned the big bucks.

"Thomas and Grace bought this beautiful home in Maryland," I said, unable to resist the urge to cut her off. "She has a kitchen nook and everything, girl."

I then introduced Danielle to Stephanie, who, like Danielle, liked to talk about herself. I hoped their mutual self-focus would keep them occupied. Stephanie told Danielle about her wedding plans, clearly pleased to have someone to brag to, while Melbourne and Andre talked sports. Marcus's mother was kind and helpful, which made Grace wonder if she had judged her mother-in-law too harshly. I assured her it was nothing more than an act.

While the men gathered in the living room to watch football on Marcus's satellite dish, the women prepared for the gift exchange. Once everything was ready, we called the men in. Marcus, wearing a Santa hat, handed out the gifts. Marcus's father received a golf bag and balls, celebrating his retirement from medical school. Danielle got a gift certificate to a body shop. Thomas received a joke book—my idea. Marcus received some ties and gag gifts from Mel, which I didn't find amusing, especially with his upcoming wedding to Stephanie. The gift exchange wrapped up around eleven. Mrs. Collin thanked me for the party and her gift without even opening it.

"Leave the dishes; I'll do them," Marcus said.

"When?" I asked, skeptical.

"Tomorrow," he replied, kissing me. He scooped me up in his arms, and we headed to the bedroom.

He laid me down and began to undress me, his energy surprising me after all the cooking. As he kissed his way from my breasts to my navel and back, he moved slowly, savoring each touch. When he turned me over, he found that spot on my neck that always made me crumble. Eventually, he bypassed the preliminaries and was inside me in an instant. The crescendo was slow and drawn out. Fatigued, I whispered how much I loved him. Shaking me slightly, he asked if I had heard him.

"No. Too tired, Marcus. Tomorrow morning, first thing."

"Not that. But damn, am I that good?" he teased. Then, handing me another gift, he said, "Anyhow, Merry Christmas."

"What's this?" I asked, my curiosity piqued.

"A little something I saw and wanted to give to you," Marcus replied, handing me a green box wrapped in a red ribbon.

Rubbing my face, I sat up in bed and turned on the light by the nightstand. I was never good at refusing gifts. I carefully tore off the wrapping and looked at him, confused.

"More keys, Marcus? What are they for?"

"I bought us a house, Racquel."

I sat up and proceeded to jump up and down on the bed, damp spot and all. "The only thing is I have to sell the apartment."

"I don't care," I said, my excitement barely contained. "When can I see it?"

"We can drive over on Sunday. I have the painters finishing up."

"Dag, I guess you can keep a secret. I had no idea. I love you, Marcus Collin." I no longer felt tired, my mind buzzing with decorating possibilities. I could not wait to see our new home. It would need a lot of work, but I was up for the challenge.

Chapter 23

Marcus

"Passing from the right hand, through the legs, to the left, back to the right, and then—jump shot."

"The eleventh row? Stop lying. Her father actually sprung for something like that. I married the wrong woman."

"Swoosh! The three-pointer went in for the win. Sweet, you had to be there."

"I am jealous," Melbourne said.

"I knew you would be."

As I talked, five crumpled-up pieces of paper lined my desk. The trash bin was strategically placed away from the desk, near the office door. "We would have won the game if Alan Huston had kept his head. Miller elbowed him, they scrambled, and both were ejected from the game." I landed three papers in the trash, missing two. I picked up the last two and went for double or nothing.

"Yo, I gotta get back to work. Holler at you later. We're still on for the gym, right?"

"Yeah, see you later, man. You're one of the few excuses I have to get away from non stop yapping."

"Cool, man. Later." Pressing the intercom, I asked my personal assistant to come in. She had worked for me for two years and still watered down my coffee and handed in reports the day they were due, not the days before like I asked.

"Good morning, Mr. Collin. Enjoy the holidays?"

"Yeah, things were nice."

"My coffee needs to be brewed a bit longer, and is the financial report due next Monday ready? I need it to be perfect before the presentation, which is why I asked for it early—and why I hired an assistant."

"No, it isn't. I am finishing up and it will be on your desk this afternoon."

"If it wasn't for your son, Matthew, you'd be fired. Why do you always wait until the last day?"

"Mr. Collin, don't even joke about firing me or something like that."

"Anyway, how was your holiday? And seriously, can you brew my coffee a little longer, please?"

"My Christmas was fine. Matthew was spoiled rotten; he had so many gifts. He loved the football helmet you gave him—he refuses to take it off, even at bedtime. He made you a thank-you card." She handed me a white card with a blue crayoned smiley face drawn on the top. I had taken a liking to her son when she brought him to work one day. He was a nice kid who behaved well during his visit.

She had complained that she didn't have childcare and fed me her line about unreliable people in her life, afraid she would have to quit the only job she loved. So I gave in, letting her bring him in for two days. Luckily for her, she found someone. She was a young, single mother who needed to keep the job. The child already had one non-working parent; he didn't need two. One day, I envisioned having a child of my own, possibly in my third year of marriage. Racquel and I had wanted to wait.

My ringing phone made my assistant exit with the coffee cup in her hand. "I'll change this stuff," she said, closing the door. It was my father, and he wanted to meet me later. It was rare that we went out for drinks, so I knew he was going to say something I didn't like. As I drove to the nearest bar, I saw my father already there, sitting at a table, motioning me over.

"Cancer? How is that possible?" I asked my father.

"Well, Marcus, it's in remission now." I didn't know too many people who lived healthy lives with it—or lived at all past a year. Skipping the sugar coating I knew my father would try to put on the situation, I asked, "How long does she have?"

"Marcus, I'm not sure, but the important thing is that for right now, her cancer is in remission, and she's as healthy as she's going to be. And she doesn't want anyone to know."

"Why didn't someone tell me something? Why was I in the dark about this? Dad, I understand what you mean, but Racquel wouldn't celebrate the fact that Mom's ill. I know they find it hard to get along."

"But—" My father stopped me before I could explain how I had everything under control.

"I think Racquel is a lovely person, but you need to respect your mother's wishes. Don't, don't say anything until we know more," he said, his voice firm yet gentle. "I know how you feel, Marcus. I've spent over twenty years with her. She's my partner, my other half. I don't know what I would do if I lost her. But let's not dwell on the negative—Gloria's a strong woman. She'll beat this." He wiped his face. "I'm telling you so that you're aware of what's going on."

"Monica has been helpful to her, so once in a while, she comes to the house when I'm not there. I never saw her as much as I do now, even when you two were married. And I see what you mean about her. I wanted to talk to you, but you're a man, and sometimes a man has to make his own mistakes, learn from them, and then correct them."

My father shook my hand and hugged me as I left. What he didn't say in words, he expressed through paternal affection. I left the bar feeling stunned, leaving my father there to sit and reminisce over happier times with his Gloria.

Racquel

The bright all white frosty room looked so sterile. I sat with my knees knocking. I was nervous.

"Racquel Middleton, the doctor will see you now," the receptionist informed me from behind her desk.

"Thank you," I replied, feeling my nerves in a jumble. I followed the assistant to the back room of the doctor's office. I was instructed to undress, so I carefully took off my dress and hung it on the available hanger. The gown I put on was stiff and blue, and the office was chilled by central air, despite it being only forty-two degrees outside. I left my bra on but had to remove my panties. Sitting in the cold, white room, I stared up at the blinding sanatorium light, wondering if my EPT test was correct.

Dr. Careen Alma had been my gynecologist since I returned to New York. It was because of her that I insisted every guy I ever dated and planned to be intimate with get tested, especially with the AIDS virus being so prevalent in communities of color.

After the invasive check-up, she smiled as she pulled off her rubber gloves. "Racquel, you are going to have a baby! I'm so happy for you. You're officially eight weeks, nearly two months along."

It was confirmed—I am pregnant, I reflected.

Speechless, I dressed and walked to the front of the office. Smiling, I hugged and thanked the doctor. As I headed to my parked car, happy tears began to fall, and by the time I drove home, I was crying hysterical, joyful tears. Once home, I took a shower, still in a state of disbelief.

I'm going to tell Marcus tonight, I thought. *How should I tell him?* I was nervous and giddy as I prepared dinner. I made sure to have cold orange juice in the fridge—no more chardonnay or merlot for me, at least not for a while.

When I heard the click of the door, I knew Marcus was home. His face was stormy as he sat down in his La-Z-Boy, clearly troubled by some inner conflict. *Maybe my news will cheer him up,* I thought.

"How was work?" I asked, leaning down.

"Fine."

"Marcus, are you okay? Is there something you want to talk about?"

"No. I'm exhausted. I'm going to take a nap."

"I cooked dinner," I said, completely disappointed. A monkey wrench had been thrown into my plans.

"I'll eat later," he promised, and off to bed he went, leaving me to sit by myself. After it was established that I was pregnant, the symptoms hit me full force. I felt more sluggish and nauseated than before. My arms and legs refused to cooperate that morning. I called my assistant to let her know I was running late and asked Rita to pull up all the documents I needed to work on that day. I had taken the train instead of driving because my car was in the shop.

Once inside the subway, I wished I had brought nose plugs; it smelled of raw sewage, urine, unwashed bodies, and garbage. The disgusting odors mixed together, and I don't know how I made it to work. Between the stench and the heat, I closed my eyes, gripping my bag firmly, swaying like someone who had too much to drink. As for finding a seat on the train, forget it—every man, woman, and child was out for themselves.

A kindly old E.F. Hutton gentleman offered me a seat by the third stop. Sitting down and relaxing, I slightly dozed off, miraculously waking just before my Grand Central stop.

Then the rat race began. A multitude of people charged through the subway tunnels to their respective destinations. Herded to the stairwell, I stepped up from the subway and breathed in the morning city's fresh, albeit smoggy, air.

"Free at last, thank God Almighty, I'm free at last." Well, not entirely—the corporate world enslaved me on a completely different level. "Damn, I need my car back, fast."

I thought as I walked to the office building. Upon entering, I glanced at the clock above the receptionist's desk—I had finally arrived at a quarter to ten.

Once inside the office, I sat behind my desk and scooted the wastebasket closer, just in case I couldn't make it to the bathroom. My breakfast traveled up, then back down, and then up again. Checking around for stashed saltine crackers, I called Grace to share my joyous, nauseated feeling with her.

"Girl, why didn't you warn me?" I asked.

"Warn you about what?"

"You know, the sickness and being tired all the time."

"You're pregnant!" she guessed. "Congratulations!"

"Yes, I am," I told her. "I'll be two months along by the end of the week."

"Racquel, stop playing. When did you find out? What did Marcus say?"

"He doesn't know yet. I can never find the right time."

"Girl, you better make the time before you know it—you'll be showing," Grace said.

"I know, but his mother has been sick, and I thought I should wait a bit until she feels better. Once she's better, she'll be more receptive to the fact that she's going to be a grandma."

"Anyway, how is Taylor?"

"She's changing every day. Are you coming to her second birthday party? You missed the first one."

"I was on my honeymoon, remember? And her birthday is four months away."

"Excuses, excuses," Grace playfully teased.

"How is Thomas?" I asked. "Since you both got married, he's starting to behave more like you. He's not the same stuffy person we met that day. And you're a lot more calm since you married him."

"What can I say? Opposites attract."

"I wonder, did he ever catch that guy who stole our purses?"

"No, he hasn't. I should bug him about it tonight."

"I'm only kidding, so don't bother him. Now let me get to work for real. I'll call you after I've told him."

The painters had finished painting our new home, and like a kid in a candy store, I couldn't wait to see it. I didn't feel like throwing another party, so I wanted to wait until after the New Year to invite our friends over for dinner. I wanted everything to be perfect.

We had a master suite with an en-suite bathroom, two extra bedrooms, a bathroom in the hallway, one in the family room, and another in the den. The basement, which Marcus decided to turn into an "I Wish I Was Still a Bachelor Pad" for him and the guys, was to have a black and gold pool table, a mini bar with black marbleized Formica, and his large sixty-inch screen television.

Well, I thought, if we worked as hard as we did, there was nothing wrong with splurging a little. Usually, I handle everything myself, but this time I broke down and called someone who knew exactly what they were doing for the window treatments I had in mind.

The current living room set in the apartment was black leather. Marcus had already decided that it would go into what I called his "no women allowed" room. We donated all the furniture we weren't keeping to Goodwill. Marcus informed me that it was a good tax write-off.

I was so happy when the kitchen remodeling was finished, as it meant we could finally move in. It took about three weeks. Everything was changed except for the kitchen nook. After turning off the lights in the apartment and handing over the keys, I happily reflected on how we had bought the house before the baby arrived.

On our first night settling in, I inspected every detail to ensure it was just right. I had gone food shopping earlier that day and stocked our Whirlpool fridge. As I pulled out the ground beef, I wondered, "What should I cook?" Then it hit me: Mother, Father, we forgot to buy a stove!

Chapter 24

Marcus

I surprised Racquel with the house and let her decorate it to her heart's content. I told her she could decorate everything the way she wanted, except for the basement. For that room, I asked her to use only basic colors like white and black. Slate gray was an option I'd consider.

"But please, don't let my company walk into any lavender or pink bathrooms, okay?" I added. Knowing Melbourne, he would probably make a joke about it every time he saw it, so I decided it was best if she didn't touch it at all. "Just leave it white. A crack in the sink is no problem."

"I heard my mother has decided to retire from her position as the director of miscellaneous functions at the church," I told Racquel over dinner, which consisted of turkey sandwiches.

"Marcus, I don't think that's what it's called. You mean she's giving up her deaconship position."

"Whatever. Pass the mayonnaise. Are you coming?"

"Why is she retiring?" Racquel asked.

I wanted to tell her that the cancer was in remission and that's how we wanted to keep it, but I didn't.

"She hasn't been feeling well, and this role at Holy Trinity zaps most of her energy."

"That role at Holy Trinity helped our friends, Steven and Timothy, go to school, remember?"

"Oh, that reminds me. I ran into Tim last week. He's looking to join the big leagues. I still keep in touch with Steven too. Working in legal aid is keeping him broke. The only real reason he became a lawyer was to make money. Anyway, he asked about your cousin Grace. I told him she was married and had a daughter. How did that saga finally end, anyway?"

"She caught him with a girl from the same dorm in college."

"Same dorm? Say WORD?"

"Syllable," Racquel replied.

"Come on, Racquel, relive our youthful days with me. Say WORD."

"WORD."

Good, I had managed to get her to laugh. With a peck on the cheek and the words "I love you," I headed out the door before she could ask any more questions about my mother's health.

On the Sunday of my mother's retirement, Racquel and I arrived at the church early and sat in the front as we were directed. My mother wanted to retire quietly, hoping to keep her illness private. Reverend Steele had to persuade her to accept an award before she stepped down from her position.

The award ceremony was held after the regular service. My mother and father sat to my right, and Racquel sat to my left. Coming up the aisle to sit behind us was Monica, whom my mother had invited. What was she thinking? I glanced over to my left, hoping Racquel wouldn't make a scene. I was ready to explode, but Racquel remained as cool as a cucumber, and I was proud of her.

My ex-wife kissed my mother on the cheek. "How nice to see you, Gloria," Monica purred.

"I have a gift for you," she said, handing a gift-wrapped box to my mother.

"Monica, you shouldn't have," my mother responded.

"Marcus, darling, how are you?"

"I'm fine. My wife and I are fine. Thank you." I hardly attended church unless dragged there by my wife or mother, so it didn't make sense that Monica had become a regular, especially since she was Catholic.

I leaned over to my father. "Pop, Racquel has a headache, and I'm taking her home."

"I don't blame you, son," he said, patting my leg.

"Tell my mother I'll call her later." I stood up, taking Racquel by the elbow. "Babe, I have a headache. Let's go home."

"Marcus, Marcus? Where are you going? You're going to miss the ceremony," my mother called after me as I turned back.

We exited through the side and left via the back door. "Racquel, where do you want to go for dinner? My treat," I offered. A marriage can be challenging enough without any additional stress.

Instead of calling, I decided to visit my mother. Her reception was as warm as always, but I had a purpose for being there that night. We walked over to the kitchen table. As I looked around the spacious room, I noticed that even in her kitchen, pictures of me were on the walls. She wore her family like a symbolic badge of honor.

My mother offered me some leftover dinner, but I mentioned that Racquel and I were planning to go out.

"Doesn't that girl ever cook?" my mother said, sounding irritated.

"Look, Mom, that's why I'm here. We need to talk," I said, holding her hand as we sat across from each other at the kitchen table.

"Is there a problem with Racquel?" she asked, standing up to put a kettle on the stove.

"Not at all," I answered, sitting down with my empty cup in hand.

"Marcus, she's not the woman for you. I've known you all your life. I've taken care of you since you were a boy."

"Mom, I'm a grown man now and capable of making these decisions for myself," I said, shaking my head.

"Well, if you thought your marriage to Monica was a disaster, this one will be a catastrophe," she said, retrieving the kettle and pouring hot water over her tea bag. Her reaction toward Racquel seemed unlike her usual self.

Blowing on and then calmly sipping her hot peppermint tea, she asked, "Who is this woman you've given your name to? No, excuse me, our name."

"Mom, her name is Racquel. She's the same person from the church we attend."

"Marcus, this girl just dropped out of nowhere." She lifted her now-empty porcelain teacup and turned the handle, as if her statement was perfectly ordinary. I deliberated for a long moment before answering.

"No, Mom, you're wrong. She's not an opportunist seeking marriage for stability like you think. She's one of the kindest and most intelligent women I've ever known. I'm trying to build something with her."

"She's not good enough for you, Marcus."

"Mom, I'm not a kid anymore, and I can't just sit back and watch you sabotage this. I love you very much, but please don't destroy the only chance I have with Racquel. For the last time, I do not love Monica. In fact, I dislike her even more now than when we were married. Please stop meddling. Please."

My mother stood up and walked over to the sink, pretending to wash dishes. In that moment, I did what I had never been able to do as a child—I silenced her. I had the last word, but I felt defeated, knowing my words had fallen on deaf ears. There was a disconnect between how I delivered my message and how it was received.

Pushing back my chair, I went to my stubborn mother and kissed her on the cheek before leaving to return home to my wife.

That night, my mother was admitted to the hospital. I felt a pang of guilt for leaving her ceremony because I was angry with her. The need to teach her a lesson and show her that I wouldn't tolerate her disrespect toward my wife no longer mattered. I couldn't forgive myself if something happened to her, especially when we weren't speaking as we should. Overcome with guilt, I rushed to her side to be there for her.

Racquel

As I approached the Chemotherapy Unit, I hesitated for a moment. I had brought along a bouquet of silk flowers from the gift shop since real flowers were not permitted in her unit. I was determined to put aside the last insult she had given me.

"Hello, Mrs. Collin. How are you feeling today?" I asked, setting the yellow daisies on her table.

"What do you think?" she snapped. "Are you blind or something, child? Don't you see these things coming out of my arm?" There was no common ground. Not only were we oceans apart, but it felt like we were worlds apart.

Although it wasn't the right time, it was past time to be firm. I needed to stand my ground.

"Mrs. Collin, if you didn't need my help, why am I here? I certainly didn't come to engage in a verbal debate with you in your condition," I said, my patience wearing thin. "That wouldn't be good for your health." 'Our health,' I thought. She was even more cantankerous now that she was ill. Mrs. Collin was prejudiced against me, and no amount of cajoling, silence, diplomacy, or rudeness seemed to change that. From her perspective, the outcome would only vilify me in my husband's eyes.

"I'm tired. Close the door on your way out," she said.

I reached my last option and had to be direct. "I don't understand why Marcus keeps trying to bring us together."

"Let me tell you about the man you married," she said, pounding her now frail l chest for emphasis, "my son." "We have a bond that overrides any flimsy piece of paper. It's cultural, spiritual, and runs through our blood. It's called family. No woman can come between that—not now, not ever."

"Don't try to analyze our bond. Our marriage doesn't need validation from you to exist. We love each other."

"What are you talking about, girl? My son needs a strong woman with a strong background, not some rootless thing like you! I am his mother; I know him and what he needs."

Tears stung the back of my eyes, but sheer will kept them from falling. Her venom felt unfair and misplaced. "Mrs. Collin," I interjected, "I'm sorry. It was never my intention to upset you."

"True, you are his wife now, but remember this: a man can have a thousand or ten thousand wives, but he only gets one mother. Remember that," she said.

"Now you're being dramatic," I said, as my patience fizzled out for the second time. "My problem isn't with my husband's mother, but with the way you, his mother, disrespect me and our marriage. Since we met, you've never had one kind word to say to me—not once." Picking up my suede gloves from the chair, I told her that I would never interfere with their relationship. I am secure in my marriage and have no desire to cause problems between them.

"I am not here to be your enemy, only your son's wife," I reminded her.

"Then why did my son leave in the middle of my ceremony?" she asked, arms folded.

"That's between you and your son. It has nothing to do with me."

"What do you know about giving birth to and raising a son?" she asked, her eyes narrowed. "To care for a child for nine months, inside of you, to raise him his whole life, and then suddenly be put aside and forgotten. Since you came into my son's life, everything is about you. You've stolen his love away."

I then saw clearly what was in front of my face.

"Marcus loves you. This is self-pity talking," I said. "His love and respect for you are part of the reason why I love him. Instead of being proud of doing your job as a parent, you've clung on, making him choose. But, Mrs. Collin, he is no longer a boy. Isn't it written in the same Bible you carry to church every Sunday that a man leaves his family and cleaves to his wife?" I pointed to my chest. "Me."

"How dare you," Mrs. Collin said, her voice rising. "How dare you talk to me like you understand. You understand nothing. Get out! I wish Marcus had never married you. Here I am, sick on my deathbed, and you're harassing me."

At her venomous attack, I simply shook my head from side to side.

She was angry—angry that she was in that hospital bed and I had come at the perfect time to be her outlet for misery.

"Mrs. Collin," I began slowly, "I love Marcus, and we love each other."

"I wanted to be his wife, and that's it. I did not sign on to be your whipping girl."

"This conversation isn't going as I planned," I continued, my tears finally flowing. "We could have had a better relationship. I wanted to be the caring, helpful daughter-in-law."

'This conversation is over. I am tired Racquel please leave. It is only by chance that you are my daughter-in-law"

"Something," I said, not caring that tears were streaming down my face, "that you would not accept." I came only to help, and no, you never needed to ask. At that, she fell silent. For once, her tongue was still. Having said all I could, I left her hospital room.

Walking down the corridor, my son's movements swirled in my stomach. I wanted so much to share my joy with her. His movements were so fierce; he seemed to demand that I tell his grandmother of his existence.

My pride, however, would not allow it. I placed my head on the steering wheel, my hands resting on my abdomen, nausea dry heaves. I took deep slow breaths. By the time I started the car and the key turned in the ignition, I had recovered. My baby had stopped rolling, and I drove home. Once there, I soaked in the bathtub filled with bubbles to clear my mind, then crawled into bed. Emotionally weary, I fell asleep.

When I woke up, it was dark. I felt nauseated. Why was it called morning sickness if it only struck at night? Giving my stomach a moment to settle, I opened the fridge. Lazy from oversleeping and not wanting to cook, I was relieved it was Marcus's turn to handle dinner. I microwaved leftovers and turned the ringer back on.

Eating in bed had recently become a habit; we had a bathroom in our master bedroom, so in case of sickness, I didn't have to run far. I replayed the day in my mind, wondering what I could have said differently. The last thing I wanted was to anger an ill woman, even if she was a thorn in my side—my mother-in-law.

I got up to check my answering machine. Marcus had called twice, Rita, my assistant, had called, and Taylor had left a message. Tonight, I told myself, I would tell him. I hoped he would be as happy as I was. Three months along, and I had barely shown. My face didn't even have the telltale signs yet.

Doctor Alma had confirmed my suspicions a few weeks ago. I was ecstatic and cried as I left her office—actually, I cried a lot after that. The only drawback was that my emotions were wreaking havoc on me. Marcus was getting on my nerves all the time. Things I normally overlooked now upset me, and we argued over nonsense.

I tidied up the house and waited for him to come home. I waited and waited, but by 3 a.m., I took it for granted that he was still at his mother's. I watched television and then went back to bed. In the morning, I woke up to an empty, cold left side of the bed. And brushed my teeth, showered, combed my hair, and dressed for work. Before heading out the door, I called Mrs. Collin's home.

"Hello? Hello?" It was Monica, why did *she* have to be there.

"Hi," I answered, my voice shaky.

"Is Marcus there?"

"Hold on. He's in the shower. Would you like to call back?"

"I'll see him later. Just tell him his *wife* called. Thank you."

I managed to carry that off, but then I fell apart before work. By the time I arrived at the office, my face was drained of color, my lips salty from tears, and my feet felt like lead as I walked around.

"So when are you due?" Cathy asked.

"In May. How did you know?"

"Come on, I'm thirty-eight and have two of my own."

"I'm three months along and haven't told Marcus yet. There never seems to be the right time to tell him."

"Mrs. Collin, call on line one."

"Excuse me," I said to Cathy, and thanked Rita as I picked up the phone by her desk.

"Hello, Mrs. Middleton-Collin here. How may I help you?"

"Hey, baby. Sorry about last night. My mother was discharged at six."

"Hold on, Marcus. Let me transfer this call." I put him on hold to give myself a moment to gather my thoughts.

"Hi Marcus, I called you this morning. Didn't Monica tell you?"

"What? Monica wasn't there this morning."

"I must be mistaken," I said, feeling frustrated, and slammed the phone down on the receiver. He called back immediately.

"Racquel, what the hell is your problem? My mother is ill, possibly dying, and you're going insane. That was the nurse, goddamn it. You see why I didn't include you—I don't need the aggravation." I was stunned into silence. 'I was mistaken.'

"Marcus, baby, I apologize. I have something important to discuss with you. Can you pick me up from work?"

"I can't; I'm working late."

"I know you're stressed, but when the woman answered and said you were in the shower, I got the wrong idea."

"She doesn't sound like Monica. How could you get the wrong idea? It's not a good time for you to start tripping."

"Marcus, I have something really important to tell you. Please pick me up from work?"

"Okay, alright. I'll pick you up at seven."

"Seven?"

"You know, I haven't been to work in two days. I have to catch up."

"Alright, make it eight. You can park in the garage; I'll tell Orphe to put the car in lot seventeen." I thought Cathy wouldn't mind.

After an argument, it is not the best time to tell your husband you're expecting. Next week I'd be four months along; the next chance might have been on the birthing table.

Marcus arrived at seven forty-five. Most of my co-workers had left for the day. I had ordered Chinese take-out, which was now sitting on my desk. The card I bought earlier was slightly damp from my nervous hands. The cigar I purchased the day before was tucked away in my desk. When Marcus walked into my office, he looked tired as he sat down in the chair across from me.

"What's so important you couldn't tell me over the phone?" he asked, a bit on edge. Okay, he's somewhat grumpy, I thought.

"Sweetheart," I began, trying to be gentle. "Are you hungry?"

"Nope," he replied, clearly determined to be difficult.

"I have something for you," I said, pushing forward.

"What?" he asked. I poured red wine for us, and he wondered if this was some sort of celebration. "Sort of," I answered.

I took out the cigar, which the Arabic tobacco store manager swore was Cuban, and handed it to him. He looked at me, then back at the cigar.

"Honey, you shouldn't have," he said, though his reaction remained neutral. I slid the envelope across the desk to him. He opened it, still puzzled, and finally got the message. Inside it read: "Congratulations, you're a dad."

He looked at me closely, then said, "Nah," though he was smiling. He reached across for me, knocking over both glasses. "How? When? Where?" he asked, eager for details.

"I am so happy, Racquel," he said, his excitement evident.

"Marcus," I exclaimed, swatting him playfully. "How many months?"

"Three months and a week," I answered.

"I can't wait." He picked up the phone and started to dial.

"Who are you calling?"

"My parents."

With one finger, I disconnected the call. "Let's wait. After all, your mom's not well. Let's keep this between us for now." I wanted to enjoy this moment with Marcus without it being overshadowed by her bitterness. Our celebration continued on the dining room floor later that evening.

I sat atop him, and in a flurry of clothes, we reached our peak and spent our excitement together. As if reminded of the reason for our celebration, Marcus stood and gently pulled me towards our room. There, we resumed our celebration on the softness of our bed.

Chapter 25

Marcus

My father's sister, Mildred, had been my mother's best friend back home, and though she preferred not to share, I reached out to her. After leaving numerous messages, she finally called me back. I hoped she might contact my mother's family. Aunt Mildred was distressed by the news and informed me that there was no one else to reach out to. Given that she and my mother were the same age and had known each other even before my mother met my father, she would have known if I had missed anyone. During times like these, families should come closer.

Aunt Mildred assured me that my mother wouldn't have wanted anyone contacted. Cancer was a horrible commonality between Racquel and me, as her mother had also succumbed to it. At one point, I refused to accept it. Anyone but my strong, resilient mother. She had hardly been sick a day in her life. The signs were unmistakable: she continued attending church regularly, held a full social calendar, and only had to make periodic trips for chemotherapy when it wasn't in remission. It wasn't until months later that it became apparent she was walking her last mile.

She called me to her bedside at home. My father had arranged for her to be cared for there instead of in the hospital. Her room, made warmer by a small heater positioned by her bed, was a comfort in her final days. Peeking in to see if she was awake, she beckoned me closer with her frail hands. Since her diagnosis, she has aged ten years. Her once long hair was now dull and sparse, a casualty of the chemotherapy. Her lips barely moved and closed the door. She strained to talk. I sat by her, wanting to sooth her, but afraid to touch and harm her.

"Son, she started, let me tell you a story."

"No ma. Tell me later, save your strength."

"No, I have to tell you now," she wheezed. Then she started to tell me something I'd never forget. To this day it stays with me.

"One day," she started, "this couple decided to have a child but it was no easy task. When the woman finally conceived, a female child was born. They were disappointed. A son would have been more useful for farming. But a female child had her uses. Growing up this girl had certain duties to perform.

She cooked and cleaned and was very proper. Because she was taught to be. The couple did not allow any misbehavior where she was concerned. She was beaten.In the old days children were beaten within an inch of their lives if caught out of line. Talking out of turn was a guaranteed lashing. Looking angry about it was another whipping. The girl as a result became contrite and obedient."

I tried to understand where all of this was going. At the present time, I felt that she had some school girl confession to get off her chest. I interrupted her. I did not want my mother to suffer mentally like she suffered physically these past few months. But she hushed me by putting her fingers to her cracked lips. Her exacerbated breathing continued as she continued.

"One day this proper child met a young man. He was nineteen and the girl was sixteen. She fell in love with him. At first of course, everything was innocent, holding hands and sneaking kisses. But by then the relationship changed. When it changed, the girl found out that she was breeding."

"Breeding mom?"

"You know, breeding, getting pregnant, having children." My mother was annoyed at my ignorance at her use of the word breeding. Now fully aware, where the story was leading. My face was grim and I was silent.

"Once slim as a reed, the girl's body was changing and she did not notice. She was always tired and therefore beaten for laziness. Her housework was always unfinished, causing another beating. But what alerted the mother of her condition was the unexplained illness and steady growing roundness of her stomach."

"Mom," I interrupted for a second time, "You don't have to continue."

Through the sheen of tears in her eyes, she said she must, and so, went on.

"The boy was sent elsewhere to live with relatives instead of being forced to marry. Marcus, if this grandchild is a boy, please name him Brandon. It's something I'd like you to consider. Alright?"

She spoke with the urgency of someone making a final wish. I didn't refuse and promised her I would. I wasn't sure how I was going to ask Racquel, but I promised to try. Once I explained, I was sure she'd agree. How did my mother know Racquel was expecting, I wondered? The connection between us was something I'd always cherished.

" Wait, how did you know?"

"Her face is changing. I'm an old woman; I know these things," she said softly.

Chapter 26

Racquel

By the fifth month, I was starting to enjoy my pregnancy. My son's swirling ceased to feel weird and became more wondrous than anything. My annoying morning sickness had subsided somewhat, and I cherished the quiet moments of relaxation. Evenings when Marcus went to the gym or visited his mother were spent in fragrant baths.

What I enjoyed most were the oil massages Marcus gave me when we were together at home. I had never felt more sensual than when he rubbed warm oil over my expectant body. I had always heard that a woman was never more beautiful than when she was creating life, but experiencing it was far more magical than I had imagined.

Though my figure changed little, my breasts had become fuller and heavier. Marcus remarked on how he had helped them grow, playfully cupping each one in his hands and kissing them softly. "Don't get too comfortable," I teased him, indicating to my generous chest, "they deflate." He responded with a grin, "I have magic powers. Abracadabra, stay!" He playfully held them with his "magic hands" and said, "Trust me, next year they will be here."

"You are so silly," I told him, hugging him tightly to convey the love I felt.

Marcus chose a Sunday to tell Mrs. Collin about the baby, hoping she would be more receptive. Looking back, I hadn't spoken to her since I called her that following day to apologize for my behavior.

Not that she didn't deserve a telling off, but the timing was wrong. We should have had that conversation long ago.

When I told her about my pregnancy, she wasn't surprised at all. "You both certainly didn't waste any time," she said. Then, in complete contradiction, she mentioned she had wondered what took me so long, which made me dismiss her initial comment. She claimed she had guessed from the weary hangdog expression I wore. Marcus later informed me that she wanted to name our child, which I was determined to avoid. Not even on her deathbed would she have a say. I had names picked out already: Susan for a girl, in honor of my mother, and Robert or Trevor for a boy.

On Monday, I was supposed to meet my father for dinner, but he canceled. He had promised his son, William, to attend his basketball tournament. He rescheduled for later in the week.

"Mrs. Middleton-Collin, Jackie Hallowell is on line three."

"Thanks, Rita." I retrieved the phone. "Hey, Jackie, how are Brianna and Parker?"

"Fine. I heard you're expecting."

"Yes, girl, I'm five months along and counting. What's new?"

"Danielle had her baby last night."

"About time!"

"She called me this morning. She had a girl, and named her Cherelle Allison Hodges."

"Nice, not too complicated."

"You know, she refused to let her mother see the baby."

"Well, she had her reasons."

Seeing a chance to gossip, Jackie added, "Remember when her mother sold her Christmas presents to buy drugs? If it wasn't for her grandmother telling Reverend Steele, Danielle wouldn't have had a Christmas that year. The presents were replaced with church-donated gifts. And remember when her mother came to church high as a kite?"

She was fully dressed in an orange robe, with a roller stuck in the back of her head, and wearing pink flip-flops. Oh, it was such a shame.

"How could I forget? Danielle locked herself in the church bathroom and wouldn't come out," I said, trying to stay optimistic. "Maybe her mother has changed."

"Not likely, Racquel. A leopard can't change its spots," Jackie replied, remaining   pessimistic. "She's probably a hot mess right now."

"Anyway, did she tell you how Andre handled the whole delivery room thing?" I asked.

"He fainted. While she was pushing, he was carried out on a stretcher."

"What was all that talk he gave at Christmas dinner, saying he'd be ready?" I asked. "Anyway, my father canceled dinner. William, his son, is having a basketball tournament. Why don't we meet at my job after work and head over to the hospital?"

"Okay," Jackie agreed.

"My car is in the shop; they're changing the motor oil. I hope you're driving."

"I'll pick you up. I leave work at five."

"Okay, I'll be downstairs. Talk to you later."

"Later, girl," she said before hanging up.

How on earth did she know I was expecting? News traveled fast at Holy Trinity. If you want to keep something a secret, don't let

Jackie Hallowell find out. Punching out the last details of the company's new client in the computer, I closed it out and packed my things to leave. Jackie was waiting impatiently downstairs.

"Come on, Prego. I'm lucky I didn't get a ticket waiting for you. What hospital is she at again?"

"Harlem Hospital."

"What's she doing up there?"

"Andre works there, remember?"

"What is this, the season for babies? First Grace, then Danielle, now you."

One thing about Jackie: when she was in the mood, she could talk your ear off. At the moment, she was going on about a new sister who joined the church, Sister Blanche Armstrong. The bashing of Sister Blanche went on nonstop.

"She's always in my husband's face. If she needs advice, she should seek it from the other sisters. My husband can't help her," Jackie said, her eyes squinting and neck jerking.

"Girl, you're right," I said, enduring her tirade as she pulled into the parking lot. She parked and stopped at the information desk on the way to her room. I went into the gift shop to buy "It's a Girl" balloons. I noticed Andre on the wall, holding an intense conversation with a woman. Jackie spotted him too.

"Hey what's up Andre, I was just on my way up visiting your new baby girl

and fiancée Danielle." I can always count on Jackie to make an uncomfortable

situation more so.

"Tell her I'll be up in a minute," Andre answered. As soon as the elevator

doors closed, we both looked at each other shaking our heads. Jackie was the first to comment. "That trifling nigga', he is nothing but a big time flirt."

"Racquel, please. We both know he's a bum. Anytime a man holds his baby and is caught up against the wall with another woman, he's a bum. My husband knows better. He would never do such a thing. And lord knows I'm crazy, so he's blessed me with a man who better not even try it."

We stopped at the nurse's station, then headed midway down the hall to Danielle's private room. She was lying down as we entered.

"How are you doing, Danielle? Were you sleeping? If you're tired, we can come back."

"No, it's these painkillers. They're making me drowsy."

"What's up, Danielle?" Jackie asked, then inquired, "Where is Andre?" Jackie knew exactly where he was.

"He's out having a cigarette. He promised not to smoke around me or the baby."

"That's very considerate of him," Jackie replied, raising her eyebrows with a hint of sarcasm.

Danielle, used to Jackie's prying, turned to me. "I heard you were expecting, Racquel. How far along are you?"

"Five months."

"How was the labor?" I asked.

"I can't begin to describe it," she admitted. "Do you have a high pain threshold? Let me not scare you with the details. Everyone's labor is different, depending on the person."

"Come on, y'all, let's see little Cherelle," Jackie said, standing up. Danielle, dressed in pink satin pajamas with a fluffy robe and slippers, slowly waddled down the hall. "There she is," Danielle said proudly, pointing to a name card in the first row, third aisle, written in pink marker.

"She's adorable," I said.

"Cherelle weighed seven pounds and eleven ounces, and she was twenty inches long. I think she'll be tall," Danielle said.

"Are you guys still planning on getting married?" Jackie asked, her curiosity evident.

"We might," Danielle said with a noncommittal shrug. "It doesn't matter anymore."

"Have you changed your mind, Danielle?" I asked as we walked back to the room.

"I'm educated, I make good money. I could raise this child on my own if I wanted to. Andre and I plan on it, but I'll be fine if we don't."

I thought to myself that this was the most rational and unabsorbed thing she had ever said. It was uplifting to hear her speak so confidently. It also meant she was aware of Andre's ongoing issues.

"I hate to break up the party, but I have to go home and cook before my husband and kids get back," Jackie said.

We all knew she had a husband, but Jackie's frequent mention of it was getting on my nerves. If Grace had been around, she might have joked that Jackie seemed so amazed she even had a husband that she felt the need to say it every chance she got.

Not wanting to endure another ride with Jackie, I gave her a hug and said I'd see her next Sunday. I then called Marcus and asked him to pick me up. He was doing overtime at the office.

I stayed for another two hours without mentioning her mother or Andre. I was sure that those were topics she preferred to keep private.

Even though I have forgiven my father, it took a deep inner strength to do so. I couldn't ask her to do the same, as her situation was different. Marcus picked me up from the hospital.

"Who does the baby look like, her or Andre?" he asked as I waddled to the car. I had told him how beautiful Danielle's baby was and how she somewhat resembled her mother, though it was hard to tell.

"Babies aren't beautiful right away," he said.

"Yes, they are," I argued.

I then told him that Andre and Danielle had changed their minds about getting married immediately.

"What you mean to say is that he changed his mind," Marcus said. I didn't want to admit it, but he was right. "Having that baby brought Danielle back to reality. I really believe that, with or without him, she'd be fine." Changing the topic to food, I said, "Honey, my daughter and I are hungry. Feed us."

"Suzann said she wants her daddy to cook for us."

"Daughter? Who said we're having a girl?"

"I did."

"Racquel, please don't give our child any girl names unless you're sure it's a girl. I don't want any confused boys running around playing with dolls and asking to go to dance class. Nah, none of that."

"Marcus, it might be a girl," I said, hoping so that I could name her after my mother, Susan Ann.

"I really don't think it's a girl. I was programmed to have soldiers and that's it," he said with a wink.

"You are so archaic," I told him with a smile.

"This is true," he agreed.

Chapter 27

Marcus

It was amazing to watch my wife's body change and grow with our miracle inside her. It was equally depressing to see my mother's body wither and struggle to renew itself. I wished for the impossible dream of seeing my wife and mother grow closer. However, my mother's embittered behavior about her health and everything else made that unlikely. In contrast, Racquel glowed with life and her happy, chipper emotions about being pregnant clearly annoyed my mother. My mother told Racquel that she wasn't doing anything special, that millions of women had been pregnant before her.

Arguments ensued, leaving me caught in the middle. I didn't want to invade my mother's privacy, but I knew that the constant bickering was affecting both her health and Racquel's. The family dog, Blaze, chased a furry stuffed animal around the kitchen. Racquel quickly recognized it as a sweater, suspiciously similar to one she had given my mother for Christmas, which I had helped her pick out. My mother insinuated that Racquel had schemed to marry me, her trapped son. Racquel, who had reached her limit, did what she had done frequently during her pregnancy—she cried. I yelled at both of them.

"For once, be a man and support your wife," she said, adding that she would never step foot in my mother's house again unless she showed Racquel some respect.And I was speechless. There was nothing I wouldn't do for either of them, but I couldn't protect them from each other. Racquel hopped into her car and drove off, while my mother's lips quivered with anger, even though she had started the whole mess. I avoided going home to prevent another argument. Instead, I spent time with Melbourne and had a few drinks. I was dealing with enough and had no intention of mediating their squabbles. If two mature women couldn't sort out their own issues, there was little I could say to help. My role was just to keep them apart.

When I returned to the home I paid for, I was greeted with icy silence. Whenever Racquel moved around, she slammed doors and cabinets. I called out, "Racquel, come here, let's talk." It was time to tell her. "Please, come and sit down," I said, patting my lap.

"There's something I should have told you months ago. My mother is dying from cancer." I held up my hand to forestall her questions. I needed to say it myself, to hear it in my own voice.

"Her cancer was in remission, as you know, but it came back and spread throughout her body. I know you and my mother don't see eye to eye, but with her progressing disease, she will only lash out more. A lot of what she says isn't meant personally. She's angry because she's dying and because she's missing out on time with a grandchild she's waited a lifetime for. I'm asking you to put up with her for my sake."

"I am so sorry, Marcus. I had no idea what you were going through," Racquel said, her tone softening.

I thought my mother had been looking sideways at her long before she got cancer.

"Honey, I'll try," Racquel acquiesced.

Chapter 28

Racquel

"It's a boy!" Dr. Alma exclaimed as she looked at the sonogram. "One month away, and you couldn't wait, huh?"

"Nope, we decided to find out and tell his mother. I still plan to surprise him on the day of the baby shower."

"A baby shower you're not supposed to know about?"

"My cousin Grace let it slip. I'm too sneaky for her, but she begged me to act surprised."

"You're coming, right?"

"Yes, I am. Marcus told me about it last night, and I happen to be off that day. I must be the only obstetrician/gynecologist who's attended a patient's baby shower."

"Come, it will be fun." I secretly hoped Marcus's mother would behave herself. I also wondered if Marcus might be open to helping her seek counseling for her recurring illness. It could be beneficial, but I worried he might not be receptive to the idea and could even be annoyed that I suggested it.

On the way home, I stopped at the fruit stand. Lately, I've been eating for three, not just for a woman expecting a child. Passing the store, I was tempted by vanilla wafers calling my name and potato chips begging, "Please buy me, buy me." Healthy roughage or artery-clogging snacks—I contemplated. In the end, the apples won, and I put the bags of cookies and chips back on the shelf.

It felt good coming home to a house instead of an apartment. Everything was organized and had a permanent place. Homeownership meant stability and a sense of permanence that I hadn't felt before. The organized spaces and settled environment provided a comforting structure, reflecting the security and comfort I had always longed for. Being settled here gave me a deep sense of belonging and control, making each day feel more grounded and fulfilling.

Instead of champagne I celebrated that thought with a glass of carrot juice Marcus had made that morning. The pulp floating in the liquid was unappealing—why couldn't he make apple juice or something? I told him I'd drink it to avoid hurting his feelings, especially since he had eaten the cheesy grits I'd prepared for breakfast one morning, despite his adorably grimace of distaste. I left the room, came back with a camera, and snapped a picture of his funny face. His mother had suggested herbal teas from "back home," but I had to put my foot down against those bitter brews. After Marcus went to the gym, I spent a lot of time working around the house as I neared my due date. During one of my breaks, I called Grace to speak to Taylor. "What's up, Grace? Is my little cousin awake?"

"Hold on, I have to drag her away from the purple dinosaur."

"Hi, hello," said fifteen-month-old Taylor, the only word she could say.

"Hi, Taylor. Now put Mommy on."

"Racquel, what's up? I forgot to tell you a guarded secret about exercising after the baby. It's a sitting-down exercise. You can do it anywhere you sit. First, clench your pelvic muscles."

"Between your pelvic muscle exercises and Aunt Lynn's lemon water, I'll be tighter than the cap on a medicine bottle."

"Racquel, I'm telling you, it works."

"Anyhow," I said, dismissing the old wives' tales, "It's a boy, so decorate the place in blue."

"Hold on," I told her, "Marcus just got home. I have to go." I turned off the cordless. Marcus entered with bags in his hands.

"How was your day?"

"Fine."

He wrapped his arms around my waist. "How are jelly bean number one and jelly bean number two?" He bent down and lovingly caressed my protruding tummy. I cherished these moments of tenderness, especially while his mother's illness weighed heavily on his mind.

"My mother has been feeling weaker lately, so she sent her gifts ahead."

"Where are they?" I asked, excited to receive my son's first gifts from one of his grandparents. I unwrapped a beautiful light blue and white hand-knitted blanket, along with a bundle of receiving blankets and a hundred-dollar gift certificate from F.A.O. Schwarz.

"My mother has more stuff for the baby when he's born."

"Can you call her and thank her for me?"

"You can call her yourself. I had a long talk with my mother. We came to an understanding, and things are going to be different." I wished he would tell me more so I could understand better, I thought.I called his mother to thank her, and she told me I didn't need to thank her for doing something for her grandchild. Letting down her guard, she mentioned that making the baby's blanket hadn't taken long and that maybe, one day, she'd show me how. Her softening mood encouraged me to drop my own guard and express that I'd love to learn. Inspired by her unexpected kindness, and out of Marcus's earshot, I told her that the baby was a boy. She was silent for a moment before claiming she had to go fix her television. Just when I thought it was safe to be nice, her response reminded me of her usual demeanor.

The baby shower was held the following week. As requested, Grace had decorated everything in blue. Marcus acted as if he was taking me to dinner, then walked into Aunt Lynn's house claiming he needed to pick up a camera. Marcus was genuinely surprised, just as I pretended to be.

"Why are the decorations blue?" he asked, grinning from ear to ear. "Are we having a boy?"

"Yup," I said, smiling up at him.

Thomas even came, knowing men are usually outnumbered at baby showers and feeling sorry for Marcus. Danielle was there with Cherelle, though Andre wasn't. Delores, my father's wife, attended with her daughter Dana. She hugged me and said she was glad to meet her older sister. I felt honored and commented that it was nice to meet a sister and have a stepmom. Delores hugged me back and congratulated us. It felt wonderful to be surrounded by so much love. Before I had a chance to get emotional, Taylor walked over and handed me a gift for the baby—a cute teddy bear with glass eyes named Gruff.

"How cute, thank you, Taylor."

"Where is Mrs. Collin?" Jackie asked, eager to start gossip.

"She's not feeling well. She gave me the gifts for the baby last week."

"That's nice of her," Jackie said, clearly disappointed by the lack of juicy scandal.

"You have everything you need, except the baby," Marcus said as he and Thomas carried everything to the car.

After having baby showers at both home and work, all I had to do was wait until my son was ready to come out. The decision to name him Brandon came after much pleading from my husband.

The decision to name my son Brandon came after Marcus begged and pestered me day and night. Every morning, he would place his hand on my stomach and say, "Good morning, Brandon," or kiss my belly and say, "I love you, Brandon." Seeing how strongly he felt about it, I decided to give in. Eventually, I joined in and began referring to the baby as Brandon as well.

Chapter 29

Marcus

I was at work when I received the call. Racquel hadn't made it to work; her contractions had begun at eight that morning. After experiencing so many false labor pains, I advised her to stay home and take it easy. By eleven, she called, asking me to come home.

I took the rest of the day off and rushed through downtown traffic from midtown towards the bridge. Though I didn't pray often, I found myself praying to make it home in time. As I arrived, I saw Racquel getting into a waiting taxi, overnight bag in hand. I quickly helped her out of the taxi, paid the driver, and let him drive off. Panting and breathing heavily, she moved slowly toward my car.

"Don't worry, I'm here. Everything is under control," I said, trying to soothe her.

"Are you in a lot of pain?" I asked.

"Hold my hand," she said. I regretted not prioritizing Lamaze classes over overtime, though she had studied the tapes.

"Everything is fine," I said, speaking slowly.

"I am in pain, Marcus, not illiterate," Racquel whispered.

I parked next to the ambulance and rushed into the hospital, my heart racing. "What's the rush?" an intake nurse asked.

"My wife is in labor," I replied.

"She's in the car; she can't stand."

"Sir, uhhh you can't park there," another nurse said.

"I'll move it once she's admitted and upstairs."

"Yeah, but what if another ambulance comes?" one of the nurses asked, clearly dedicated to her job.

"Then tow it," I snapped, my patience running thin. "Now call a doctor or something, because I'm ready to deliver this baby myself."

Noticing my anxiety, the same nurse informed me that it was only the beginning stages.

"She still has a way to go," she added. "Her contractions are ten minutes apart, if that."

"There's more?" I thought, mentally kicking myself for not watching the *Miracle of Birth* tapes with her.

After I registered Racquel at the hospital and wheeled her to a room, I started to pace. I called my father, who reiterated what the nurse told me—we had a long wait. Once Racquel was changed into a gown and hooked up to the fetal monitor, we listened to Brandon's heartbeat.

"He's a feisty one," I said, trying to distract her from the pain. I stroked her hair and thanked her for agreeing to name the baby Brandon.

"My father and Delores want you to call them right after he's born," she said.

"I will. How about your aunt? Do you want her here?"

"Later," she replied, bracing herself for another contraction. Her friend, Doctor Alma, entered the room.

"Hello, Marcus. Hi, Racquel," she said, noticing my wife writhing in agony. "I'm going to give you a sedative, okay? We talked about this before, remember? You said no epidural. Try to relax, okay, hon?"

"Okay," Racquel said, rolling her eyes back and biting her lips. A sedated Racquel was able to relax. I called my father again to voice my concern.

"Dad, is this normal?"

"This is the normal process, son. It will all be over soon."

The scream down the hall sounded like Racquel's. I quickly hung up and rushed back to her side.

"Dr. Alma, is it normal for her to be in this much pain?" I asked, scared on Racquel's behalf.

"Marcus, listen to the sounds around you," she said. And she was right—every woman in the place was screaming their heads off.

"The baby is coming," Racquel announced. I returned to her side, and with two hard pushes, my son, red-faced and swollen, entered the world.

He was the most beautiful child I had ever seen. Racquel held him to her chest, repeating over and over again that he was worth it. The doctor and nurses cleaned her up and swaddled our son in a blanket. I took Brandon in my arms as Racquel, exhausted from giving birth, drifted off to sleep. He slept in my arms while my wife, weary from the ordeal, rested beside us.

"Thank you, Doctor." I then turned to Racquel, who was sleeping peacefully. "Thank you," I whispered, humbled by my wife's strength.

After the nurse took the baby to the nursery, I called everyone we knew. Her Aunt Lynn was upset that I hadn't called her earlier, while my mother was thrilled to hear that Racquel had named our son Brandon and asked me to thank her. Grace and Thomas said they were on their way to New York to meet the new addition to the family.

With Racquel still sleeping, I went to the gift shop to buy some flowers and balloons. I couldn't get over the incredible creation. Life, created by us, now rested in the nurse's arms. "Wow," was all I could keep saying. Melbourne and his wife Stephanie came by later that night.

"How was it, man?" Melbourne asked.

"I can't explain it, man. Amazing, I don't know."

"Stephanie's talking about having children."

"Really? Man, it's a beautiful thing if you want kids." I wished I had more words to describe it, but even with a college degree, I couldn't fully express what I had seen and felt. It was a miracle.

We had named our son *Brandon Trevor Robert Collin*. It was a big name to live up to, but I felt confident that he would.

I wanted to spend our first day home with the baby quietly, but so many guests came and called that it was hard to do. Brandon was three days old, and he already had most of my features on his little face. A son—I never imagined that a boy who used to play basketball with imaginary friends would one day grow up to have a child of his own. Yet, here I was, holding my son.

Brandon had his own room, but we kept a bassinet next to our bed. Racquel hadn't put him down for a second since we brought him home. Her father stopped by briefly to see him and was honored when Racquel told him that Robert was one of his middle names.

By day four, things began to settle down. I watched my son sleep, swelling with pride as I imagined my little football player's future. College football, then on to the pros, and if he wanted to be a doctor or lawyer, all the better. But athletes these days raked in more money. "I'm going to teach you everything I know," I whispered to my sleeping son.

I had been almost worried we'd have a girl. I could picture it—she'd run into dogs because, well, I had been a dog. But I had a boy, and that thought vanished.

I called my mother and made plans to bring Brandon to see her by the end of the week.

Chapter 30

Racquel

Twelve hours of labor, before Brandon emerged. I was not convinced. I'd live through it but after giving birth I was sure that he was the most beautiful baby that anyone has ever seen. For all of that pain, my son was quiet and continued to be silent, when Dr. Alma swatted his bottom to hear his lungs. He is already strong I thought. As Brandon was placed on my chest he opened his curious eyes for the first time, and looked at me. He has strength and intelligence just like his father I thought.

When the nurse came to take him to the nursery I did not want to let him go yet I needed the rest. Marcus is not a man who cried, when he was happy or sad for that matter, however, he beamed. Strutted around like he did all of the work and laid a kiss on my temple as I rested and leaned close to say thank you for my son in my ear. Dog-tired, I dozed for half the day, until my cell phone started ringing.

"Hello?"

"How is my little cousin? Where is he, and who does he look like?"

"Thank you. I'm fine," I answered.

"I'ma get to you in one minute."

"Brandon is fine. He is in the nursery. He looks a lot like Marcus."

"I'm sure he is a cutie. How was the labor?"

"I was good for the first seven hours then lost it. Girl I screamed, sung, clapped my hands and slapped my husband. You name it I did it and said it. And I took one look in my son's face and said he was worth it, every hour."

"My mother called right before Marcus did. She already told me you had the baby," Grace said.

"She's on her way and should be there now," I replied. "After she plays her numbers, of course. She'll probably start playing Brandon's birth date too, just like she does with Taylor's every week."

"She finally hit last week—for three hundred," Grace added.

"Finally! It only took her twenty-nine years. With the way she plays, she should be winning every day. She spends nearly a hundred dollars a week."

"She already sent Taylor her half, but I had to tell my mother that next time, we want sixty percent, and she gets forty. I did do all the work, after all." We both laughed at that.

Marcus

My mother's health was on a steady decline. She was too weak to walk around by herself anymore. Despite just having given birth, Racquel offered to clean up her house. I had hired a cleaning woman, and my father had hired a nurse to handle everything else. On the days he was home, he took care of her himself.

Racquel and I finally arrived with the baby for his first visit with my parents. My mother was sitting in Dad's recliner, propped up with pillows, a cloth diaper draped over one shoulder—ready for her grandson. Racquel gently placed Brandon in my mother's arms.

"Hi, Brandon, sweetheart," she cooed softly. The hat she wore covered her hair, which was still growing back from her last round of chemotherapy. Ever fashionable, her light-colored blouse matched her headgear. The brim dipped low, covering half her face as she bent over my son. She spoke quietly, as if only Brandon could hear her, making it seem like no one else was in the room.

Racquel handed the flowers she had brought for my mother to my dad. He preened the flowers and placed them in a tall, wide glass bowl. My mother broke her reverie to ask Racquel about the labor, then added that if Racquel had taken the prescribed teas, her pain would have lessened considerably. Returning her gaze to

Brandon, she remarked on his resemblance to me, though she added that it was really too soon to tell.

"He is a beautiful boy. You both did well."

Unable to hold Brandon any longer, she passed him to me after Racquel snapped a picture. I studied her in silence. How does it feel being a father? she asked me, but I couldn't answer her. My mother seemed to have aged in just a matter of days.

Once vibrant, her skin now held an ashen pallor, and she was frail, with even the slightest activity draining her. For a moment, I completely forgot her question.

Racquel covered for me, saying she believed I would be a great father.

"Oh, this will be a piece of cake," I said, gesturing to Brandon with a smile.

My wife and I exchanged a glance. She then excused herself to help my father, who had been in the kitchen. When they reentered the living room, my father's eyes were red and watery. He asked to hold the baby. My mother handed him a diaper cloth.

"He is handsome," my father said, his voice thick with emotion.

"Hold the baby's head, Trevor," my mother instructed.

"Gloria, sweetheart, I've held a baby before, and I've dropped one maybe… zero times," my father replied with a loving tap of affection.

He cooed to the baby, telling his grandson to listen to his mommy and daddy, and maybe one day, he would take Brandon for ice cream.

After handing the baby back to Racquel, I helped my father take my mother upstairs to bed. They were about the same size—both slim and average in height—yet somehow, he had managed to bring her downstairs earlier. Knowing my mother, she probably insisted on coming down to look as healthy as possible. We stayed until after ten that night before deciding it was time to bring Brandon back home.

It was the fifth night with Brandon in the house. He woke up three times, twice before the sun came up. Racquel's decision to breastfeed him kept his cries to a minimum. I usually got up with her while she changed his diapers, nursed him, then rocked him back to sleep. As her hair fell over her shoulder like a veil, I felt in that moment that I had made the right decision to remarry. She was the one. I knew it even back then when I used to pull her ponytails and run. The feeling was so strong in my chest—a deep sense of love and protection I had never felt for anything or anyone before.

When we visited my mother, I could see the genuine sadness and concern on Racquel's face. Even though I knew they had their differences, Racquel had put them aside for that day. They were two very strong-minded women, and I loved them both. I was proud that day, in particular, because they had finally reached a ceasefire.

The following day, my father called to tell me that my mother, Gloria, had passed. I wanted to cry, but I couldn't; I hoped he had made a mistake. I wanted him to check again, to find that, by some miracle, she was still breathing. But I had to face reality. Her body was tired, she told me so. Was there anything more clear than her saying it? My mother was truly gone.

Chapter 31

Racquel

She went to sleep and never woke up. It was a peaceful passing. Arrangements had already been made, and although things were a little chaotic, she had the foresight to prepare most of it months in advance. A cream suit in her size was ready, along with a set of pearls. Since her own hair had grown back, she had no need for the wig; the instructions were to use it only if there was no one to do her hair. She knew her time was near.

Her casket was pearl white with gold-tone handles and a dark blue interior. I hated to admit it, but she had taste—she was a diva. My only task was to ensure that her son and husband did not fall apart. I was making strides with Mr. Collin, but I was failing miserably with Marcus. He took her passing very hard. Despite the fact that it was anticipated given her illness, it was still a sad homecoming.

I thought about the woman who had shrouded herself in godliness while overlooking all the basic principles. The fact that there were so many things left unsaid bothered me. She had deprived me of the chance to change my opinion of her.

Marcus allowed me to help with the wake and funeral, which made me feel a bit better. He was so consumed by his misery that he didn't know whether he was coming or going.

I was not surprised by the turnout. Every charity and organization she had served, all the parishioners, and even Milford and Denise with their children showed up. The United States Virgin Isles Support Organization, which Mrs. Collin had been a member of since 1979, was also present. I could never know Mrs. Collin the way Marcus did—because she was his mother—but I was sincerely upset for his and Brandon's loss. She had held on long enough to see her grandson. At that moment, my baby was being held by my father's wife, Delores.

She didn't mind while I ran back and forth, trying to get mourners to sit and start the elegy. After the choir sang 'Our Father,' the attendees settled down, and a brigade of people seemed to come to the podium.

One person from each organization she had supported said a few words about her before a reading from the Bible. I was unaware of how many lives she had positively impacted. The Chadmeyer's Funeral Home was literally packed with flowers. Despite our estrangement, she was capable of kindness. Why she had disliked me so much remained a mystery. As I walked past her casket, I saw a sardonic expression of disdain lingering on her brows, even in death.

I looked intently at her chest to make sure she was not breathing. The funeral director had done a first-class job; it was hard to tell she wasn't merely sleeping. When it was time for Marcus to give the eulogy, he appeared unable to speak and seemed to be hyperventilating.

"Doctor Collin, Marcus doesn't look so well. I've spoken with Pastor Steele, and if it's alright with you, I'll read whatever Marcus wrote," I offered.

Standing before the crowd, I gave the performance of a lifetime. I searched my heart and found something meaningful to speak about. Even though she hadn't shown much kindness to me personally, I discovered she had her virtuous qualities. I finished as Marcus regained his composure.

Earlier, a woman I had never seen before had been wailing in the back; she had fainted, and Grace's old boyfriend, Steven, had carried her away. Thanks to Mrs. Collin, Steven had been able to get into law school. He was also devastated by the loss of a beacon of light like Gloria Collin. After Marcus's speech, the reverend returned to the podium.

The woman, now composed but hiccupping repeatedly, had taken a seat. Later, I learned that she was Marcus's aunt, Mildred, his father's sister, who had come over from Saint Thomas for the funeral.

"She seemed pretty broken up, Marcus," I said.

"They were close friends," he replied.

Mildred approached us in the foyer, leaning heavily on her cane as she introduced herself to me.

"Gloria was right, Marcus, your wife is very pretty," Mildred said, her eyes watery as she watched me.

"She said that?" I asked, unable to believe it. It didn't sound like something Gloria Collin would have said.

"Yes, she did," Mildred confirmed. "Marcus, can you please get me some water? My throat is dry," she requested, sending him away.

"Racquel, my dear, I can only imagine what you're both going through. Come, child, sit. I'm old, and my legs aren't what they used to be."

I followed her to a bench, wanting nothing more than to retrieve Brandon and avoid discussing my husband's mother. "Here," she said, handing me a letter addressed to her from Mrs. Collin.

"I don't think I should," I said, trying to return it.

"Well, I think you should," she insisted, handing it back to me.

"You don't understand. We never really got along, and I shouldn't read it if it's personal."

"You can never be what she was to Marcus, and vice versa. She was his mother, and you are his wife. It's as simple as that. He chose you to build a life with, to be the mother of his child. No one can take that from you. I am fully aware of how she felt, and I'm here to tell you that her protective feelings concerning her son had nothing to do with you."

"I don't understand," I said, feeling lost.

"Read it later," was her only reply.

Settling down for the night was proving difficult. My son had gas, making him hard to soothe. Marcus's face was glum, and he had bought a bottle of whiskey. Within five minutes, half of it was gone. I gave him space until he reached for a second bottle. This behavior was unlike Marcus. I sat next to him, gently taking the glass and the second bottle from his hands.

I held him, though he wouldn't hold me back; he seemed numb and immune to my tenderness. When he finally spoke, his words were slurred and angry.

"Are you happy now? Is this what you wanted?" he accused.

His words were harsh and, given the situation, almost cruel.

"Marcus, you don't know what you're saying. I understand how you feel. I lost a mother once, remember?"

"You've never had a mother or father. How could you understand?" His voice was filled with bitterness. "You're to blame with all your bickering. My mother was right—I should have never married you."

I drew back, feeling his words sting more deeply than any physical blow. Trembling, I handed him back his whiskey and glass.

Letting him drown in his own pity and grief, I watched as the man with the laughing obsidians was replaced by an angry drunkard. It was hard to reconcile the lips that once said "I love you" and promised, "I will never let you go," after a night of intimacy, with the hurtful words he was now spewing.

My first instinct was to hit him as hard as he had hurt me, but I didn't want that kind of destructive relationship. Instead, I drew upon the brassy strength Aunt Lynn had instilled in me and, with the serenity worthy of Susan Ann Middleton's daughter, I turned to him and said, "Now, wait a minute. Not once did I ever put your mother in her place after she cussed me out," I said, my voice steady despite the turmoil inside me.

"I left that up to you to handle, but not once did you say a word in my defense. I even named my son Brandon for her sake—you should know that I didn't have to."

"She mistook my tolerance for submissiveness and continued to disrespect me, just like at your father's party." The drunken stranger who was once my husband looked away.

"What? Was I not supposed to know that Monica was there, trailing behind you? I could go through a laundry list of grievances, but I won't. I am the one you took those vows with. I am not going to let you disregard me as if I have no feelings just because you're feeling miserable. I am no one's stepping stool, not hers and certainly not yours. When you are ready to come to your senses and apologize instead of drowning yourself in a bottle, I will be down the hall with Brandon."

The legs that carried me to my son's room wobbled; I still reeled from his insult. I wanted nothing more than to pack up and leave the husband I had supported, who apparently did not appreciate it. Marcus had never spoken to me like that before. If he wanted to drink himself to oblivion, that was his choice.

Was I happy about her passing? I asked myself honestly. No, I was not. My husband lost a mother, my son lost a grandmother—this was no occasion for celebration.

I placed Brandon in his bassinet by our bed, then prepared his things for the next day's burial. I laid out Marcus's black suit and my black dress. Ten minutes passed, and Marcus made no move towards our bedroom.

Pretending to watch the late-night news, I fed the baby. Still no sign of Marcus. To hell with him, I told myself, as I tried to sleep. Tossing and turning, I pounded my pillow, imagining it was my stubborn husband's head. Sleep eluded me, and by three in the morning, there was still no sign of Marcus. I put Brandon down after his 4 a.m. feeding, hoping he would not be late for his mother's funeral, which started at nine in the morning.

My husband was depressed and roamed the streets, and I was almost out of my mind with worry. Searching the baby bag, I told myself, "I will not panic. If he's not here by six, I'll call Trevor." Then I found the letter Marcus's aunt had handed me at the wake. It was in the bag under the diapers. I walked into the dining room and paused to click on the standing lamp.

I took the letter out of the envelope and unfolded it. The letter, addressed to Mildred Collin, was clearly in Gloria Collin's handwriting. As I read, I shook my head slowly, confused and reluctant to believe that Gloria was anything other than the strong, resolute woman she had always appeared to be. The letter detailed the life of a frightened girl, thrust into adulthood by the birth and subsequent death of her child. I had no idea of the true feelings hidden behind Mrs. Collin's tough exterior. In the end, she asked Mildred to seek my forgiveness. There was no way to undo the hurt caused by her harsh words and gestures.

She had acknowledged her own harshness, though it had come too late to change the past. A part of me wanted to leave the past behind, but another part of me held onto the pain. Despite everything, the right choice was to forgive.

Right then and there, I dropped to my knees and prayed for a mother-in-law I hardly knew, hoping her spirit had finally found peace. I asked God to guide her son back home, to a place where he would always be loved.

Marcus

My mother's passing was anticipated, but it was still a shock. In the back of my mind, I had hoped she would pull through, but this time, it didn't happen. My father and I were at the doctor's office when we learned her cancer had returned and spread to her lymph nodes. That was two months ago. She passed away just a week after my son Brandon was born.

Her death hit me like a gut punch, leaving me feeling like a lost child. Despite knowing she had been ill for a while, the reality of her absence was unbearable. My father and her doctor had done everything medically possible, but it was her time to go. Why couldn't she have lived into her late eighties instead of dying at fifty-nine?

When my father called to tell me, his voice was so distraught and trembling that it felt surreal, like an out-of-body experience. I felt numb.

The realization that I would never see her again didn't fully hit me until I arrived at her wake. Racquel spoke at the wake, which I'm sure took a lot of courage given their relationship. I managed to add to what she had already said, though my own emotions were on edge.

When the casket was closed over my mother, I couldn't bear to leave. My chest felt constricted, but I refused to cry. "This can't be happening," I thought, gazing up at the ceiling as if seeking answers from a higher power. My father eventually persuaded me to leave and drive Racquel and Brandon home.

Once we were back, I went out to the liquor store, seeking solace in a bottle. Cheap or expensive, it didn't matter. At that moment, all I needed was the burning liquid to flow through me and ease the ache. The guilt of all those times I took my mother for granted, or failed to say "I love you," added to my pain. If only I had one more day, I would listen to her when she wanted to talk. I'd make an effort to understand her old-fashioned ways from the island.

My wife was awake, holding our baby. She didn't say anything but embraced me, and together we cried. I knew I needed to apologize. When I finally did, she put aside the calculator and the stainless steel frying pan she had been holding. I raised my eyebrows in confusion, and she explained that she had been calculating child support payments and that the pan had my name on it. I ducked, and she laughed softly. With a touch of newfound courage, I held her close and asked, "Were you really going to hit me?"

"No, of course not. I would never hit any woman and I love you too much,"

I love you too, she said and hearing those words felt like a balm to my wounded soul. I thought to myself, "Mom, she was the right choice." Gratefully, I leaned in to kiss her, reaffirming that Racquel was my wife, my partner.

Epilogue

y mother, Susan Middleton, always said that you could never change your past, only your future. With that in mind, I set aside any lingering resentment toward Mrs. Collin. The idea of staying angry at a deceased woman seemed absurd.

"Where are we going, Mommy?" Brandon's small voice broke through my thoughts.

"Where we go every year," I replied, "to see Grandma."

Clutching Mildred's letter, I kept my eyes on the road as I drove to the cemetery. Brandon sat in his car seat, clutching a pot of flowers with his tiny hands. Visiting the cemetery was something I dreaded, but I had made it a tradition to visit my own mother's grave once a year. This year, I decided to also visit Mrs. Collin's resting place. Marcus was unaware of my annual visits to his mother's grave for the past two years.

My conscience had been troubled. Marcus and his mother never resolved their differences while she was alive, and we had never fully settled ours. It was only after reading Mildred's letter that I began to understand the depth of Gloria's struggles and the tight hold she had on Marcus. I made my peace with her a year after her passing.

The revelation about Marcus's brother was a shock to us both. Marcus had felt deeply betrayed and mistreated, not just by his mother's family but by Gloria's own inability to protect her child. I, too, was appalled to learn of the circumstances surrounding Gloria's first son, Brandon's death. Born prematurely, he had suffered due to a lack of proper care, including the failure to clear his lungs of fluid and mucus—a basic procedure any midwife should know.

Standing before Gloria's gravesite, I felt a profound sense of injustice and sorrow for the pain she had endured.

I placed a pot of flowers on the headstone, which read:

Gloria Ann Collin, Devoted Wife and Dearly Loved Mother.

Gently, I touched my stomach, feeling a wave of anticipation. Marcus and I were expecting again the following year. God had blessed us with twins: one I named Glory Anne, and the other he named Suzann.

Our son Brandon was two years old at the time and old enough to attend daycare. His class consisted of eleven children from various racial backgrounds, which appealed to me as a parent.

I believed that if the world could become a better place, it would be through the diversity and understanding fostered in our children. Brandon had a crush on a little Caucasian girl named Holly.

I couldn't help but notice her eyes seemed set too far apart and too close together, a peculiar observation. This was a contradiction, as I hadn't yet begun to discuss issues of race, yet the awareness of it was present in my thoughts. Was I turning into my mother-in-law, I hoped not.

The End